Social Networks and Music Worlds

Social networks are critical for the creation and consumption of music. This edited collection, *Social Networks and Music Worlds*, introduces students and scholars of music in society to the core concepts and tools of social network analysis. The collection showcases the use of these tools by sociologists, historians and musicologists, examining a variety of distinct 'music worlds', including post-punk, jazz, rap, folk, classical music, Ladyfest and the world of 'open mic' performances, on a number of different scales (local, national and international). In addition to their overarching Introduction, the editors offer a very clear and detailed introduction to the methodology of social network analysis for the uninitiated.

The collection builds upon insights from canonic texts in the sociology of music, with the crucial innovation of examining musical network interaction via formal methods. With network analysis in the arts and humanities at an emergent stage, *Social Networks and Music Worlds* highlights its possibilities for non-scientists. Contributions hail from leading and emerging scholars who present social network graphs and data to represent different music worlds, locating individuals, resources and styles within them.

The collection sits at the nexus of sociological, musicological and cultural studies traditions. Its range should ensure a large scholarly readership.

Nick Crossley is Professor of Sociology and co-founder/co-director of the Mitchell Centre for Social Network Analysis at the University of Manchester. His most recent book is *Networks of Sound, Style and Subversion: The Punk and Post-Punk Music Worlds of Liverpool, London, Manchester and Sheffield 1975–1980*, Manchester, Manchester University Press.

Siobhan McAndrew is an economic historian and Research Fellow at the University of Manchester. Her DPhil examined the evolution of institutions providing opera in modern Britain. She also researches religious and value change in contemporary Europe, and has written on the effect of recession on suicides for the SCHMI 'Hard Times' programme.

Paul Widdop is Research Fellow in Culture, Leisure and Sport at Leeds Metropolitan University. His main research interests are in the sociology of taste and consumption, focusing on exploring how social networks impact upon behaviour in the fields of music and sport. He is also interested in the importance of place and neighbourhood effects in these fields, especially in relation to their mediating role in developing cultural lifestyles and cultural communities.

Routledge advances in sociology

Social Networks and Music Worlds

**Edited by Nick Crossley,
Siobhan McAndrew and Paul Widdop**

Routledge
Taylor & Francis Group

LONDON AND NEW YORK

First published 2015
by Routledge
2 Park Square, Milton Park, Abingdon, Oxon OX14 4RN

and by Routledge
711 Third Avenue, New York, NY 10017

Routledge is an imprint of the Taylor & Francis Group, an informa business

British Library Cataloguing-in-Publication Data
A catalogue record for this book is available from the British Library

Library of Congress Cataloging-in-Publication Data
Social networks and music worlds / edited by Nick Crossley, Siobhan
McAndrew, Paul Widdop.
pages cm
  1. Music–Social aspects. 2. Social networks–Great Britain. 3. Social
sciences–Network analysis. I. Crossley, Nick, editor of compilation.
II. McAndrew, Siobhan, editor of compilation. III. Widdop, Paul, editor
of compilation.
ML3916.S655 2014
306.4'842–dc23   2014005762

ISBN: 978-0-415-71888-2 (hbk)
ISBN: 978-1-315-86779-3 (ebk)

Typeset in Times New Roman
by Wearset Ltd, Boldon, Tyne and Wear

Printed and bound in the United States of America by Publishers Graphics,
LLC on sustainably sourced paper.

Contents

Figures

Tables

Contributors

Roberta Comunian is Lecturer in Creative and Cultural Industries at the Department of Culture, Media and Creative Industries at King's College, London. Dr Comunian's work focuses on the relationship between arts, cultural regeneration projects and the cultural and creative industries. She is currently leading an AHRC research network exploring the connections between higher education and the creative economy and has published extensively on the career opportunities and patterns of creative graduates in the UK.

Nick Crossley is Professor of Sociology and co-founder/co-director of the Mitchell Centre for Social Network Analysis at the University of Manchester. His most recent book is *Networks of Sound, Style and Subversion: The Punk and Post-Punk Music Worlds of Liverpool, London, Manchester and Sheffield 1975–1980*, Manchester, Manchester University Press.

Tim Edensor is Reader in Cultural Geography at Manchester Metropolitan University. He has research interests in urban and rural cultures, industrial heritage and ruins, and materiality, among others. His most recent book is *A World of Cities: Urban Theory Beyond the West* (with Mark Jayne; Routledge 2011).

Martin Everett is Professor of Social Network Analysis and co-founder/co-director of the Mitchell Centre for Social Network Analysis at the University of Manchester. He has published widely on social network analysis and contributed to numerous methodological innovations within the approach. His most recent publication, co-authored with Stephen Borgatti and Jeffrey Johnson, is *Analysing Social Networks* (Sage 2012).

Alessandra Faggian is Associate Professor at The Ohio State University, AED Economics Department and co-editor of *Papers in Regional Science*. Dr Faggian's research interests lie in the field of Regional and Urban Economics, Demography, Labour Economics and Economics of Education. Her publications cover a wide range of topics including migration, human capital, labour markets, creativity and local innovation and growth.

Ruth Finnegan is Emeritus Professor in the Faculty of Social Sciences at the Open University, where she was a founding member of the academic staff.

Among other academic honours, she is a Fellow of the British Academy. Originally a classical scholar, then anthropologist (and amateur musician), she has conducted fieldwork in Sierra Leone, Fiji and England during her extensive career. She continues to research extensively into the comparative sociology and anthropology of artistic activity, communication and performance.

Karim Hammou is a researcher at the CNRS and member of the Centre for Sociological and Political Research of Paris (CRESPPA). He is interested in commodification processes and social hierarchies in popular music. In 2012 he published a history of French rap music (*Une histoire du rap en France*, La Découverte). He is currently working on dilemmas and contradictions of status in 'urban music'. More information about his research can be found on his research blog (in French): http://surunsonrap.hypotheses.org.

Paul Hepburn is a political scientist and Research Associate at the Heseltine Institute for Public Policy and Practice, University of Liverpool. His PhD, on the role played by social and online networks in local governance, was awarded in 2011. He researches in e-democracy and e-government, alongside an investigation into the social impact of the great recession, for the Social Change Harvard–Manchester Initiative (SCHMI) study on 'Hard Times'.

Fay Hield is a lecturer in Music and Director of the Music Management MA at the University of Sheffield. Alongside teaching, Fay records and performs folk music. Her recent project, *The Full English*, took inspiration from a newly created digital archive of folk music, and earned the titles of 'Best Album' and 'Best Group' at the BBC Radio 2 Folk Awards 2014.

Sarah Jewell is a lecturer in Economics at the University of Reading. Her research interests lie in the fields of Labour Economics, the Economics of Higher Education and Life Satisfaction. She has published in journals such as: *Oxford Economic Papers*, *Regional Studies*, *Feminist Economics* and *International Review of Finance*.

Siobhan McAndrew is an economic historian and Research Fellow at the University of Manchester. Her DPhil examined the evolution of institutions providing opera in modern Britain. She also researches religious and value change in contemporary Europe, and has written on the effect of recession on suicides for the SCHMI 'Hard Times' programme.

Susan O'Shea is a sociology lecturer at the University of Manchester. A serial Ladyfest organiser and SNA user, her research looks at gender inequalities in music worlds, cultural production and participation. Mixing methods and mixing beats at the edge of the analogue–digital divide, Susan is one half of the dark electronic duo, Factory Acts. Their first EP is due out with AnalogueTrash Records, summer 2014.

Nigel Richards currently works in coordinating HIV prevention and treatment and related sexual health services for black and minority ethnic groups in the

UK during the daytime but at night transforms into a regular of the open mic scene in Manchester and the north of England. He was previously in charge of the Centre for Applied Research based at the University of Mauritius and worked in poverty reduction in southern Africa.

Rachel Stevenson is a PhD student in the Department of Sociology at the University of Manchester. Her doctoral research explores the structures of covert social movement networks. With Nick Crossley, she has recently published work in the journal *Social Movement Studies* on the changing network structure of the Provisional IRA.

Paul Widdop is Research Fellow in Culture, Leisure and Sport at Leeds Metropolitan University. His main research interests are in the sociology of taste and consumption, focusing on exploring how social networks impact upon behaviour in the fields of music and sport. He is also interested in the importance of place and neighbourhood effects in these fields, especially in relation to their mediating role in developing cultural lifestyles and cultural communities.

Foreword

Ruth Finnegan

Another book about music, divine and, yes, human too.

And what a delightful feast this proves to be. Human indeed, as the well-briefed contributors here – the up-to-date references alone are worth the price – demonstrate so well with their rightly judged suspicion of the slick 'community' notion and their cautious but constructive use of the social scientists' old 'network' tool, here further developed and put to new uses (not of course without a side glance at Becker's classic 'music worlds' concept). It is a book all social scientists with even a passing interest in music and art should read forthwith.

As I too found, while struggling to find a way to present the 'hidden' musicians of Milton Keynes way back in the old but after all not-so-changed world of the 1980s, striving to be analytic but not without some measure (not overly romanticising I hope) of celebration for those wonderful local creators and creative listeners in an English town, bedrock of our culture, the social scientific outsider's approach to music is a hard and still – amazingly – a sometimes lonely road. It is delightful to find it so sensitively and knowledgeably trodden here.

But the writers are also themselves immersed in music: this is no philistines' book. So the divine? That too shines through, as for the immortal products of the muses it ever must.

Old Bletchley
5 February 2014

Acknowledgements

Much of the research for this book was funded by 'Music Communities', AH/J006807/1, an Arts and Humanities Research Council project funded under the cross-council 'Connected Communities' programme. The editors would like to thank the AHRC for their support.

1   Introduction

*Nick Crossley, Siobhan McAndrew and
Paul Widdop*

As Christopher Small's (1998) felicitous term, 'musicking', suggests, making
and enjoying music are social activities, patterned by convention and involving
multiple relays of interaction between those involved. These activities tend to
cluster along stylistic and/or geographical lines. In much early sociological work
on popular music this clustering was captured by the concept of sub-culture or,
more precisely, 'working class youth sub-cultures' (Clarke *et al.* 1993; Hebdige
1988). This work remains important and instructive but the concept of subculture, at least in the dominant formulation of it, posited by members of Birmingham's Centre for Contemporary Cultural Studies (Clarke *et al.* 1993; Hebdige
1988), is problematic. It focuses only upon 'popular' forms of music, having
nothing to say about the 'elite' forms against which the popular is at least tacitly
pitted. It focuses almost exclusively upon the activities of audiences and consumers of music, abstracting them from and neglecting musicians and such
'support personnel' as promoters, managers, etc. And it is demographically
skewed towards working-class youth (admittedly affording a focus upon racial
and gender differences in later work (McRobbie 1991; Gilroy 1992; Jones
1988)), precluding any understanding of musical enthusiasm and participation
among older and middle-class individuals (Bennett 2013; Bennett and Hodkinson 2012; Smith 2009). These limitations have prompted a number of attempts,
in recent years, to devise a different model for theorising the abovementioned
clusters, a model which incorporates the positives of 'subculture' without suc-
cumbing to its weaknesses (Bennett 1999; Hesmondhalgh 2005). Three alternatives in particular have achieved prominence: 'scenes' (Straw 1991; Shank
1994; Bennett and Peterson 2004), 'fields' (Bourdieu 1993; Savage 2006) and
'music worlds', a concept which builds upon Howard Becker's (1982) work on
'art worlds' (Finnegan 1989; Lopes 2002; Martin 2005, 2006a, 2006b).

There are considerable overlaps between these conceptions and whichever
one we opt for the literature on the others will remain a useful resource. There
are differences between them, however, and in earlier work we argued in favour
of 'music worlds' (e.g. Bottero and Crossley 2011; Crossley 2015; McAndrew
and Everett forthcoming), a choice to which we adhere here. This book is
intended to contribute to and expand the 'music worlds' research agenda. Individual contributors vary in their attachment to the concept but most work at least

loosely within its parameters and all, in our view, have much to contribute to an understanding of music worlds.

As noted above, the identity and boundaries of a music world are often demarcated by reference to musical styles. We refer to the jazz world, the folk world and the punk world, for example, or to various sub-divisions within or cross-cutting these broader styles: e.g. the trad jazz world, the folk-rock world, the sludge metal world, etc. Beyond style, as we also noted above, worlds may be demarcated by geography: e.g. the Manchester music world, the French music world, etc. And style and geography often intersect: e.g. the Liverpool jazz world, the Birmingham metal world, etc. Indeed, even within the same broad style and city, we may find distinct music worlds, separated by sub-style and geography, as Samuel Gilmore's (1987, 1988) fascinating work on art music worlds in New York demonstrates. Furthermore, as Bennett and Peterson (2004) say in their (complementary) work on 'scenes', worlds may be local, translocal (including but not exclusively national or global) and increasingly also virtual.

Beyond style and geography, worlds often vary in structure and other sociological properties. Some are enduring and institutionalised. Others are transient and informal. Some are big, others small and so on. The music worlds concept is intended to capture and facilitate analysis of this variation. It is not a prescriptive concept. It is a sensitising concept which invites open-minded empirical inquiry and comparison.

Underlying all of this variation, however, is collective action (Becker 1974, 2008). Music worlds are forms of collective action, akin to social movements. They entail interaction between a population of social actors with overlapping musical interests who conspire, in different ways and combinations, to make their preferred forms of music happen. Agency is central (music worlds involve people doing things together) but interdependence between participants and an unequal distribution of the resources typically involved in musicking generate constraints and power imbalances which they must work within and around. As such, music worlds assume a structure, albeit a structure which, due to the impact of inter-agency, is inherently dynamic and subject to change: structure-in-process.

Becker suggests various elements of music worlds that might be focused upon in sociological analyses, including their constitutive conventions, the distribution and mobilisation of their key resources (e.g. money, skills, equipment) and the physical spaces where music is performed, rehearsed and recorded. Other writers who take Becker's conception as their point of departure, including Ruth Finnegan (1989) in her classic study of the distinct but overlapping music worlds of Milton Keynes, and Paul Lopes (2002), who analyses *The Rise of a Jazz Art World* in the USA, have added to this list. One very central component of any music world for Becker, however, which sociological analysis must address, is the network formed by the interactions of its participants. Music worlds have a reticular structure and this demands sociological investigation. It is the networked character of music worlds that we are particularly interested in this book.

Networks and worlds

All of the contributions to the book examine the role of networks in relation to music worlds, in most cases drawing upon formal 'social network analysis' (SNA). We offer an introduction to SNA in Chapter 2 (see also Borgatti *et al.* 2012; Scott 2000; Wasserman and Faust 1994), affording those unfamiliar with it the necessary background to engage fully with subsequent chapters. For present purposes we will elaborate at a more general level upon the significance of networks and network analysis for music worlds and our understanding of them. We begin by considering the various ways in which music worlds can be said to be networks.

Music worlds and networks

The first way centres upon a key theme in Becker's (1982) work: the division of labour involved in most forms of musicking (see also Small 1998). As collective action, musicking typically requires coordination between multiple participants, running along various relays and forming a network. Different roles are performed by different people who must communicate and coordinate their respective contributions. The coordination between players in a band is an obvious example of this but musicians must also coordinate with a variety of 'support personnel', including managers, promoters and technicians, who must also coordinate with one another. And both musicians and support personnel must coordinate with audiences who also have a role to play, turning up to performances (in the right place at the right time), buying recordings (in both cases funding everybody else) and, often via the mediation of critics but not always in agreement with them, bestowing meaning and value upon what they hear. Listening and hearing, like all forms of perception, are activities. They engage with auditory stimuli, shaping and thereby contributing to the form of what is heard (Dewey 1980; Merleau-Ponty 1962). In this way they enter into the process of music-making. Furthermore, it is the audience who bestow the status of music upon what they hear (or not) (Dewey 1980; Small 1998; Becker 1982); audiences are among the actors who contribute to the classification of musical genres (DiMaggio 1987, 2011); and they give further life and meaning to music by means of the often innovative ways in which they use and deploy it (DeNora 2000; Willis 1990).

We could explore the division of labour involved in musicking much further, extending our focus to consider instrument-makers, music shops, the cleaners and administrative staff employed at venues and many more besides but the point is clear enough. Musicking is not a solitary activity. It involves its participants in a network of others with whom they must coordinate, and this network is therefore central to a proper understanding of it. It is also worth noting at this point that much of the importance which Becker attaches to 'convention' relates to the need of participants to coordinate their activities with others. Mutual adherence to conventions, from 12-tone scales and standardised tunings to outlets for ticket sales and pecking orders among roadies, makes coordination easier.

Beyond the division of labour involved, networks are implicated in music worlds in the form of various relations of influence, support, antagonism, etc. within the 'communities' which particular musicians, support personnel and audiences form; relations which impact directly upon individual 'moral careers' within the world and the career of the world itself. The existence of 'musical communities' has long been recognised within sociology, predating the above-mentioned work on youth subcultures. 'Community' is an unfortunate term, however, both because it suggests cohesion and cooperation, which we do find in music worlds but usually intermingled with competition, conflict and factions (dominant and subordinate), and because it fails to capture structural differences within and between music worlds: e.g. the different positions that participants occupy, such as being central or marginal, and variations in cohesion and cen-tralisation both between different worlds and within the same world over time.

'Social network', as defined in SNA, avoids these problems. It does not pre-judge the nature of ties between participants. It allows for competition and con-flict as well as cooperation, further allowing that cohesion and cooperation may have negative as well as positive effects, and that conflict, competition and mar-ginalisation may have positive as well as negative effects: e.g. conflict may spur musicians on both to rehearse hard and innovate, producing better music, and relative isolation may remove musicians from strong social influences and demands for conformity, facilitating innovation. 'Social network' allows us to think relationally without committing ourselves to a cosy communitarian picture of the world or indeed any picture (Crossley 2011). Furthermore, it both allows that different worlds may be 'wired' in different ways, with different participants enjoying different patterns of connection within them, and allows us, by means of the tools of SNA, to capture, measure and analyse these variables (see Chapter 2).

We should add that the networked character of music worlds is not restricted to their human participants nor SNA to the analysis of human networks. The many sites of activity within a music world, which Becker (2004) begins to explore in his essay 'Jazz Places', for example, from rehearsal spaces to venues, festivals, record shops, studios and so on, are often linked, both through arrange-ments between their owners and the flow of bands, audiences and others between them. Similar styles may take root in spatio-temporally distant venues and events, for example, because of the flow of the same artists or audiences between them. To give another example, songs may be linked through practices of cita-tion and borrowing. And the official bodies and corporate economic actors involved in a music world may be linked through shared members/directors. Each of these 'nodes' is important to a proper understanding of music worlds and so too are the interactions and networks between them.

Social capital

Music worlds do not just happen to be networked. Connection between participants, which, to reiterate, will vary both within and between specific worlds, involving ties which, as Simmel (1906, 1955) says of ties more generally, involve an ambivalent mix of positive and negative elements, is essential to the existence of a world. It is connection, for example, which facilitates communication and thereby coordination. Audiences arrive at the same venues as the bands they wish to see, on the same evenings, because communication allows for coordination between them. Furthermore, connection generates emergent properties which both characterise music worlds in particular ways and facilitate forms of action, on various scales, which would not otherwise be possible; forms of action which make the world what it is. Whatever its flaws, and there are many (Fine 2001), the concept of 'social capital' encapsulates much of this. For our purposes this concept can be understood in two ways.

On an individual level, participants may enjoy indirect access to certain resources necessary for their participation, by means of their connection to others who enjoy direct access, as in Nan Lin's (2002) conception of social capital. Making the acquaintance of an individual who sits on a radio playlist committee may afford one the opportunity to indirectly influence that committee, for example, while befriending a studio engineer may be a route to free studio time.

Beyond this, as James Coleman's (1990) more structural conception of social capital suggests, dense and closed networks in particular tend to generate incentives for cooperation, trust and mutual support among their members, even when those members might in other respects find themselves in conflict or competition. Members of such networks often depend strongly upon one another. This can be a cause of tension but it requires that they strive to maintain a good reputation as reliable, trustworthy, helpful, etc. They cannot afford to do otherwise because the costs, in terms of sanctions from others, will deprive them of what they need to achieve their own musical ambitions. Over time these pressures may be internalised, giving rise to a sense of duty and community (Mead 1967). Furthermore, participation in collective action may give rise to a collective identity, solidarity and *esprit de corps* (Blumer 1969). Even where actors remain purely strategic in orientation, however, it is often in their best interests to cooperate.

This, in turn, facilitates activities conducive to the flourishing of a music world that would not otherwise be possible: e.g. sharing of equipment, rehearsal space, know-how and information; 'leg-ups' for less established by more established artists; and acceptance of and support for experimentation with sounds, looks and lifestyles which might invite hostility in the 'outside world'. Indeed, Coleman (1988) suggests that dense and closed networks play a crucial role in the cultivation of 'deviant lifestyles', allowing for the emergence of deviant constructions of reality and incentive systems, and insulating their participants from harsh sanctions in the wider world which might otherwise bring them back into line. He illustrates this with examples of self-sacrifice in sport and politics (e.g. suicide bombers). There is no shortage of examples in music worlds, however. From inter-racial mixing and drug-taking in early jazz worlds, through the obsessive pursuit of obscure records and freaky dancing in Northern Soul, to the peacock fashions of Teds, punks and Goths and the persistence of metal heads and prog rockers in the face of widespread ridicule, music world participants are often 'different' and their networks, the networks of their music world, will often encourage and support this difference, counteracting any 'corrective' influence from wider society.

This may be progressive. Dense networks are conducive to stylistic innovation. However, it may be a matter of conserving traditions in a context of widespread change. Socio-linguistic research by Milroy (1987) and Bott's (1957) classic sociological study of family forms, for example, both suggest that traditional cultural forms tend to survive best in the context of dense and closed networks, resisting a pressure to change which may be proving irresistible in other contexts. In a musical context this may mean preserving musical forms when they (inevitably) fall from grace within the mainstream, holding them in abeyance until they (equally inevitably) become fashionable again. Describing what happened to Northern Soul, which had emerged in the context of a dense network of enthusiasts and venues, when the popularity it enjoyed in the early 1970s began to wane, for example, Nicola Smith observes:

> Once again ignored by the mass media and by the public majority, the scene was kept alive by word of mouth and the continued passion for the music by a relatively small number of existing fans.
>
> (Smith 2012: 161)

She adds that 'Today the scene has overcome a decline in popularity' (ibid.) and begun to thrive again. Smith does not use the word 'network' here but reference to 'word of mouth' is clearly suggestive of a network keeping its members 'in the loop' and primed for participation.

Diffusion, taste formation and social space

Networks are also important mechanisms in the generation of the shared tastes which define a music world. There is a growing body of literature suggesting both that tastes are formed within networks, as an effect of mutual influence, and that, as a consequence, tastes diffuse through networks (Becker 1996; DiMaggio 2011; Erickson 1996; Lewis *et al.* 2008; Lizardo 2006; Mark 1998, 2003). This may be a matter of actors passing on the taste for pre-existing musical forms or, in the case of more innovative worlds, of actors collectively generating both new forms and the taste for them (albeit usually on the basis of pre-existing shared tastes). Alternatively, it may be the taste for particular formats of musical production/consumption that is transmitted: e.g. live versus recorded music, MP3s versus vinyl, big concerts versus small clubs, etc.

Exactly how tastes are acquired in social interaction remains under-researched. Many mechanisms may be involved and they may combine differently in different instances. For illustrative purposes we suggest seven mechanisms:

1 *Exposure*: a taste may pass from one actor to another through the simple fact of the first actor introducing the second to a style of music they have not previously encountered: e.g. playing a record which has instant appeal.

2 *Co-participation*: actors may 'go through the motions' of musical appreciation, because their friends are, finding in the process that they actually like the music. A liking for dance music may be acquired in the process of dancing in a club with friends, for example, and a liking for folk singing may be acquired by accompanying an insider to a folk club and taking part.

3 *Aesthetic instruction*: liking a form of music may require or at least be enhanced through background knowledge and know-how which is transmitted in a more explicit way than in co-participation. Audiences may need to know what to listen for or how to listen and respond. Like a football fan, they need to understand 'the game' and acquire a stake in it in order to feel moved by it. This could be a matter of the 'internal meaning' of the music (e.g. the way in which different pieces play with musical conventions and expectations) or the external meaning attached to music within a particular world: e.g. learning to associate particular musical styles with social or political values/identities which one already holds.

4 *Choice heuristics*: actors may find themselves overwhelmed with equally enticing possibilities for musical enjoyment, resolving the difficulty of choosing between them by emulating the choices of others, especially where those others appear to derive pleasure from their choice.

5 *Secondary benefits*: beyond the ease involved in following the example of friends, pursuing one musical path over another may be anticipated to create greater opportunities for sociability, status or another extrinsic reward.

6 *Association*: music may bring pleasure because it has become associated with positive relationships and/or other pleasurable experiences shared with others.

7 *Suggestion*: early sociologists such as Tarde (1903) and Cooley (1964) both identify 'suggestion' as one among a number of mechanisms of imitation/contagion. The concept is poorly explained and a little mysterious but we include it here as a possibility which, like our other mechanisms, stands in need of further elucidation and empirical investigation.

Though analytically distinct, none of these mechanisms are mutually exclusive and most are likely to work in conjunction with several of the others. The decision to emulate another will result in exposure, co-participation and perhaps aesthetic instruction, for example, which may result in the development of a genuine taste for whatever type of music is involved. Furthermore, over time this may be found to bring secondary benefits, such as linking the individual to a group in which they have friends and enjoy status, and may become associated with positive experiences enjoyed with this group.

These processes of taste formation and diffusion may be overlaid by the structuring effect of wider social divisions. It is widely observed, for example, that actors are disproportionately likely to form ties with others of a similar social standing to themselves (e.g. actors in a similar income bracket, with a similar level of education, of a similar age and ethnic background, etc.), a process which Lazarsfeld and Merton (1964) call 'status homophily' (see also Blau 1974, 1977; McPherson 2004; McPherson *et al.* 2001). Mark (1998, 2003) has used this observation to explain the further, much discussed observation, associated with Bourdieu (1984) in particular, that particular musical tastes tend to cluster in particular positions in 'social space'. There is no necessary or inherent connection between particular social positions and the liking for particular types of music, Mark insists (see also McPherson 2004). However, musical preferences tend to become located in specific demographic niches because, first, they pass from person to person through sociable contact and, second, relations of sociable contact tend to be status homophilic.

This argument marks a significant advance on the currently dominant Bourdieusian framework because Bourdieu is very unclear as to why particular tastes become lodged in particular regions of social space, sometimes seeming to suggest, problematically and despite insistence to the contrary, that there is a necessary 'fit' between tastes and social positions. Those low in economic capital, for example, are condemned to certain tastes on account of their proximity to 'necessity'. Furthermore, where Bourdieu tends to focus exclusively upon economic and cultural/educational inequalities in his analysis of these matters, Mark's perspective is open to the importance of divisions based upon a wide range of statuses, including age and race, both of which appear to be among the strongest predictors of taste and certainly stronger than economic and cultural 'capital' (Bennett *et al.* 2009).

Music and network formation

The direction of traffic between ties and tastes is not all one way, however. Shared tastes are often a basis upon which actors are brought into contact and, having made contact, may help to build enduring bonds between them. Scott Feld's (1981, 1982) concept of network foci addresses the first element in this process. Actors often share interests and tastes with others in their networks, he argues, not only because of mutual influence between them but also because their shared tastes and interests drew them together in the first place, to common events and time–spaces.

The jazz enthusiasts in a particular town are likely to know one another, for example, because they will attend the same clubs and events, and perhaps also hang out at the same specialist record shops. Furthermore, when they do meet the likelihood of them forming a meaningful bond is increased by the fact that they have a shared interest (jazz) to talk about and a shared identity (jazz enthusiast), both of which are foregrounded by the fact that they meet at, for example, a jazz club. In conversation each will reward the other's preference for jazz, affirming her identity as a jazz lover, exchanging information and rendering the interaction positive in a manner which incentivises further contact.

The structure of the book

As noted earlier, our understanding of networks derives from the tradition of formal social network analysis (SNA) and most of the contributors to this book draw upon the concepts, techniques and measures of this tradition. In the next chapter we offer an introduction to SNA for the uninitiated (see also Scott 2000; Wasserman and Faust 1994; Borgatti *et al.* 2012). This is intended to provide readers with sufficient background knowledge to engage fully and critically with the analyses and arguments which follow in subsequent chapters.

In Chapter 3 Nick Crossley compares the network structures of the post-punk worlds of Liverpool, Manchester and Sheffield as of 1980. The aim of the chapter is to identify both similarities across the networks, which indicate stable and perhaps necessary features of such worlds, and also differences whose various causes and effects can be explored. At a methodological level, the chapter reflects upon the possibilities for and advantages of taking a comparative approach to network and world analysis.

Moving on from post punk, in Chapter 4 Siobhan McAndrew and Martin Everett explore gender inequality within the classical music world, combining social network analysis with both qualitative analysis and a more straightforward statistical approach. Specifically they consider whether women occupy a distinctive position in the network formed by a variety of types of cooperation between composers and they consider whether women, responding to the particular obstacles and constraints they experience as women, adopt a distinctive strategy in the pursuit of musical success.

In Chapter 5 Paul Widdop examines how networks impact upon consumption. It is widely acknowledged that a shift has occurred in the cultural consumption patterns of the middle and upper classes. Where once tastes and preferences were based around rigid rules of exclusion, they are now based on an openness to a variety of cultures across both the high and popular genres (the 'omnivore thesis'). Social and educational gradients in omnivorousness have been found across Europe, Australia and North and South America: having broader tastes is associated with higher social status, social class and education, gender, youth, and geographical location. What is less understood is how an individual's position within social networks, and their social capital, affect their cultural tastes. It seems plausible that musical omnivores benefit from having a broader and more diverse social network, within which they display their cultural knowledge for social approval and to access the social resources embedded in their social networks (social capital). Using large-scale social survey data on cultural participation, Widdop tests whether this relationship between taste and network diversity and density exists. He explores whether there are well-defined omnivorous patterns in music consumption in England, whether they are socially stratified, and the effect of social capital and social network position on musical taste.

As noted above, music-making involves cooperation and coordination between multiple parties. And yet it displays very fluid forms of organisation. This combination has stimulated a vast literature focused upon situations where people are not formally bound to each other. In Chapter 6 Karim Hammou shows how SNA facilitates analysis of such situations. Drawing upon the concepts of both world and scene he explores patterns of collaboration in francophone rap music.

In Chapter 7 Susan O'Shea takes up the issue of homophily, focusing specifically upon the salience of sexual identities in the formation of networks involved in three separate Ladyfest festivals. She uses longitudinal network data on the musicians and activists associated with the festivals. In addition, she discusses the historical development of Ladyfest as a movement, the movement's core values and its musical influences. Her work also draws from ethnographic, feminist and action-research methodologies, illustrating by example how such methodologies can be integrated with SNA in the context of a mixed method approach.

Chapter 8, by Tim Edensor, Paul Hepburn and Nigel Richards, reflects upon Manchester's vibrant open mic world. It explores how the social networks of open mic participants inform the production of creativity and conviviality, and the expression of alternative values. Formal social network analysis methods are used to render visible and understandable the connections between performers and other attendees. Edensor, Hepburn and Richards examine how such connections alternatively constrain or facilitate routes to employment, collaborative music-making, leisure, and social opportunities. This chapter sees SNA methods used alongside an observational study into the ethics and etiquette of open mic culture, particularly the ways in which participants welcome newcomers, give moral support and musical advice, and encourage a wide range of musical expression without exercising judgement about style and ability. Edensor, Hepburn and Richards also consider the significance of physical geography for Manchester's open mic network, mapping the pubs that host its events, from central Manchester to suburban sites and beyond.

In Chapter 9, Roberta Comunian, Alessandra Faggian and Sarah Jewell explore the connections and dynamics linking higher education and music careers. An emerging literature on the role of higher education in the creative economy reveals that while higher education institutions develop human capital for careers after graduation, creative graduates also face great difficulties in entering the professional networks and employment opportunities of the creative sector. Popular writers and journalists have recently begun to note the increasingly elite backgrounds of those working in the arts and media, and among performing pop musicians. Drawing on statistical data on graduates and their employment after graduation, this chapter examines the factors associated with achieving a music career, and success within that career. It explores how the networks formed via selective education and training give musicians advantages in their post-university life. The statistical analysis is given additional nuance through a focused set of interviews with music graduates, those working in the music industry hailing from subjects other than music, and practitioner-teachers in higher education.

In Chapter 10, Fay Hield and Nick Crossley explore Sheffield's folk singing world. The network of participants in this world, they show, is very dense and the demographic profile of participants is quite specific, at least with respect to age and educational level. Combining network analysis with insights from Hield's earlier ethnographic work on this world, however, they are able to explore an interesting age-based partition which is integrally linked to recent innovations and developments in this local music world.

The final chapter, written by Siobhan McAndrew, Paul Widdop and Rachel Stevenson, explores the duality of musicians and groups in the British jazz world. Using John Chilton's *Who's Who of British Jazz* as their source, and exploiting the detail it affords on individual career histories and musical backgrounds, they compile a network involving some 900 musicians and representing the most central figures in British jazz from its genesis to 2003. Jazz is a fascinating case study for network analysis because band line-ups are often very fluid, with musicians playing in many bands within the same period and moving through many more over time. With information on the ties between individual performers and their ties to bands, McAndrew, Widdop and Stevenson identify the most central musicians and bands, distinct communities within the network, and assess the significance of centrality versus marginality for musical innovation and audience esteem.

References

Becker, G. (1996) *Accounting for Tastes*, Cambridge, MA, Harvard University Press.

Becker, H. (1974) Art as Collective Action, *American Sociological Review* 39(6), 767–76.

Becker, H. (1982) *Art Worlds*, Berkeley, University of California Press.

Becker, H. (2004) Jazz Places, in Bennett, A. and Peterson, R. (eds), *Music Scenes*, Nashville, TN, Vanderbilt University Press 17–30.

Bennett, A. (1999) Subcultures or Neo-Tribes, *Sociology* 33(3), 599–617.

Bennett, A. (2013) *Music, Style and Aging*, Philadelphia, PA, Temple University Press.

Bennett, A. and Hodkinson, P. (eds) (2012) *Ageing and Youth Cultures*, London, Berg.

Bennett, A. and Peterson, R. (eds) (2004) *Music Scenes*, Nashville, TN, Vanderbilt University Press.

Bennett, T., Savage, M., Silva, E., Gayo-Cal, M. and Wright, D. (2010) *Culture, Class, Distinction*, London, Routledge.

Blau, P. (1974) Parameters of Social Structure, *American Sociological Review* 39(5), 615–35.

Blau, P. (1977) A Macrosociological Theory of Social Structure, *American Journal of Sociology* 83(1), 26–54.

Blumer, H. (1969) Collective Behaviour, in McClung-Lee, A. (ed.), *Principles of Sociology*, New York, Barnes and Noble 166–222.

Borgatti, S.P., Everett, M.G. and Johnson, J. (2012) *Analysing Social Networks*, London, Sage.

Bott, E. (1957) *Family and Social Network*, London, Tavistock.

Bottero, W. and Crossley, N. (2011) Worlds, Fields and Networks, *Cultural Sociology* 5(1), 99–119.

Bourdieu, P. (1984) *Distinction*, London, Routledge.

Bourdieu, P. (1993) *The Field of Cultural Production*, Cambridge, Polity.

Clarke, J., Hall, S., Jefferson, T. and Roberts, B. (1993) Subcultures, Cultures and Class, in Hall, S. and Jefferson, T. (eds), *Resistance Through Rituals*, London, Routledge 9–79.

Coleman, J. (1988) Free Riders and Zealots: The Role of Social Networks, *Sociological Theory* 6(1), 52–7.

Coleman, J. (1990) *Foundations of Social Theory*, Cambridge, MA, Belknap Press.

Cooley, C. (1964) *Human Nature and Social Order*, New Brunswick, NJ, Transaction.

Crossley, N. (2011) *Towards Relational Sociology*, London, Routledge.

Crossley, N. (2015) *Networks of Sound, Style and Subversion: The Punk and Post-Punk Worlds of Liverpool, London, Manchester and Sheffield 1975–1980*, Manchester, Manchester University Press.

DeNora, T. (2000) *Music in Everyday Life*, Cambridge, Cambridge University Press.

Dewey, J. (1980) *Art as Experience*, New York, Perigee.

DiMaggio, P. (1987) Classification in Art, *American Sociological Review* 52(4), 440–55.

DiMaggio, P. (2011) Cultural Networks, in Scott, J. and Carrington, P. (eds), *The Sage Handbook of Social Network Analysis*, London, Sage 286–300.

Erickson, B. (1996) Culture, Class and Connections, *American Journal of Sociology* 102(1), 217–51.

Feld, S. (1981) The Focused Organisation of Social Ties, *American Journal of Sociology* 86, 1015–35.

Feld, S. (1982) Social Structural Determinants of Similarity among Associates, *American Sociological Review* 47, 797–801.

Fine, B. (2001) *Social Capital versus Social Theory*, London, Routledge.

Finnegan, R. (1989) *The Hidden Musicians*, Cambridge, Cambridge University Press.

Gilmore, S. (1987) Coordination and Convention, *Symbolic Interaction* 10(2), 209–27.

Gilmore, S. (1988) Schools of Activity and Innovation, *Sociological Quarterly* 29(2), 203–19.

Gilroy, P. (1992) *There Ain't No Black in the Union Jack*, London, Routledge.

Hebdige, D. (1988) *Subculture: The Meaning of Style*, London, Routledge.

Hesmondhalgh, D. (2005) Subcultures, Scenes or Tribes? *Journal of Youth Studies* 8(1), 21–40.

Jones, S. (1988) *Black Culture, White Youth*, London, Macmillan.

Laing, D. (1985) *One Chord Wonders*, Buckingham, Open University Press.

Lazarsfeld, P. and Merton, R. (1964) Friendship as Social Process, in Berger, M., Abel, T. and Page, C. (eds), *Freedom and Control in Modern Society*, New York, Octagon Books 18–66.

Lewis. K., Kaufman, J., Gonzalez, M., Wimmer, A. and Christakis, N. (2008) Tastes, Ties and Time, *Social Networks* 30, 330–342.

Lin, N. (2002) *Social Capital*, Cambridge, Cambridge University Press.

Lizardo, O. (2006) How Cultural Tastes Shape Personal Networks, *American Sociological Review* 71, 778–807.

Lopes, P. (2002) *The Rise of a Jazz Art World*, Cambridge, Cambridge University Press.

Mark, N. (1998) Birds of a Feather Sing Together, *Social Forces* 77(2), 453–85.

Mark, N. (2003) Culture and Competition: Homophily and Distancing Explanations for Cultural Niches, *American Sociological Review* 68(3), 319–45.

Martin, P. (2005) The Jazz Community as an Art World, *Jazz Research Journal* 2. Online, available at www.equinoxpub.com/journals/index.php/JAZZ.

Martin, P. (2006a) *Music and the Sociological Gaze*, Manchester, Manchester University Press.

Martin, P. (2006b) Musicians Worlds, *Symbolic Interaction* 29(1), 95–107.

McAndrew, S. and Everett, M. (forthcoming) Music as Collective Invention: A Social Network Analysis of Composers, *Cultural Sociology*.

McPherson, M. (2004) A Blau Space Primer, *Industrial and Corporate Change* 13(1), 263–80.

McPherson, M., Smith-Lovin, L. and Cook, J. (2001) Birds of Feather: Homophily in Social Networks, *Annual Review of Sociology* 27, 415–44.

McRobbie, A. (1991) *Feminism and Youth Culture*, London, Macmillan.

Mead, G.H. (1967) *Mind, Self and Society*, Chicago, Chicago University Press.

Merleau-Ponty, M. (1962) *The Phenomenology of Perception*, London, Routledge.

Milroy, L. (1987) *Language and Social Networks*, Oxford, Blackwell.

Savage, M. (2006) The Musical Field, *Cultural Trends* 15(2–3), 159–74.

Scott, J. (2000) *Social Network Analysis: A Handbook*, London, Sage.

Shank, B. (1994) *Dissonant Identities*, Hanover, NH, Wesleyan University Press.

Simmel, G. (1906) The Sociology of Secrecy and Secret Societies, *American Journal of Sociology* 11(4), 441–98.

Simmel, G. (1955) *Conflict and the Web of Group Affiliations*, New York, Free Press.

Small, C. (1998) *Musicking*, Middletown, CT, Wesleyan University Press.

Smith, N. (2009) Beyond the Master Narrative of Youth, in Scott, D. (ed.), *The Ashgate Research Companion to Popular Musicology*, Aldershot, Ashgate 427–48.

Smith, N. (2012) Parenthood and the Transfer of Capital in the Northern Soul Scene, in Bennett, A. and Hodkinson, P. (eds), *Ageing and Youth Cultures*, London, Berg 159–72.

Straw, W. (1991) System of Articulation, Logics of Change, *Cultural Studies* 53, 368–88.

Tarde, G. (1903) *The Laws of Imitation*, New York, Henry Holt and Company.

Wasserman, S. and Faust, K. (1994) *Social Network Analysis*, Cambridge, Cambridge University Press.

Willis, P. (1990) *Common Culture*, Boulder, CO, Westview.

2 What is social network analysis?

An introduction for music scholars

Nick Crossley, Siobhan McAndrew and
Paul Widdop

In this chapter we offer a brief introduction to the fundamental concepts and techniques of social network analysis (SNA) used by most of the contributors to this book. Our primary aim is to provide readers who are unfamiliar with SNA with the necessary background knowledge to fully engage with the book. Those who wish to go further and use SNA in their own research will need to read more widely. However, we hope that the book will inspire music and culture scholars to consider using SNA and to this end we extend our remit slightly by both discussing some of the questions that SNA allows us to address and briefly introducing some of the main software packages that network analysts typically use: e.g. UCINET,[1] Pajek,[2] PNet[3] and Siena.[4]

Readers who wish to learn further about SNA should consult one of the excellent textbooks in the area. We briefly review our preferred teaching texts at the end of the chapter.

Networks and network analysis

As we noted in the Introduction to this book, 'musicking' is collective action. It involves connection and interaction between social actors. On a very basic level, for example, individual musicians interact both with one another, with a variety of support personnel, such as promoters, managers and studio engineers, who also interact with one another, and with audiences, who again also interact with one another and with support personnel. In addition, connections exist on other levels: works borrow from other works, the organisations involved in the music industry interlock in different ways and venues, cities, festivals and countries are all linked by the flow of artists and works between them.

Standard social scientific methods of data gathering, albeit perhaps tweaked slightly, allow us to elicit data regarding these interactions, ties and flows, and we may use standard methods of data analysis when trying to make sense of these data. SNA need not be a standalone methodology. As the contributions to this book testify, many network analytic studies mix methods. However, standard techniques of data analysis, at best, focus upon individual ties and have no way of storing or analysing data concerning the structures constituted by multiple simultaneous ties. That is to say, they have no way of analysing the social networks that musicking both draws upon and creates.

A social network has two basic elements and an optional third:

1   a set of **nodes** (also sometimes called 'vertices');
2   a set (or sets) of **ties** (also sometimes called 'relations', 'connections', 'edges' or 'arcs');
3   optionally, a set of **node attributes**.

Nodes are the objects within a network which are connected to one another (or not). In the context of a particular study it is crucial to define and demarcate one's node set appropriately, in a way which is meaningful for that study and will allow one to answer one's research question. From the point of view of the analytic routines involved in SNA, however, anything might count as a node if defining it thus is meaningful in the context of the wider study. One's node set might be all of the musicians active in a particular town; all of the high-capacity venues in a country; all of the record labels represented in the UK Top 40 during 1978; all of the top charting records or bands during that year. To reiterate, anything can count as a node if defining it thus is meaningful in the context of a particular study.

Similarly, any type of connection can count as a **tie** if treating it as such is meaningful in the context of the study. In relation to bands we might link those who play on the same bill and/or those who share members. In relation to venues we might want to know about any arrangements they have for sharing resources or costs or we might be interested in the flow of bands between them (venues are linked by bands who play in them). Furthermore, it may make sense to survey multiple types of tie within the same study. Thus, within the same set of musicians we may want to know (1) who has ever played live together, (2) who has ever recorded together, (3) who socialises together outside of their music-making activity and (4) who was friends with whom before they became involved in making music. Again, SNA is very flexible in this respect but analysis is only meaningful if we focus upon a connection which we believe to be important for some reason (relating to our broader understanding of the music world in question). Knowing which musicians have played together might be meaningful, for example, if we are interested in the diffusion of particular playing styles or if we believe that who one has played with influences one's likelihood of getting further work but 'played together' isn't the right tie to focus upon in all cases.

Ties can be directed or undirected. A **directed tie** points from one actor to another and is not always reciprocated. John may admire Jane's musical ability (a tie of admiration), for example, without Jane necessarily admiring John's. She may but not necessarily. Similarly, Helen may teach or mentor Michele (a tie of teaching or mentoring) without Michele teaching or mentoring Helen. Indeed, ties such as teaching and mentoring are often asymmetrical. An **undirected tie** is reciprocal by definition and is not reducible to the attitudes or activities of one party. For example, playing in the same band: if Pete plays in the same band as

Nick then Nick plays in the same band as Pete, by definition. Playing in the same band necessarily implicates them both. Similarly, if Phil has co-written songs with Sally then Sally has co-written songs with Phil. Like playing, co-writing necessarily involves both parties.

Ties can be conceptualised in binary terms, as either existing or not but they might also be weighted and they can be weighted in either ordinal or interval terms. If we ask musicians to rate their admiration for other musicians in their node set on a scale of 0–5, for example, we will have an ordinal weighting. If we actually count how many times two musicians have played together then we have an interval weighting.

The above examples involve 'positive' ties but we may focus upon negative ties too. For example, a recent survey by the Federation of Entertainment Unions (2013) points to the existence of bullying in the music industry. This might be the basis for a social network analysis. We would look at who bullies whom. Similarly, we might track the networks of rappers who publicly diss one another in the music press or in their songs. In many cases we would do this in exactly the same way that we would study positive ties. As noted above, the analytic routines of SNA are indifferent to the nature of ties and that extends to their positivity or negativity. However, in some cases network analysts want to study negative and positive ties together, exploring issues of 'structural balance' (i.e. if my friend is in conflict with a third person does that increase the likelihood that I will have a negative tie towards that person and/or decrease the likelihood that I will have a positive tie with them?). de Nooy (2008), for example, was interested in the balance of positive and negative reviews in a network of literary author-reviewers. Special techniques exist for this type of work.

Node attributes are additional bits of information that we have about nodes. If our nodes are individual musicians, for example, then we might want information about the instrument they play, whether they play more than one, how long they have been playing, whether they are professional, semi-professional or amateur, etc. In addition, we might want to know their gender, ethnicity, age, annual income, etc. If our nodes are venues we might want to know their capacity, any admission restrictions, whether they sell alcohol, etc.

Network data are gathered, for purposes of SNA, by means of surveys. 'Survey' does not necessarily mean 'questionnaire', however. Questionnaires are only one form of survey. We might survey a set of recordings, for example, by purchasing them all and systematically noting certain of their properties. We might survey venues or bands by looking them up on the internet and getting information in this way. A survey is simply a systematic way of verifying (in this case) the existence or not of ties of a specific type between all members of a particular node set, and perhaps also certain properties of those nodes. Note, however, that it is as important to be clear about where ties do not exist as where they do.

Whole network data, graphs and matrices

Network data are typically gathered in one of three forms. Much of what we say in this chapter is relevant to all three and we distinguish them below. For sake of brevity and clarity, and following the lead of the wider literature, however, we base most of our discussion around one in particular: 'whole network' data.

To gather whole network data we identify a particular set of nodes (e.g. all of the jazz musicians gigging in a particular town during 2013, or every UK music festival in the UK in 2005 with a capacity greater than 10,000 people); we decide upon the type or types of tie that we are interested in; and we conduct a census survey[5] of ties between every possible pairing of nodes in the set. If we have 10 nodes in our set and we exclude reflexive ties[6] that will mean checking for the existence or not of either 90 directed ties[7] or 45 undirected ties.[8]

Whole network data are stored in adjacency matrices such as the (very small) matrix represented in Table 2.1. Note that the top row and left-hand column of the matrix each list the same nodes, in the same order. Every node has both a row and a column and their row intersects both with their own column (an inter-section which runs along the diagonal of the matrix, from the top left to the bottom right) and with the columns of every other node: e.g. John's row inter-sects with his own column, with Jane's column, Mike's, Lucy's, etc. Con-sequently, each node's column is intersected both by its own row and the rows of every other node. These intersections are where we record the relations between nodes. Thus, John's relation to Frank is recorded where his row inter-sects Frank's column.

In Table 2.1 ties are binary. They either exist or they do not. We record this by way of 1s and 0s. If two nodes are tied in the way we are interested in then we put a 1 at their intersection, if not we put a 0. If ties were weighted then the numbers in the matrix would reflect the weighting and might have a much wider range. If John has recorded with Helen on seven occasions, for example, and that is the tie we are interested in, then we would put a 7 at the intersections of their rows and columns.

If ties are undirected then each is recorded twice in the matrix. The tie between John and Jake in Table 2.1 is recorded both in the cell where John's row intersects with Jake's column, for example, and the cell where Jake's row

Table 2.1 A hypothetical adjacency matrix (undirected and binary data)

	John	Jane	Mike	Lucy	Jake	Frank	Helen
John	0	1	0	0	1	1	0
Jane	1	0	0	0	1	0	0
Mike	0	0	0	0	1	1	0
Lucy	0	0	0	0	1	0	1
Jake	1	1	1	1	0	1	1
Frank	1	0	1	0	1	0	1
Helen	0	0	0	1	1	1	0

intersects with John's column. This double entry system allows us to capture unreciprocated ties in directed data and to record their direction. If John likes Jake's playing but Jake does not like John's (perhaps he has never heard it), for example, then we would put a 1 where John's row meets Jake's column but a 0 where Jake's row meets John's column.

In many cases it is not meaningful to ask whether a node has a tie to itself (a 'reflexive tie') and for this reason SNA software generally[9] ignores the value in the diagonal that runs from the top left of the matrix (where John's row intersects his column) to the bottom right (where Helen's row intersects her column), unless instructed otherwise. If we are interested in relations of collaboration, for example, we want to ignore the diagonal because it makes no sense to ask if a person collaborates with their self. Reflexive ties might be meaningful, however, and can be included. If our tie was 'plays music written by', for example, then reflexive ties would be meaningful because some musicians only play music written by other people, some only play music which they have written themselves and others do a bit of both.

Software packages typically allow data to be input in a matrix format such as Table 2.1. Many (including UCINET) have their own spreadsheet editor interfaces to facilitate this and a number (again including UCINET) accept Excel spreadsheets. Filling out a spreadsheet for an adjacency matrix can be a lengthy process, however, especially if node sets are big. For this reason a number of easier data entry formats are possible in most cases (which the software will then use to construct an adjacency matrix).

Adjacency matrices record network data in a systematic way which facilitates a range of analytic routines (see below). They are not very visually appealing, however, and even quite strong patterns are difficult spot. For this reason we sometimes visualise networks as graphs like that in Figure 2.1. At its simplest a graph will represent nodes as small shapes (e.g. squares), all of the same size and colour, connected by lines where they enjoy a tie. We have decided to be a little more fancy in Figure 2.1, however. We have coloured nodes according to their gender (grey = males, black = female); we have given them different shapes to represent the instrument which they play (square = guitar, up-facing triangle = fiddle, and circle = bass); and we have sized them in accordance with their annual income (bigger node = higher income). Note that Jake, the male fiddler, both earns the most and has the most connections (he is connected to everyone else). Perhaps there is a correlation between number of connections and size of income? Perhaps number of connections is affected by gender? These are questions we might ask and address using SNA if this network was a bit bigger and based on real data.

We refer to such diagrams as 'graphs' because they have the form of what mathematicians who work in 'graph theory' refer to as 'graphs' (they are sometimes called network diagrams too, however, and also sociograms). Graph theory is a branch of mathematics devoted to the analysis of structures such as that represented in Figure 2.1. and the fundamentals of SNA derive from cross-fertilisation between social science and graph theory.

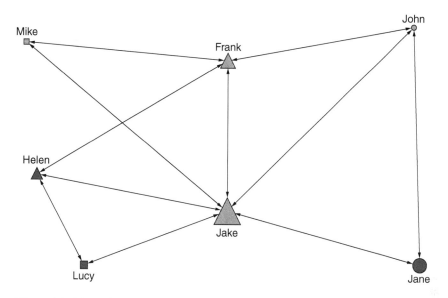

Figure 2.1 A hypothetical network graph (based on the data in Table 2.1 and additional node attribute data).

This explains some of the terminology of SNA. In addition to graphs, for example, the reference to 'adjacency' in 'adjacency matrix' derives from graph theory (nodes which are connected are said to be 'adjacent') and we sometimes call nodes 'vertices' and ties either 'edges' or (where directed) 'arcs' (many people use 'edges' whether ties are directed or not). This might be confusing at first but there aren't many terms to learn and they are quickly picked up.

The direction of an edge is visualised on a graph by way of an arrow head. Technically the edges in Figure 2.1 are undirected (or at least they are perfectly symmetrical) and the heads therefore serve no function. Ordinarily we would remove them as they make the graph busier than it needs to be and therefore more difficult to understand. We have left them on, however, for illustrative purposes.

Graph theory operates with a different conception of space to the one that we ordinarily use when visualising data in, for example, scatterplots. In a scatterplot space is defined by horizontal (x) and vertical (y) axes. The 'position' of a point refers to its location along each of these axes, the distance between points is the difference between their 'score' for each axis and is clear from their location on the plot, and those points found towards the middle of the plot are the most central. In graph theory and therefore in SNA, by contrast, space is mapped entirely in connections. The position of a node refers to its pattern of connections and the proximity of any two nodes is measured by reference to the length of the **path** (see below) connecting them. Two nodes which are directly connected are closer to one another than two which are only indirectly connected via a third party, for example, irrespective of where they are located in the plot. Furthermore, the distance between two nodes which have no path connecting them is undefined and indefinable, irrespective of their co-location within the same plot. How close to the top or bottom of a plot a node lies, how far to the right or left, how proximate to this or that other node has no meaning in graph theory and therefore no meaning in SNA.

At least that is the theory. In practice the software packages which network analysts use to draw graphs employ algorithms which locate nodes on the basis of certain principles – usually they are located close to those with which they share a similar profile of ties, using multidimensional scaling or a similar method. However, there are different algorithms, which give different layouts. Each can only approximately locate nodes according to its chosen principle. And analysts will often manually alter layouts in any case, either for aesthetic purposes or to illustrate a point which they wish to make (they are perfectly entitled to do this and the software packages make it very easy to do).

This must be taken into account when we visually inspect graphs. It is easy to be misled, particularly when first starting out. Graphs give us an instant impression of certain gross properties of a network: e.g. how 'dense' (see below) it is, whether it includes very well-connected nodes (**'hubs'**) or completely unconnected nodes (**'isolates'**), whether it includes clusters of nodes with apparently distinct patterns of connection, etc. This can be useful for purposes of preliminary analysis and graphs are often great means for demonstrating findings in both written texts and verbal presentations. However, there are many properties of networks that can't usually be seen in a graph and even those which we think that we can see may be more apparent than real. For both reasons we need more precise ways of analysing the properties of networks.

Levels of analysis

Properties of networks can be identified at five basic levels: (1) the whole network; (2) sub-sets of nodes; (3) individual nodes; (4) the dyad; (5) the triad. The latter two levels are particularly important in statistical approaches to SNA and we deal with them separately in a section devoted to that. Here we will briefly summarise the first three.

Properties of whole networks

These include:

1   **Order.** This is the number of nodes in the network.
2   **Density.** This is the number of ties in the network, expressed as a proportion of the total number of ties that are possible. As noted earlier, for example, a directed network with 10 nodes (where reflexive ties are discounted), potentially involves 90 ties. If we find evidence of 35, therefore, we have a density of $35/90 = 0.39$. If the same network is undirected then there are

potentially 45 ties. To measure the density we would divide the actual number of ties in the network by 45.

3   **Paths** and **path lengths.** A path is a chain of connections which links two nodes. Path lengths are measured by the number of ties (referred to as 'degrees') they involve. In Figure 2.2, which is taken from Crossley's (2015) work on the punk and post-punk worlds of Liverpool, London, Manchester and Sheffield, for example, Don Letts (bottom right) has no direct tie to Malcolm McLaren. He is linked to Andy Czezowski, however, who has a direct tie to McLaren. Letts is therefore linked to McLaren by a path of two degrees (Letts's link to Czezowski is one degree, Czezowski's to McLaren is the second). Furthermore, though neither Letts nor Czezowski has a direct tie to Johnny Rotten, McLaren does, putting Letts at a distance of three degrees from Rotten (Letts > Czezowsky > McLaren > Rotten) and Czezowsky at two degrees. Letts may have had no idea of the existence of Rotten at this point in time but if Rotten were to catch the flu he would be in danger of catching it because there is a path between them along which the virus could spread. More relevantly, if Rotten is fronting a great band or writes a great song, Letts is likely to hear about it.

4   **Geodesic distance.** There are often several possible paths between two nodes, of differing lengths. Although McLaren and Rotten are directly tied, for example, we could also trace various long and circuitous paths between them if we were so inclined. Usually it is the shortest path between two nodes that we are interested in and we call the length of this path, measured in degrees, the geodesic distance. The geodesic distance between McLaren and Rotten is one degree because they are directly connected. The geodesic distance between Letts and McLaren is two degrees.

5   **Components.** A component is a sub-set of nodes each of whom is at least indirectly connected to each of the others by a path. In Figure 2.2 there are five components. Three of these (to the top left of the graph) comprise individual nodes who have no connection to anybody else in the node set (isolates). One comprises the four founder members of The Vibrators, who were soon to come under the influence of punk but hadn't yet as they had no connection to any punks. Finally there is a big component comprising everybody else.

6   **Average geodesic distance.** If we add up the geodesic distances separating every possible pair of actors in the network and divide by the number of pairs we get the average distance, which gives us a good idea of how far information and new ideas (and flu viruses) typically have to travel in the network before everyone has access to them. In the network in Figure 2.2 a number of path lengths are 'undefined' because there are a number of components and, by definition, there is no path between them. The network involves 'structural holes', as Ronald Burt (1992) calls them (Burt believes that nodes can profit greatly where they manage to bridge such holes). Average geodesic distances only make sense where all nodes are connected by a path. However, we could perhaps measure average geodesic distances

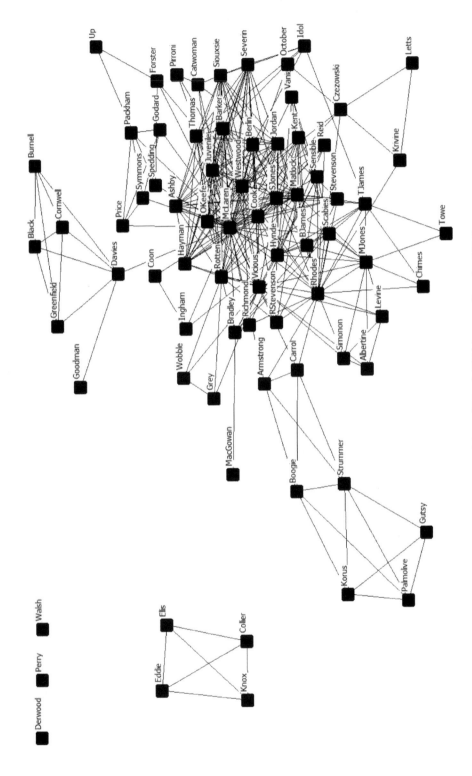

Figure 2.2 The key players in London's emerging punk world, as of March 1976 (source: Crossley 2014).

within each of our components or at least within each of the two which involve more than two nodes. This would be a meaningful and might be a useful thing to do if we were particularly interested in a component or in the activities of its members.

7 **Diameter.** Alternatively, we sometimes measure the width of the network by taking the longest of its geodesic distances. This is called the diameter of a network.

Properties of sub-networks

Sub-sets of nodes are typically distinguished in one of two ways:

• **endogenously**, by reference to distinctive patterns of connection: e.g. they form a component or they form a subset of nodes all of whose members are tied to each of the others (a '**clique**'). Even if not directly connected to one another, moreover, nodes may be tied to many of the same others ('**alters**'). Bands may be connected to the same manager, promoters and audiences, for example, even if they are not connected to one another, and this common pattern of ties may be significant. Where two nodes are tied to exactly the same alters, irrespective of any contact between them, we say that they are **structurally equivalent**. In practice it is very uncommon for two nodes to share exactly the same alters but some may have a similar profile of ties (**approximate structural equivalence**) which we can capture using one of various clustering algorithms);

• **exogenously**, by reference to attributes such as gender or ethnicity.

Endogenously defined subgroups are often of interest because their existence may tell us about conflicts and power structures in a network, or because we might expect different sub-groups to behave differently, either because their members are subject to different influences within the network or because their position in the network enables/constrains them in different ways and to a different extent. If we are specifically interested in structural equivalence (or one of a number of other forms of equivalence which are defined in the literature) then we would ordinarily pursue this through a branch of analysis referred to as **blockmodelling**.

To blockmodel a network we use a form of cluster analysis to partition its node set into blocks, blocking nodes whose position in the network is equivalent (according to one of the recognised definitions of equivalence). We then use these blocks as nodes in a reduced representation of the network. Blocks are linked to one another on the basis of the ties between the original nodes clustered within them. An analyst may link two blocks where one each of their constituent nodes is tied. Often, however, the threshold for regarding blocks as tied is higher and rests upon a density value; that is, the analyst requires that a certain proportion of all possible ties between the constituent nodes of their respective blocks is reached before deeming the blocks themselves tied. Blockmodelling can be a useful way of discovering underlying structural patterns (of connection) in a network which are difficult to see when individual nodes are the focus. Its usefulness depends, however, upon the extent to which such underlying structures are there to be discovered.

Another very common form of sub-group analysis centres upon the **core–periphery structure**; that is, a common pattern in networks in which we find a subset of nodes who are very densely tied to one another (**the core**) compared to the rest (**the periphery**). Ties within the periphery are relatively sparse and so too are ties between core and periphery. In the classic core–periphery structure, however, the periphery nodes are better connected to the core than they are to one another. In a **core–periphery analysis** we try out different ways of partitioning our nodes into two sets (core and periphery) in an effort to find the partition which best approximates this description (UCINET has an algorithm for this). This generates a density matrix, akin to Table 2.2, which we can use to judge whether our partition has the properties of a core–periphery structure.

For example, Table 2.2 tells us that the best fit to a core–periphery structure that we can get by partitioning the network illustrated in Figure 2.2 involves a core of 18 members whose density of ties to one another is 0.89 (89 per cent of all ties between them are realised) compared to only 0.06 within the periphery and 0.09 between core and periphery. This is a clear core–periphery structure.

The next step of our analysis, were we doing this for real, might be to: (1) look at who is in the core; (2) reflect upon the likely impact of a core–periphery divide upon actors situated either side of it and upon the network as a whole; (3) seek out the mechanisms which have allowed this structure to form; (4) consider whether core membership is associated with any node attributes and, if so, explore the significance of this: e.g. are men disproportionately represented within the core? If so why? And with what consequence?

This brings us to exogenously defined subgroups. They are often interesting precisely because they may enjoy more or less advantaged positions in the network. In addition, in many cases shared attributes or identities increase the likelihood of connection between nodes, a phenomenon termed 'homophily' (Lazarsfeld and Merton 1964; McPherson *et al.* 2001), although there are obvious exceptions, such as gender in heterosexual sexual relations (which are heterophilic). Various tests can be used to ascertain whether specific node attributes impact upon network position and/or whether ties within a network are homo/heterophilic.

Table 2.2 Core–periphery density matrix (derived from the network in Figure 2.2)

	Core	Periphery
Core (*n*=18)	0.89	0.09
Periphery (*n*=57)	0.09	0.06

Properties of nodes

Key examples of node level properties are the various types of **centrality**. Nodes may be more or less central than one another and, to develop the above point, nodes which share particular attributes (e.g. females) may be more less central on average than their counterparts. There are many ways of measuring a node's centrality within a network but the four main ones are:

1 **Degree.** A node's degree is the number of ties it has within a network. In Figure 2.1, for example, Jake has the highest degree (=6). He is the most degree central node in the network. Frank, John and Helen each have a degree of 3, and the three others each have a degree of 2. Typically we are only interested in the most and/or least degree central actors. In a big network we may calculate the mean degree and focus only upon actors who are, for example, one or more standard deviations above (or below) it.

2 **Eigenvector.** Sometimes being connected to someone who has a high degree is as beneficial or more beneficial than having a high degree oneself. Eigenvector centrality captures this. It is a measure of the extent to which a node is connected to others who have a high degree.

3 **Closeness.** A node's closeness is the sum of the path lengths connecting it to every other node in the network, normalised and inverted so that higher scores indicate shorter distances. Like average path length, this measure only fully makes sense in relation to components, and as with degree (and betweenness) we are usually interested in rank orderings, particularly the highest and lowest scoring nodes.

4 **Betweenness.** This is a measure of how often a node falls along the shortest path connecting two other nodes, such that they might 'broker' between these parties. Nodes which bridge 'structural holes', as defined above, will typically have a very high betweenness because they are the link-point between all nodes on either side of the hole.

   A high centrality in any of these forms can equate to a high level of constraint by the network and may drain a node's resources – having a lot of friends can be hard work – but it may also bestow considerable advantage and opportunity. Central nodes are usually in a better position to mobilise the network to their advantage and more central actors, by whatever definition, are often regarded as more important and influential by network analysts (although this will depend upon the type of tie defining the network).

5 **Ego-net density.** Though not a measure of centrality, ego-net density is also sometimes a useful node level measure. We calculate it by isolating, for each node, the other nodes to which they are connected and the proportion of the potential number of ties between these others which are actually present. If Phil has five contacts in an undirected network, for example, there are a possible ten ties between them. If we find that, in fact, there are seven ties between them then Phil has an ego-net density of 0.7. A high ego-net density tends to go hand in hand with a low betweenness. It can indicate

that a node is highly constrained in the network: most of the others to whom it is connected are connected to one another, affording the node little opportunity for managing the flow of information about herself within the network (a state of affairs which Goffman (1961) found to be very distressing for the inmates of total institutions) or for playing their contacts off against one another. On the other hand, however, social support may be stronger and the node may benefit both from the solidarity of a close-knit group and from the control that is exercised over their alters. If my friends are friends with one another then I have an incentive to be cooperative and prove trustworthy in my dealings with them (doing otherwise would invite sanctions from all of my friends and give me a bad reputation, which would be an impediment in my future interactions with them) but they have the same incentive and the effect of that is beneficial for me. I have friends whom I know I can rely upon and trust, and this enables me to act in ways I might not dare in different circumstances.

Average node level properties as whole network properties

Mean averages of node level measures are sometimes used as whole network measures and **average degree** and **average ego-net density** (also sometimes referred to as the **clustering co-efficient** or, when it is weighted by degree, **weighted clustering co-efficient**) in particular are sometimes used as correctives to (whole network) density. The density of a network tends to be sensitive to the number of nodes in it, at least if type of tie is held constant. A participant in a music world comprising 50 nodes might be expected to have a meaningful tie with a high proportion of them, for example, but a participant in a music world comprising several thousand could not. Consequently, density will be lower in the world with the larger order. This reflects something real about the network but it might be misleading. We might imagine that nobody really knows anybody else in the bigger network, for example, and that everybody is really well connected in the small world, when in fact average degree is the same in both – a fact we will only know if we measure average degree. Similarly, we might interpret low (whole) network density to mean that that the network lacks the cohesion which would facilitate collective action when most nodes are actually embedded in quite dense clusters at the local level – a state of affairs which the clustering co-efficient would pick up.

Basic SNA software packages

The two main basic SNA software packages, UCINET and Pajek, each facilitate the various forms of analysis outlined above, and much else besides. Both are very easy to use, relying upon dropdown menus and a user-friendly interface. Pajek is free to download. There is a nominal charge for UCINET but a free trial period of several months and an online advice and troubleshooting service. Both packages come with archived data from celebrated studies to allow beginners who have no data of their own to practise and each has a textbook, written by the software authors, which seeks to introduce SNA in a hands-on way, by using it (Borgatti *et al.* 2012; de Nooy *et al.* 2005).

Dyads, triads, homophily and statistical models

The dyadic level of analysis is seldom focused upon in isolation from the triadic level these days. However, it was an important first step in early attempts to statistically model networks. Statisticians asked whether ties from one node to another (i to j), in a directed network, were more likely when there was already a tie moving in the other direction (from j to i). Of course this will depend upon the type of tie defining the network: if j likes i this will motivate him to do things to make her like him, which will probably increase the likelihood that she will like him (unless he is a pest); if j is bullying i, however, then it is very unlikely that i will be bullying j. The key point, however, is that we are beginning to think about the probability of ties between i and j and therefore moving from description of networks to the statistical modelling of them.

A dyad in a binary, undirected network can only be in one of two states. Either the nodes are connected or they are not. In a directed network that increases to four possible states, although two of those states are **isomorphic**, so that, if we are not interested in **node labels**, we would say that there are three states:

1   Neither node sends a tie to the other.
2   Both nodes send a tie to the other.
3   One node send a tie to the other but this is not reciprocated.

3 states becomes 4 if we are specifically interested in which node sends a tie to which and therefore distinguish between a state in which i sends an unreciprocated tie to j and a state in which j sends a unreciprocated tie to i. For most (statistical) purposes, however, we are not.

If, as suggested above, there is a tendency towards reciprocation in directed networks then we would expect both state 1 and state 2 to occur more often in real world networks than they would purely by chance (in networks with the same density but whose ties are randomly assigned) and we would expect state 3 to occur less often. Using this thought as our guide we can begin to think about modelling ties statistically and also about testing hypotheses regarding reciprocation.

The next step from dyadic analysis, within statistical circles, was triadic analysis; that is, analysis of all possible states of three nodes in the network. In an undirected network there are four possible states (excluding isomorphisms):

1   no ties;
2   one tie;
3   two ties;
4   three ties.

If we allow for direction there are 64 states but these boil down to 16 when we remove isomorphisms. Most software packages have a 'triad census' function which counts the number and proportion of all possible triads within the network which fall into each of the 16 possibilities. Again the point is usually to identify configurations which occur significantly more often than would be predicted by chance. Reciprocation will be part of this picture but a key addition at the triadic level is **transitivity**. In the simplest (undirected) case this means that if i has a tie to j and j has a tie to k then i is more likely to have a tie to k too: in colloquial terms, and focusing upon friendship for sake of convenience, we are more likely to be connected to our friends' friends than to alters who are unconnected to anybody else that we know because our friends typically introduce us to their other friends.

It is not only factors endogenous to network structure which affect the probability of ties. Exogenous factors may be important too, not least **homophily**. As noted above, 'homophily' refers to the tendency for nodes to form ties disproportionately with others who share a salient attribute with them. Focusing upon human nodes, Lazarsfeld and Merton (1964) break this down into **status homophily**, where nodes link disproportionately to alters with whom they share a social status (e.g. gender, ethnicity, occupational class), and **value homophily**, where they link disproportionately to alters with whom they share values, attitudes or tastes. In relation to music this might mean linking to others who like the same type of music or musical events (e.g. small versus big gigs). Not all salient similarities are categorical. In status terms, for example, we might gravitate towards others who are of a similar age to us or who have a similar income.

What counts as a 'salient similarity' may often be a difficult question to answer. If it can be answered, however, and the necessary data are available, then several methods exist within SNA for exploring and testing hypotheses regarding homophily. As with the abovementioned approaches to reciprocity and transitivity, these tests generally compare an existing network, believed to betray a homophilic bias, against what might be expected by chance in a non-biased situation, looking for significant levels of difference between the two.

Much of the statistical work referred to here and more besides can be implemented in basic SNA software packages such UCINET and Pajek. It is important that they are implemented in these packages because network data deviate from the assumptions of many standard statistical methods and therefore must be analysed with techniques which have been modified to accommodate their specificity.[10] The routines in standard statistical packages, such as SPSS, are not appropriate for network data in many cases. However, using the corrected routines in dedicated network analysis packages it is possible to run a variety of the most common statistical procedures on network data. For example, one may wish to compare centrality scores against gender using a t-test or across various ethnicities using ANOVA. One may wish to explore correlations between different types of tie within a network and/or build regression models which explain the structure of a network at any given point in time.

Statistical thinking within network analysis has developed hugely in recent years, however, and a new branch of SNA has emerged centred upon 'Exponential Random Graph Models' (ERGMs). The details of these models go beyond our remit here (Lusher *et al.* 2013). Suffice it to say, however, that they build upon the considerations regarding reciprocity, transitivity and homophily referred to above, in an attempt to model the factors, both endogenous and exogenous to network structure, which increase (or decrease) the likelihood of a tie. One of the main software packages for ERGMs is P-Net, which is free to download and comes with a clear manual and even an idiot's guide! (Harrigan n.d; see also Lusher *et al.* 2013).

Network dynamics

Networks are not usually static structures. They are constantly in process. New ties are formed, established ties are sometimes broken; some nodes increase in significance, others decrease; new nodes enter a network and others leave. We can use many of the techniques and measures outlined above, in conjunction with more narrative-focused methods, to explore and explain such changes. Figure 2.2, discussed above, for example, is one of six snapshots which Crossley (2015) uses to analyse the evolution of the London punk network between January 1975 and December 1976. Using various of the measures discussed above he charts changes in the network over this two-year period and, using standard archive-focused methods of historical sociology, he situates these changes within an explanatory narrative. Network measures and changes in them are used to raise questions which a more conventional approach to historical sociology then seeks to answer and vice versa.

Change in networks has also been a key focus within the abovementioned statistical branch of SNA, however, and a number of sophisticated methods of and software packages for modelling change in networks now exist. The best known and most widely used of these is SIENA (Simulation Investigation for Empirical Network Analysis), a free-to-download package which runs within the R environment. It is not possible to summarise the workings of SIENA within this brief overview of SNA. Suffice it to say, however, that it allows one to model change in both network ties/structure and node attributes, and allows for the fact that each may causally affect the other. That is to say, nodes may change certain of their attributes (e.g. their tastes) as an effect of **social influence** within relationships but they may also choose new partners and reject old ones in a process of **selection**, on the basis of their attributes: e.g. forming new ties with alters who share a salient attribute and breaking ties with others who do not. Moreover, attributes can be either fixed (e.g. race) or potentially changeable (e.g. musical likes).

Other types of network data

Our focus hitherto has been upon 'whole network' data. Other types of network data exist, however. In what follows we will briefly outline two of them: ego-net data and two-mode data. Much of what we have said above applies to these other types of data but there are differences and we will spell these out as far as we can in the space available.

Ego-nets

An ego-net is a network centred upon a particular node (ego). It includes that node, all nodes tied to that node ('**alters**') in the way specified by the researcher and all ties which exist between alters. Optionally it may also include attribute data on both ego and alters.

Defined in this way, a whole network is comprised of ego-nets (each of its constitutive nodes has or is an ego-net) and we can extract individual ego-nets from a whole net. In Figure 2.3, for example, we have extracted the ego-net of Billy Idol from the punk network represented in Figure 2.2. It follows that, at a purely technical, mathematical level we can do everything that we would do in an ego-net analysis in the context of a whole network study, to the ego-nets which comprise our whole network. Indeed, we have already introduced a number of ego-net measures in our discussion of whole networks. We have discussed ego-net density, for example, and the concept of degree centrality which we discussed earlier is effectively a measure of ego-net size. There are many other measures for ego-nets (see Burt 1992) but all can be implemented on the ego-nets which comprise a whole network.

However, ego-net data is not only gathered in the context of a whole network. We might gather ego-net data *instead* of whole network data. To do so we would still identify the node set or population of interest to us but rather than attempting a census of all nodes in that population we would take a sample, using one of

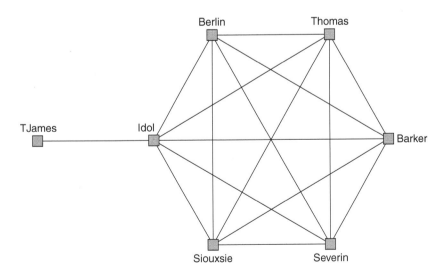

Figure 2.3 Billy Idol's ego-net (extracted from the network in Figure 2.2).

the recognised sampling strategies used in standard survey or qualitative research. This would not allow us to reconstruct the whole network, as we would have no information regarding the ties or attributes of the majority of nodes, but if our sample was representative we could infer back from the sample to the wider population as happens in sample surveys more generally.

We might conduct a random sample survey of all musicians registered with the Musicians Union, for example, asking them about the other musicians with whom they have collaborated in the last two years. If we also ask them about collaboration between their alters (which of their alters have collaborated in the past two years?) then we have ego-net data. Alternatively, if we were interested in the consumption of music we might gather a random sample of a whole national population, asking people both about their ties and about their musical tastes and consumption.

It is increasingly common for ego-net or related questions to be asked on big national surveys as the importance of social networks has become more obvious. Often these bigger surveys do not ask about ties between the alters who egos nominate when filling out the survey, and in this respect they fall short of what many network analysts would regard as ego-net data. However, they often elicit data on the size of ego-nets and on composition. It is common, for example, to use 'position generators' (which ask respondents whether they know anybody in any of a range of occupational and other positions) or 'resource generators' (which ask who, if anybody, they could turn to in order to access particular resources) to get a sense of who people have in their ego-nets and how 'well connected', in this sense, they are. Similarly, they may be asked to indicate the gender, race, age, etc. of their alters, allowing the researcher to test for status homophily.

There are three advantages to this type of ego-net research. First, it affords a means of analysing big networks. If we are interested in a relatively small population of actors, such as participants in a local music world or orchestra, then it is feasible for us to conduct a census survey of our node set and we can do whole network analysis. If we are interested in bigger populations, however, then a census survey will not be possible, ruling out whole network analysis. Ego-net analysis is still possible, however, because it only requires that we sample the population that is of interest to us.

Second, where it has been gathered using one of the sampling strategies more ordinarily used in survey research, ego-net data meets the assumptions of standard techniques of statistical analysis and modelling. This means both that these techniques can be employed, where desirable, and that ego-net research can be bolted on to projects which have a wider and more varied agenda. Often networks are one of a number of factors of interest to researchers, and research-ers want to integrate their network focus, at the level of both data gathering and data analysis, with a focus upon other issues. This is far easier with ego-net research than whole network research, at least if the researcher's other priorities require a sample survey, because ego-net research meets the assumptions of and 'fits' with a standard sample survey methodology (as noted above, whole network data violates the assumptions of standard statistical approaches). Having said that, a whole network study often fits nicely with a historical or ethnographic case study approach, so the decision about what sort of network data to gather (whole network or ego-net) should take into account the wider data gathering strategy of the researcher (in addition to the object of study).

The final advantage of ego-net research relates to what Simmel (1955) calls 'intersecting social circles' and what White (2008) calls network domains or 'net doms'. Both writers observe that in modern societies most people interact and form ties across a number of distinct 'social circles' or 'domains' whose membership, with the exception of them, does not overlap. For example, an amateur musician will be active in a specific music world but they will also probably have a family, neighbours who they are friendly with, a circle of old friends from school, friends from work, etc. They are a point of intersection between these different worlds but they are most likely the only point of intersection in many cases. Their fellow musicians won't know their work colleagues and neither will know their family members. These intersecting circles are much easier to tap into via ego-net research because the individual is the focus of the research and they may nominate alters from each of the social worlds in which they are engaged if we ask them. Whole network research, by contrast, tends to define its node population by reference to a single world and must do so to remain manageable.

In Crossley's aforementioned work on punk, for example, all nodes were key participants in London's emerging punk world (or the post-punk worlds of Liverpool, Manchester and Sheffield) and this is reflected in the ego-nets that we can abstract from his whole networks. We assume, for example, that the six alters identified in Billy Idol's ego-net above (Figure 2.3) are only a fraction of the individuals with whom he had regular contact. The six represent the subset of his ego-net that were key participants in the punk world but we assume that he had a mum and dad, friends from school, friends from university (he was a student living outside London during the very early months of punk's emergence), etc. These other ties may not be relevant and for the sake of his (whole network) research Crossley had to assume that they were not, bracketing them out, but they may have been. It is perfectly conceivable, for example, that Idol's contacts from outside the punk world fed him ideas which he used within it. An ego-net approach, involving an interview with Idol, might have allowed Crossley to explore this.

However, ego-nets can be similarly misleading and involve a considerable loss of information with respect to the structure of any particular world in which an individual may be involved. Looking at Billy Idol's ego-net, for example, we would be tempted to conclude that he is a bridge between Tony James (to the left) and five others to the right. Adding a little context, namely that James was involved in London SS, who were one of the key bands in the emerging London punk world, and that the five others were the nucleus of the Bromley Contingent, who were central punk 'faces', we might imagine that this bridging position put Idol in a very strong position. He could broker between two key early punk constituencies, passing ideas between them and profiting from doing so. He could appropriate the innovations of one constituency and impress the other constituency with them, claiming them as his own. And he would have access to information, from one, that was not otherwise available to the other, which he could trade for status or favours. However, we do not need to add very much more of the network to see that this picture is misleading.

If we combine James's ego-net with Idol's, including all ties between their alters (Figure 2.4), we see that both James and other members of his ego-net already have access to the Bromley Contingent (and vice versa) via Steve Jones and Glen Matlock (both of The Sex Pistols). In addition, Jones and Matlock are better connected on James's side of the network. In other words, Idol's position is not nearly as advantageous as his ego-net might suggest. The picture would, of course, change further if we were to add the ego-nets of Jones, Matlock or any of the other alters in Figure 2.4.

Furthermore, we glean little about the structure of the punk world overall from Idol's ego-net. His network position could not be said to be in any way representative. If we are interested in the overall structure of a world then there is no substitute for whole network analysis.

Two-mode data

Two-mode data involves two different types of node (two modes) and relations across them. For example, our two types of node might be (1) bands and (2) venues, and our tie might be 'has played at'; that is, for each band within our node set we know which of the venues in our node set it has played at within a specified period of time.

Note that the ties we are focused on can only exist between a band and a venue, not between bands or between venues. If we had additional information about links between bands and/or between venues and we wished to use that too then we would have multi-level networks and would need to consider a strategy for analysing them but that is a step too far for our purposes (Wang *et al.* 2013). We will assume that we are only dealing with ties which connect one type of node (e.g. a band) to another type (e.g. a venue).

There are two reasons why we might gather this type of data. First, musicking involving lots of types of entities (e.g. human beings, studios, venues, festivals, gigs, record labels, recordings, etc.) and we might be interested in relations across them. Second, two-mode data is often easier to get hold of and for historical work may be the only data we can access. It would be very difficult to track down every high profile DJ in the north-west of England and interview them to find out about their friendships and collaborations with other DJs, for example. We might more easily identify the clubs at which such DJs typically play, access information on who actually has played there in a given period, and construct an **incidence matrix**[11] linking DJs to clubs on this basis. As with a single-mode adjacency matrix we may visualise this data in the form of a graph (see Figure 2.5).

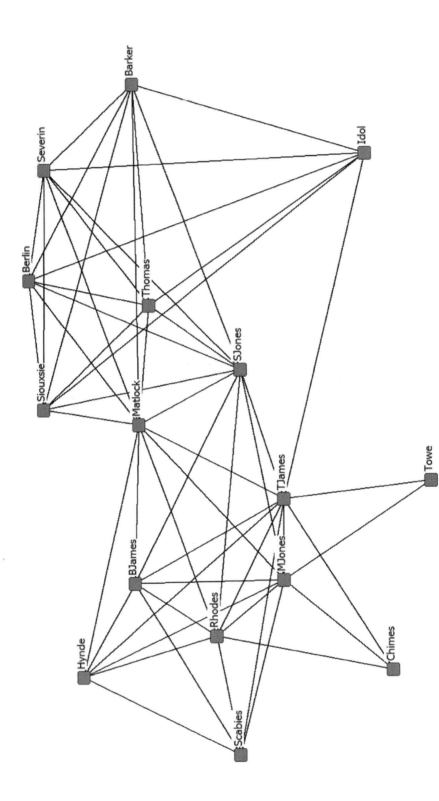

Figure 2.4 Billy Idol's ego-net merged with Tony James's (extracted from Figure 2.2).

	Frank's	Blitz	CashCow	S-Cool	Wasted	Glitterball
DJ Hot	1	0	1	0	1	0
MC Sexy	0	0	1	0	1	1
DJ Phat	0	1	0	0	1	0
DJ PJ	1	0	0	1	1	0

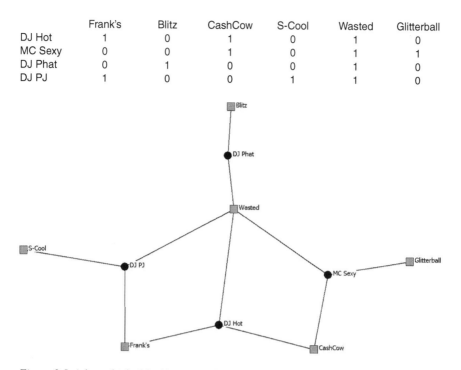

Figure 2.5 A hypothetical incidence matrix and two-mode graph: DJs and clubs.

In recent years a number of 'two-mode versions' of the whole network measures introduced above have been devised: e.g. two-mode density and two-mode degree centrality (these are available in UCINET). It is very common when analysing two-mode networks, however, to decompose or '**affiliate**' them into two single-mode networks (UCINET and Pajek each have algorithms which do this). What this means, in practice, to use our above example, is that we would create a network of DJs who were deemed to be tied when and if they had played at the same club, and a network of clubs, any two of which would be tied if the same DJ had played at both. In each case the adjacency matrix created would be weighted. A pair of DJs who had played at four of the same clubs, for example, would have a tie strength of 4. We might work with this data as weighted or convert it back to binary format on the basis of a threshold value: e.g. any ties stronger that 3 count as present, any equal to or less than 3 count as absent.

Having affiliated our two-mode network we may then analyse one or both of the single-mode networks this affords us. Indeed some researchers only gather two-mode data as an indirect way of getting the single-mode data that they are interested in. This is fine in many cases but we must exercise some caution.

The sociological logic behind the procedure is spelled out in an important paper by Breiger (1974). Briefly, and focusing upon social actors and places (or events) as his modes, he notes that actors who hang out at the same places or take part in the same events are likely to meet and form ties as a consequence of this (see also Feld 1981, 1982). Their common participation in an event is a proxy measure for their being tied in some way and this is especially so if they co-participate in a number of events. Similarly, spaces and/or events are linked by actors who move between them because those actors effectively transfer ideas, information and other such things between them. The culture at two clubs may be very similar, for example, because the bands who play in them and the audience who attend them are largely the same. Similarly, events might evolve over time because the same actors are involved in them and put the 'lessons learned' into practice at each new event. Similarities in the organisation of different illegal raves in Britain during the late 1980s and early 1990s, for example, might be explained by the involvement (in organisational roles) of the same participants in them. Similarly, any evolution in their organisational forms might be explained by those participants carrying forward the lessons learned from earlier into later events. Less glamorously, the emergence of the convention of audiences at early punk gigs spitting at bands to show their appreciation might be explained as an effect of the same audience members relaying that practice from one gig to another (where it might be appropriated by further audience members who then do the same).

The sociological logic here is good but it applies better in some cases than others. It is not obvious that DJs who play at the same club will have any meaningful tie, for example, because they won't play it at the same time and so won't meet. We must be mindful of this when using two-mode data.

Similarly, big events will generate a huge amount of 'ties' in an affiliated network but those ties are unlikely to be real or meaningful. Attendees at small folk or jazz clubs are likely to enjoy some connection, especially if their participation overlaps on various occasions, but attendees at Glastonbury and large stadium gigs, if they befriend anybody, will only befriend a tiny proportion of the others there. We cannot assume that attendees at such events know one another. In the vast majority of cases there will be no meaningful tie between them.

Furthermore, affiliated two-mode data is often clumpy because everybody who attends the same event is assumed to be tied to everybody else who attends it (creating a clump of connections). In single-mode data which is gathered in the normal way such clumpiness (which would be captured by the clustering coefficient) might be interesting. In single-mode data which is derived from two-mode data, however, it may be no more than an artefact of the way in which the data have been gathered.

Finally, it has been argued that studying single modes, when they are derived from two-mode data, involves a loss of important information about network structure. Recent work by Everett and Borgatti (2013) suggests that this can be overcome in relation to some routines by putting the two modes back together. This doesn't work for all routines but it is important where it does. Everett and Borgatti focus upon **blockmodels** and **core–periphery** analysis in particular.

In the case of a core–periphery analysis, this involves identifying the core and peripheral nodes for each of the two modes separately and then bringing them back together in a density matrix, so that, for example, the core–core cell tells us

Table 2.3 A hypothetical two-mode core–periphery density matrix (DJs and clubs)

	Core clubs (n = 20)	*Peripheral clubs* (n = 50)
Core DJs (*n*= 12)	0.8	0.34
Peripheral DJs (*n*=30)	0.04	0.07

what proportion of all possible core events were attended by the core actors. In Table 2.3, for example, the table suggests that the core DJs play most often at both the core and the peripheral clubs but less at the peripheral clubs. The peripheral DJs play less often at both but are slightly more inclined towards the peripheral clubs. If these were real data this would tell us something about the social structure of clubbing, which we might then further explore using both SNA and other methods of enquiry, both qualitative and quantitative. There is an example of a two-mode blockmodel in Chapter 10).

Summary

In this chapter we have offered a whistle-stop tour of SNA. Our primary intention has been to provide readers who are unfamiliar with the approach with a sufficient background to engage with and enjoy the chapters which follow. We also hope that we have whetted the appetite of some readers, who may now wish to try SNA out for themselves. If so then one of the texts listed under 'Suggested Further Reading' would make an excellent starting place.

Notes

1 www.analytictech.com/.
2 http://vlado.fmf.uni-lj.si/pub/networks/pajek/.
3 http://sna.unimelb.edu.au/PNet.
4 www.stats.ox.ac.uk/~snijders/siena/.
5 That is, we gather data on every node or rather every possible pairing of nodes (do they have a tie or not?) rather than taking a sample – although see our discussion of ego-nets later in the chapter for a sample-based approach.
6 As explained later in the chapter, in some cases it makes sense to ask if a node has a tie to itself. This is a reflexive tie.
7 Each of the ten nodes can send a tie to a potential total of nine others: $10 \times 9 = 90$.
8 The calculation for directed ties counts i's tie to j and j's tie to i as two separate ties. If ties are undirected this is not true. i's tie to j and j's tie to i are the same tie. We therefore halve the number: i.e. $(10 \times 9)/2 = 45$.
9 There are exceptions, particularly in blockmodelling routines, for example.
10 Standard statistical tests of significance, for example, typically assume that our data are a random sample from a population and that we wish to infer from the sample to the population. In SNA, however, we do not work with samples but rather with a census of a given population and our respondents are not randomly selected. Furthermore, standard statistical tests assume case-wise independence whereas, in a network, we precisely have dependencies (ties) between cases (nodes).
11 An incidence matrix is like an adjacency matrix except that one mode is represented by the row and the other by the columns.

References

Borgatti, S.P., Everett, M.G. and Johnson, J. (2012) *Analysing Social Networks*, London, Sage.

Breiger, R. (1974) The Duality of Persons and Groups, *Social Forces* 53(2), 181–90.

Burt, R. (1992) *Structural Holes*, Cambridge, MA, Harvard University Press.

Crossley, N. (2015) *Networks of Sound, Style and Subversion: The Punk and Post-Punk Worlds of Liverpool, London, Manchester and Sheffield 1975–1980*, Manchester, Manchester University Press.

de Nooy, W. (2008) Signs over Time, *Journal of Social Structure* 9(1), www.cmu.edu/joss/content/articles/volindex.html.

de Nooy, W., Mrvar, A. and Batagelj, V. (2005) *Exploratory Social Network Analysis with Pajek*, Cambridge, Cambridge University Press.

Everett, M. and Borgatti, S. (2013) The Dual-Projection Approach for Two Mode Networks, *Social Networks* 34(2), 204–10.

Federation of Entertainment Unions (2013) *Creating without Conflict*, available at www.equity.org.uk/documents/creating-without-conflict-report/.

Feld, S. (1981) The Focused Organisation of Social Ties, *American Journal of Sociology* 86, 1015–35.

Feld, S. (1982) Social Structural Determinants of Similarity among Associates, *American Sociological Review* 47, 797–801.

Goffman, E. (1961) *Asylums*, Harmondsworth, Penguin.

Harrigan, N. (n.d.) *PNet for Dummies*, online at www.mysmu.edu/faculty/nharrigan/PNetForDummies.pdf.

Lazarsfeld, P. and Merton, R. (1964) Friendship as Social Process, in Berger, M., Abel, T. and Page, C. (eds), *Freedom and Control in Modern Society*, New York, Octagon Books, 18–66.

Lusher, D., Koskinen, J. and Robins, G. (2013) *Exponential Random Graph Models for Social Networks*, Cambridge, Cambridge University Press.

McPherson, M., Smith-Lovin, L. and Cook, J. (2001) Birds of Feather: Homophily in Social Networks, *Annual Review of Sociology* 27, 415–44.

Simmel, G. (1955) *Conflict and the Web of Group Affiliations*, New York, Free Press.

Wang, P., Robins, G., Pattison, P. and Lazega, E. (2013) Exponential Random Graph Models for Multilevel Networks, *Social Networks* 35(1), 96–115.

White, H. (2008) *Identity and Control*, Princeton, NJ, Princeton University Press.

Suggested further reading

Borgatti, S.P., Everett, M.G. and Johnson, J. (2012) *Analysing Social Networks*, London, Sage.
  An excellent hands-on introduction to SNA which instructs readers how to implement routines in UCINET. Borgatti and Everett co-wrote the UCINET software with Linton Freeman.

de Nooy, W., Mrvar, A. and Batagelj, V. (2005) *Exploratory Social Network Analysis with Pajek*, Cambridge, Cambridge University Press.
  An excellent hands-on introduction to SNA which instructs readers how to implement routines in Pajek. Mrvar and Batagelj co-wrote the Pajek software.

Scott, J. (2000) *Social Network Analysis: A Handbook*, London, Sage.

An excellent, brief introduction to the key concepts and ideas involved in SNA and the history of the approach. This book avoids equations and mathematical notation.

Wasserman, S. and Faust, K. (1994) *Social Network Analysis*, Cambridge, Cambridge University Press.

An excellent introduction. A big book which covers the field comprehensively. Unlike Scott, the authors seek to teach the reader how to read the equations and follow the mathematical notation. They do so with admirable clarity.

3 Totally wired[1]

The network of structure of the post-punk worlds of Liverpool, Manchester and Sheffield 1976–80

Nick Crossley

In this chapter I compare the network structure of the post-punk 'music worlds'[2] of Liverpool, Manchester and Sheffield as they took shape between 1976 and 1980. I have discussed the rationale for and limits of this geographical-temporal focus elsewhere (Crossley 2015). For present purposes it must suffice to say that: selection was necessary to make my study manageable; these cities were chosen because they were key sites of post-punk innovation in the UK; I begin in 1976 because that is when punk arrived in these cities; I end in 1980 because changes in that year initiated a gradual shift away from post-punk which is interesting but beyond my scope. The punk and post-punk worlds were always in process, constantly evolving, but in 1980 developments were afoot which began to disconnect post-punk from its roots in punk, both organisationally and stylistically, heralding a move towards what Reynolds (1990) has called 'the new pop'.

The chapter continues my earlier analysis of punk and post-punk (Crossley 2008, 2009, 2015), building upon the argument therein: namely, that music worlds emerge where a critical mass of would-be participants gravitate together, forming a social network characterised by cooperation, mutual support, influence, trust but also competition and conflict. The interaction constitutive of this network facilitates the coordination necessary to a music world, generates the collective effervescence and creativity that results in stylistic innovation and facilitates the building of a collective identity, albeit contested in many instances.

I am not going to repeat the details and defence of this argument here nor retest its claims (see Crossley 2015). I am going to extend it by seeking out similarities and differences between the three abovementioned worlds, which I will use to raise questions regarding the typical structural characteristics of local music worlds and the factors which explain those characteristics. This only amounts to a very preliminary analysis but it hopefully does enough to show that such analysis is revealing and to make the case for further investigation.

Data on the three worlds and their constitutive networks were gathered by way of secondary and archival sources (see Crossley 2015). Each has generated a small industry of biographies, autobiographies, band histories, memoires, venue histories, etc. Combined with the music press and local archives, these sources have allowed me to identify both the key actors in each of the worlds (my network nodes) and any significant ties between them.

Ties, in this case, represent either longstanding friendships which predate the nodes' involvement in punk/post-punk or, more usually, some form of musical collaboration during the specified period of the study (1976–80, inclusive). Often 'collaboration' means playing in the same band but it may relate to management, production of recordings and other significant support activities.

This definition of ties sets the bar at a high level. Had I been able to survey relations of acquaintance or friendship I would no doubt have found much denser networks. Everybody within my node set, I expect, knew and socialised with everybody else to some extent. Furthermore, my node set only captures those participants whose involvement was such that they left a trace in the archive. As such it is biased in favour of musicians and organisers over audience members and undoubtedly underestimates the actual size of the worlds I am surveying. These selection biases need to be factored into the interpretation of my findings but they do not undermine the analysis. Rather, they specify what it is an analysis of; namely, networks of those participants in the specified music world who were sufficiently prominent to leave a trace in the archives and/or secondary sources. All computations and visualisations were performed using UCINET (Borgatti *et al.* 2002).

Before I introduce the networks it is important to set the scene by both explaining how music world networks are formed and briefly charting the rise of post-punk in the UK in the late 1970s.

From prog through punk to post-punk

From rock 'n' roll, through Merseybeat to the early glam rock of David Bowie and Roxy Music, pop music was a central source of identity and excitement for young people in the UK between the mid-1950s and the early 1970s. It was rebellious, dangerous and all the more attractive for that. By the mid-1970s, however, it was beginning to stagnate in the view of some. Glam rock was crumpling under the weight of safe and saccharine imitations and the main underground alternative, 'progressive rock', entertained high-cultural aspirations which alienated and frustrated a significant number of young music enthusiasts whose expectations had been formed in the excitement of earlier decades. These enthusiasts were frustrated and looking for alternatives, which to some extent they found. Among the deeper underground currents they seized upon were: reggae, krautrock, pub rock and, especially, the garage–glam fusion of such US bands as The Stooges, The MC5 and The New York Dolls (the New York 'punk' scene, often cited as a key influence, was unknown to most, with a few important exceptions[3]) (Savage 2011).

Across the country small pockets of enthusiasts sought out these alternatives, in some cases aspiring to form bands themselves and make their own alternatives. It was only in London, however, or rather it was first in London, that a critical mass of would-be innovators began to gravitate together, forming a network and, from that network, deriving the mix of cooperation, support, competition, inspiration and resourcing that would lead them to construct their own alternative: punk.

A small, 'alternative' boutique situated at the run-down and bohemian end of London's King's Road, owned by Malcolm McLaren and Vivienne Westwood, was an important focus for the generation of this network in its early stages (on foci see Feld 1981, 1982). It attracted individuals who were attached to alternative music and fashion, bringing them into contact with one another. Significantly, moreover, in addition to younger individuals seeking to form bands this network involved slightly older individuals, such as McLaren himself, whose aesthetic, philosophical and political interests would inform early punk developments and whose business savvy and resources would help to nurture and promote it.

McLaren and his friend, Bernard Rhodes, were particularly important. They worked together during the early history of punk, collaborating and cooperating in the management and promotion of various bands and events. As punk began to take off, however, their relationship became more competitive, each wanting their main band (The Sex Pistols in McLaren's case, The Clash in Rhodes's) to be its figurehead. This competition, no less than the extensive and continued cooperation between them, was a major motor in the development of punk.

The Sex Pistols were the first of the UK punk bands to play live, late in 1975, and their gigs too served as important foci for the punk network. Word spread about The Pistols among those attracted to alternative forms of music and clothing, drawing people to the gigs and into association with one another. And this newly formed network of like-minded individuals generated social capital, in Coleman's (1990) sense, which those involved, inspired by the punk activities of others, could draw upon in the generation of further punk projects. Events generated a network which facilitated and supported further events, in a continuous feedback loop. And this same dynamic established the stimulating environment in which punk took shape.

The DIY, amateur ethos of punk was an important factor in this feedback loop. Early punk culture was a call to arms: don't sit back and accept what you are given, have a go yourself. Form a band, make your own clothes, organise your own events, establish and write a zine (zine production flourished in London, Liverpool, Manchester and Sheffield during the period studied here, generating mediated networks of information flow).

Recruitment to the network, initially, was by word of mouth and thus largely restricted to the London area. However, a Pistols' gig review in the *New Musical Express* (*NME*) in February 1976 sparked interest among some disaffected music devotees outside the capital, not least because the review likened The Pistols to The Stooges. This drew outsiders to London. T.V. Smith and Gaye Advert, for example, were prompted to move from Devon to London to become involved (they formed early punk favourites, The Adverts, within months of their arrival), and Howard Devoto and Pete Shelley travelled down to the capital, from Manchester, the following week, managing to see The Pistols twice. It also took punk and The Pistols beyond London, however. Devoto and Shelley arranged for The Pistols to play in Manchester, for example, kick-starting a process of network formation there (see below) and redoubled their on-going efforts to put a band together, resulting in one of the most celebrated punk bands: Buzzcocks.

Other reviews and articles followed in the music press, each further diffusing interest about punk among those on the look-out for something different. The punk 'virus' only crossed into the mainstream, however, when, on 1 December 1976, The Pistols were interviewed on a regional (to London) teatime television show. In a now-infamous exchange the band were goaded by interviewer, Bill Grundy, and challenged to 'say something outrageous'. They did and the next morning they were front-page news across several national dailies. A 'moral panic' was soon in full swing (Gildart 2013). This closed down many opportunities for The Pistols, decimating their planned 'Anarchy' tour and contributing to the loss of their first record deal. And other punk bands, tarred by the same brush, suffered too. However, the controversy attracted many new recruits to the punk camp, encouraging the formation of further bands and local worlds. A distinctive punk world had already begun to to form in Manchester by this time, giving rise to a number of high-profile punk bands. And enthusiasts in other cities, including Liverpool and Sheffield, soon caught on too.

Over time, however, diffusion gave way to opposition and adaptation, in Tarde's (2000) sense. Significant numbers of those who had been mobilised by the energy and DIY ethos of punk began to feel that it was ossifying, acquiring a uniformity and settling upon a form which was both limited and limiting. They wanted to do something different. Les Pattinson, of Liverpool-based band, Echo and the Bunnymen, for example, comments: 'After six months of punk, everybody got bored with it and started getting into weirder things' (in Cooper 1982, 14). Linder Sterling, whose artwork, as well as her music, shaped Manchester's punk/post-punk identity, makes a similar point:

> The original punk thing ran out very quickly ... in its initial purity punk was probably just six months or so ... with Howard [Devoto] being so articulate it happened early – this sense of 'It's not right, it's not right.'
>
> (Reynolds 2009, 219)

For others punk had never been particularly attractive, even in its earlier, more fluid manifestation. What was attractive was its DIY ethos and the signal that doing your own thing might just work. Many of Sheffield's most successful post-punk bands exemplify this second relation to punk. Cabaret Voltaire, for example, predated The Sex Pistols and, notwithstanding the slightly more up-tempo and aggressive feel of their classic single, 'Nag, Nag, Nag', were not obviously influenced musically by punk. However, punk both signalled and created a structure of opportunity for them which allowed them to take what they were doing to a new level. Likewise for the formative members of The Human League, who were not particularly impressed by punk music either:

> During the punk revolution everything became possible. All the things that had seemed completely unattainable were in reach, however unlikely.
>
> (Martin Ware in Lilleker 2005, 43)

Musically, both The Human League and Cabaret Voltaire were more influenced by krautrock (Kraftwerk in particular) than The Sex Pistols or The Stooges. In this respect they exemplify an interesting dynamic: much of what came after punk was influenced by musical currents and experiments that had been inspiring the post-punk vanguard prior to the rise of punk. The punks largely took inspiration from The Stooges, MC5 and New York Dolls but, as noted above, this was only one among a number of alternative strands of music offering hope to the musically disillusioned during the mid-1970s. And when punk had run its course, in the view of the vanguard, these other influences resurfaced.

The importance of David Bowie and Roxy Music, often combined with the krautrock that was influencing them in the mid-1970s, is difficult to overestimate in this respect, particularly in the case of the 'futurists' and the New Romantics but also in the case of Joy Division, who were the very definition of post-punk for some. In the case of Two-Tone, by contrast, the primary influences were ska and reggae. And in other cases, particularly Echo and the Bunnymen and The Teardrop Explodes, the garage-psychedelia, popularised by Lenny Kaye's *Nuggets* compilation, was a key influence. Beyond these underground influences, moreover, various musical forms, from folk to funk and rockabilly, were all rediscovered and reworked, creating a diverse patchwork of DIY musical experimentation.

Positive influence and interaction within local networks are important elements in the dynamic which shifted local music worlds from punk to post-punk but the relative lack of connection between punks in different cities was also a factor. Different cities did punk differently in the first place because relative isolation minimised influence between them. As Pete Shelley explains:

> It was a bit like Australia, you know, the animals had a chance to develop in their own peculiar ways, untainted by what was happening in the rest of the world.
>
> (cited in Lee 2002, 137)

We should not overstate this isolation. Over time different city-based worlds linked up in significant ways, generating national punk and post-punk worlds. However, ties were inevitably geographically concentrated and this is one reason why, as Reynolds (2005) observes, different cities often spawned distinctive forms of post-punk too. We should understand this as a network effect. Gaps and isolation are as important as ties in network structure.

The formation of music worlds

The formation of the music worlds which cultivated these 'mutations', like the formation of London's punk world, involved recruitment within and diffusion through pre-existing networks. News of events and innovations were passed on, with participants mutually influencing and enthusing one another. The excitement generated by the first Sex Pistols gig in Manchester in June 1976, for example, set in motion a process of recruitment which ensured a much larger audience for the second one, in July:

> I've no idea of the time difference between the first and the second show but I just get the feeling that we'd all run around and said 'You've got to come, you've got to come...'
>
> (Paul Morley, cited in Nolan 2006, 72)

> I was evangelical about it, honestly. I told everybody about that band, everybody I encountered, about the Sex Pistols.
>
> (Ian Moss, cited in Nolan 2006, 72)

> Maybe it's only in a small city that you can have that kind of communication, that can take you from thirty-five people on June 4th to several hundred on July 20th. The word goes out, the word spreads.
>
> (Tony Wilson, cited in Nolan 2006, 71)

However, 'world formation' involves the forging of new ties too. Relatively few of the ties in the networks that I discuss below pre-existed the formation of the music world to which they belong and the accounts that I have drawn upon for data are replete with stories of first meetings and tie formation.

Some, but not many of these new ties were deliberately sought out, either through adverts in record shops and zines or through targeted approaches to individuals with valued skills and resources. Others were an effect of transitive closure, as individuals introduced their new acquaintances to one another. The most important mechanism of network formation, however, was what Feld (1981, 1982) terms the network focus: a place or event which like-minded individuals gravitate towards, bringing them into contact.

Liverpool's foci

The central focus of Liverpool's post-punk world between 1978 and 1980 was Eric's, a cellar-based club which hosted the lion's share of punk and post-punk gigs in the city (Florek and Whelan 2009). Everybody who was anybody went to Eric's and many important first meetings happened there. It was at a Clash gig at Eric's, for example, that Julian Cope first met Pete Wylie and, through him, Ian McCulloch, establishing the line up of The Crucial Three (see below). And that first gig was also the occasion for the formation of post-punk pranksters, Big in Japan.

Around the corner from Eric's was another key focus, Probe, a record shop in which a number of the luminaries of Liverpool's post-punk world would work at one time or another and where many would hang out. Furthermore, as Strachan (2010) observes, these two central sites of punk and post-punk activity were situated within a broader 'boho' district which also contained the Liverpool School of Language, Music, Dream and Pun: a converted warehouse which hosted various avant-garde art and theatre events, provided studio and rehearsal space for artists and musicians, and housed a small indoor bazaar (Aunt Twackies) comprising clothes and other stalls, including one run by Jayne Casey.[4] It also housed one of two tea rooms (O'Halligan's) which were also key foci for Liverpool's post-punks.

This boho enclave compares in important respects with the World's End area of Chelsea, where McLaren and Westwood set up their boutique and where many of London's pioneer punks, including the formative members of The Sex Pistols, first met and forged ties. The comparison is important because it points to the more general significance of such enclaves. If, as I have suggested, networks are crucial to the formation of new music worlds then so too are the foci which generate those networks. Individual gigs, venues and record shops might suffice for this but where they cluster, geographically, creating a wider urban space where the like-minded hang out over extended periods, network formation is clearly enhanced.

Furthermore, the appropriation of warehouse space at the Liverpool School is important and finds an echo in both Manchester and Sheffield. The industrial base of all three local economies was in terminal decline during this period, with devastating consequences for local people. One positive outcome, however, was the availability of big spaces close to the city centre where the artistically inclined could congregate and pursue their projects. As Fish puts it:

> Unlike London, where rehearsal space was expensive and difficult to find, Sheffield's industrial decline offered no end of disused factory space ideal for up and coming bands to vent their musical spleens.
>
> (Fish 2002, 88)

Manchester's foci

Manchester's early punk world was centred upon The Electric Circus, a dingy club outside the city centre which had hosted the third and fourth of The Sex Pistols' 1976 gigs in the city. The Lesser Free Trade Hall had hosted the first two but refused to do so again following the Bill Grundy debacle. The owner of The Electric Circus spotted the opportunity this provided, inviting punters to see the band which The Free Trade Hall (and also The Palace) had refused to put on, and this earned his venue the status of Manchester's premier punk club, a place where the city's punks (and some from Liverpool and Sheffield[5]) would converge, forming ties and hatching plans. That is, until it was closed, ten months later, on health and safety grounds.

A number of venues filled the gap left by The Electric Circus, including The Squat, The Oaks and Rafters but it was The Factory which was to be most closely associated with post-punk (Nice 2010). Established by Tony Wilson, Alan Erasmus and Peter Saville, who later founded Factory Records too, The Factory was a key punk and post-punk venue for the duration of its existence (May 1978–June 1980). Like Eric's, anybody who was anybody in Manchester's post-punk world congregated at The Factory.

Manchester had no equivalent to Liverpool's boho enclave. However, its punk and post-punk world revolved around a number of well-known haunts in addition to those named above, including a gay bar called The Ranch. This resonates with London's punk world, where the lesbian bar, Louise's, played a key focal role (Crossley 2015) and points to a key attribute of early punk and post-punk foci: tolerance for experimentation in clothing and lifestyle. A number of post-punk protagonists from different cities have pointed to the significance of gay bars in providing proto-punks (straight or gay) with spaces in which they could experiment with their appearance:

> like all our mates we'd come from gay clubs. Before Eric's opened, gay clubs were the only ones that would let us in, because of the way we looked. We'd kind of been into dance music in gay clubs, so we brought that with us.
>
> (Casey 1993)

In addition, most of the key Manchester bands rehearsed at one time or another at T.J. Davidson's, a converted warehouse close to the city centre which is immortalised in the video to Joy Division's, 'Love Will Tear Us Apart'. Again this was a focus for local musicians, encouraging some movement and collaboration between bands.

Sheffield's foci

Sheffield's equivalent to Eric's and The Factory was The Limit, a cellar-based club close to the university which opened in March 1978 (Anderson 2009). Like its Liverpool and Manchester equivalents it hosted most of the main punk and post-punk bands of the era, including such home-grown talent as: Cabaret Voltaire, The Human League, Clock DVA and Artery. And, like The Factory, it emerged in a context already shaped by its predecessors, namely: The Crazy Daisy (where, in 1980, Phil Oakey would recruit Joanne Catherall and Suzanne Sulley for the commercially successful incarnation of The Human League), the university's Now Society (Nowsoc) and the art college on Psalter Lane.

As this suggests, universities and colleges were also important foci and, indeed, resources. Early developments in Sheffield were centred upon Nowsoc and before that, Cabaret Voltaire, who were not students, had been granted access to the university music department to use their synthesisers – one of their first gigs was a disastrous recital at a university function. Likewise in Liverpool, two key pre-punk bands, who played a central role in the formation of the city's punk world, Deaf School and Albert Dock, were both formed by students at the art college. And much of the leading design talent in Manchester's punk and post-punk worlds came from the Poly's art department: e.g. Linder Sterling, Peter Saville and Malcolm Garrett.

The involvement of students wasn't always welcomed, however, not least because entry to their subsidised bars and venues was usually restricted to students (the Nowsoc found a way around this), breeding resentment. As Julian Cope (1994), who came to Liverpool as a student in 1976, admits, even students hated students.

Like Manchester, Sheffield had no boho enclave but as noted above it had a ready supply of disused industrial spaces which were appropriated for musical purposes. The best known of these was Western Works, a studio owned by Cabaret Voltaire and used by many of the city's punk and post-punk bands, often with The Cabs on engineering and production duties, and also a place where some would crash, watch videos and carry on drinking after the pubs had closed. The Beehive, just up the road from The Limit, was the pub of choice for Sheffield's premier post-punks:

> The place positively buzzed with musical gossip.... Everyone you talked to seemed to be in a group: Artery, I'm So Hollow, Graph, 2.3, Clock DVA, the Stunt Kites, Hula – oh yes, and Pulp. The list was endless. All these people so busy with their musical projects, their trendy clothes and hanging around looking cool.
>
> (Fish 2002, 84)

There was a hierarchy, however. Not everyone converged upon the Beehive:

> The Hallamshire, a hundred yards down the road, was more for the second stream. There was a definite pecking order.
>
> (Lilleker 2005, 47)

It is difficult to determine the exact proportion of significant ties which were forged at foci such as these but it is reasonable to assume that a high proportion were, given that these were the places where post-punk music was 'done' (my survey of the London punk world suggests that foci account for a high proportion of ties there (Crossley 2015)). However, the relation between foci and networks is two-way. Foci generate networks but interaction in networks often gives rise to events which become foci, providing the social capital which supports and facilitates organisation of these events. Furthermore, places become foci when word gets around about them. And word gets around through networks.

In addition, without denying that venues have physical and acoustic properties that shape what can happen, musically, within them (Byrne 2012, Small 1998), foci become what they are for participants in virtue of the uses to which they are put within interaction networks: e.g. booking and door policies, regulars, their identities and rituals. Most post-punk foci were dingy cellars but they became important because repeated interaction within networks of regulars gave rise to conventions which allowed these places to offer something which others did not: a safe space to experiment and hang out, free from 'townie' interference and aggression; a sense of belonging; and access to music and fashions which were largely unknown to those outside select circles. No less significantly, interactions stratified focal spaces. In some cases, as in Sheffield, different pubs served different castes (see above). In other places, such as Liverpool, elites marked out their spaces within a club:

> At the bottom of the stairs, Peter Burns and Paul Rutherford were ensconced on their thrones, the territory of floor just before the main doors. They would sit there, sometimes with Lyn [Burns] and their young acolytes, and slag people off as they entered the club.
>   ... to a girl behind me who was wearing a leopard-skin pill-box hat, 'Ay gairl, worrav yer gorra dead cat on yer 'ed for?'
>
> (Cope 1994, 32)

The structure of the networks

Turning now to the networks themselves, it is striking how similar they are in basic structural terms (see Table 3.1). Note first that they all involve a similar number of nodes. Of course the individuals captured in my survey are only the best known of those involved in each case. They are the people who were significant enough to leave some sort of trace in the archive; the inner circle. In each case there will be many participants who left no trace, and their collective size is an unknown, 'dark figure'. However, it is still interesting that the archived, inner circle of each of the three local worlds is roughly the same size. This suggests that there may be an optimum size for the inner circle of a local musical world; big enough to lend the critical mass necessary to initiate and support the events and practices of the world but small enough to facilitate efficient communication, coordination and cohesion, given the other structural properties of the networks.

Beyond size each of the networks is similar in the respect that it forms a single component with a diameter of either five (Liverpool) or six (Manchester and Sheffield) degrees. In each case, moreover, this maximal geodesic applies to only a tiny proportion of pairs of nodes. Close to 8 per cent of all pairs of nodes are connected directly in each case and a further 70 per cent are at a distance of either 2 or 3

Table 3.1 Basic network properties

	Liverpool	Manchester	Sheffield
Order (number of nodes)	131	129	130
Components	1	1	1
Density	0.08	0.08	0.07
% of pairs at 2 degrees	34	33	41
% of pairs at 3 degrees	48	37	33
Diameter	5	6	6
Average path length	2.62	2.75	2.648
Cluster co-efficient	0.79	0.79	0.77
Weighted cluster co-efficient	0.45	0.56	0.39
Average degree (SD)	9.82	10.85	9.45

degrees, giving an average path length of between 2 and 3. And average degree is, in each case, above 9, with a clustering co-efficient above 75 per cent.

These metrics have a threefold significance. First, the number of components and short path lengths are important because they suggest that information and gossip would have passed quickly around each network, other things being equal, and that musicians looking for collaborators would have been able to search the network relatively easily. Second, the figures for average degree and clustering are important because they suggest that the influence of the network upon each of those involved could have been strong. As Coleman (1988, 1990) argues, dense network clustering tends to generate norms of and incentives for cooperation, trustworthiness and mutual support, simultaneously insulating those involved from wider external influences and reinforcing cultural patterns which may appear deviant from an external perspective (see also Bott 1957, Milroy 1987, Burt 2005). Reference groups reinforce shared patterns of behaviour and situational definitions, and offer strong incentives for actors to succeed in the terms defined by the group. Furthermore, reputations, which mediate actors' relations and their access to desired goods, especially where interdependence is high, develop and diffuse quickly, giving actors an incentive to conform to shared norms. In addition, as Blumer (1969) suggests, participation in collective activities can give rise to a sense of *esprit de corps* and a basis for a collective identity which, again, encourages conformity and cooperation.

I do not mean to suggest that these music worlds were cosy communities with no competition or backbiting. They weren't. Claims and evidence suggesting cooperation and solidarity within the archive are invariably followed, in close succession, by claims and evidence of conflict and competition, and vice versa. As Simmel (1955) notes, however, competition and conflict are often positive, motivating bands to rehearse, innovate and seek out further audiences where otherwise they might have been inclined to sit back and enjoy whatever level of success they had. Furthermore, conflict and competition can be a source of what we might call negative influence: i.e. bands and artists taking on styles and identities in order to distinguish themselves from others.

Third, and finally, the similarity between the three networks across most measures is interesting because it suggests that the flurry of interactivity which generated the networks we are analysing was subject, in each case, to similar constraints and perhaps also opportunities. It is not clear at this stage what those constraints are. That must be a topic for further research. Two obvious sources of constraint, however, are the conventions and resources which, according to Becker's (1982) account, are crucial elements of music worlds, alongside networks. I will suggest below, for example, that the resources held and controlled by support personnel in a network shape networks because their relative scarcity leads those who seek them to the same source individuals, elevating the centrality of those individuals. And such conventions as inform the line-up of a typical rock band (one singer, one guitarist, one bassist and one drummer) will shape networks in the respect that musicians who play the same instrument have a reduced likelihood of ever playing together. Much as the incest taboo shapes kinship networks so too the 'one drummer per band' convention shapes musical or least rock networks.

Note, however, that the worlds are not identical in every respect. Specifically, they differ in relation to degree and betweenness centralisation (see Table 3.2). Before I discuss why this might be, these two measures, and a third, closeness, require brief elaboration.

There are many different ways of measuring and comparing the centrality of individual nodes within a network. The three most frequently used, however, are degree, betweenness and closeness. A node's degree is the number of connections which it has to other nodes in the network. Those with the most connections (the highest degree) are the most degree central. Betweenness refers to the number of times that a node lies in the shortest path connecting any two other nodes; if node A must 'go through' node B to get to node C, for example, then this adds to B's betweenness. A node's closeness is a measure of the path lengths separating it from every other node in the network. High closeness indicates short path lengths.

Degree, betweenness and closeness are individual level measures. Each node in each network has a score for each measure. This can be revealing and I return to it. However, by looking at the dispersion of scores we can also determine the extent to which a small number of nodes within a network monopolises one or more of these types of centrality. This network level measure is called centralisation and it is important because it may tell something about the balance of power and inequalities within a network. High centrality can be a burden and constraint but it often advantages those who have it and where centralisation is high that relative advantage will usually be greater.

It can be difficult to assess the order of magnitude of centralisation scores. However, when we are comparing scores, particularly across networks that are in other respects very similar, differences between them can be revealing, and in this case we see that Sheffield is significantly more centralised than either of the other two networks for both degree and betweenness.

This raises the question of why? I have a theory, centred upon 'support personnel'. Before I outline this theory, however, I must first outline and test another.

Support personnel and the primacy of the network

It might be surprising that each of the three networks surveyed forms a single component, given the quite strict definition of ties that is being used. Bands are,

Table 3.2 Centralisation of the networks

	Liverpool	*Manchester*	*Sheffield*
Degree (%)	27.48	32.65	46.10
Betweenness (%)	32.67	26.27	57.55
Closeness (%)	33.13	38.62	42.22

after all, relatively self-contained units or at least one would imagine so. Why and how would they be connected?

Part of the reason may be that many musicians, especially in the early stages of their career, often move through a variety of short-lived bands, in different combinations, forging ties with alters who will eventually play in a number of different bands. In both Liverpool and Sheffield, for example, we find several 'pre-fame super-groups': that is, groups whose members would each subsequently achieve success in different bands: e.g. The Crucial Three, a bedroom band involving Ian McCulloch (Echo and the Bunnymen), Julian Cope (The Teardrop Explodes) and Pete Wylie (Wah!); Big in Japan, whose future members went on to form The Lightning Seeds, Pink Military, The KLF and Frankie Goes to Hollywood; and in Sheffield, the early Human League, which included members of both the famous line up of the band and also Heaven 17; The Future, which included members of the early Human League, Heaven 17 and Clock DVA; and The Studs, which included most of the above plus the three members of Cabaret Voltaire.

This fluidity suggests that the network of individual musicians in an emerging music world is in some respects more important than any given band. Bands are often temporary formations within a network which both predates and outlives them, facilitating their formation and easing their demise by affording their members new opportunities. Bands come and go but the network within which they form and into which they often dissolve endures. Moreover, this fluidity allows better bands to emerge; partly because their members acquire experience but also partly because mobility between bands allows their members to try out collaborations and move on in search of more compatible alters. This fluidity is not the complete answer to the question of the connectedness of the networks, however.

Another part of the puzzle, which is not so surprising given Becker's (1982) important reflections on music worlds, is that many bands rely upon the same, relatively small set of support personnel who tend, in virtue of this, to become hubs, linking various parts of the network together. To achieve their ends bands need access to a variety of resources which they often lack: e.g. cash, managerial and promotional expertise, rehearsal spaces, studio time and expertise, etc. To access these resources they must hook up with actors who own and control them and since there are often few such participants in a local world, those participants become a link point between a number of bands.

To test this hypothesis I divided the nodes in each network into two camps, 'support personnel' and 'others'. I then compared the mean centrality scores for each of the groups, using UCINET's network-friendly t-test to establish statistical significance (see Table 3.3).

Identifying support personnel was not straightforward. Roles in music worlds, especially small, local and emerging worlds such as those analysed here, are not clear cut. Many people, including musicians, play more than one role and members of one band often play a low-level support role for another band, e.g. lugging gear or lending equipment. I therefore had to make a judgement, based

Table 3.3 Differences in mean centralities between support personnel and others

	Liverpool	*Manchester*	*Sheffield*
Number of identified support personnel	9	14	9
Degree	22.03**	13.75**	19.47**
Betweenness	736**	590**	678**

Note
**$=p<0.000$.

upon the secondary literature, as to who played a significant support role in their music world, over and above routine low-level favours and irrespective of other roles for which they may be better known for (e.g. musician). For these purposes I did not include those whose primary role was zine writers among support personnel.[6]

Deciding upon a measure of centrality also required judgement. Given what I have said about support personnel I hypothesised that, on average, they would be both more degree and betweenness central than others. My reasoning was that while each band has its own singer, drummer, etc., the same support personnel will often serve a number of bands, a state of affairs which will both give them a higher number of connections than individual band members (degree) and make them a bridge between bands (betweenness).

As Table 3.3 shows, support personnel enjoyed a significantly higher level of each type of centrality in each of my networks. My hypothesis was supported. These results are also shown in Figure 3.1, which visualises the Manchester network, sizing nodes in accordance with degree and colouring them to distinguish support personnel (black) from others (grey). Note that the bigger nodes (higher degree) are disproportionately black (support personnel).

Turning now to Sheffield's elevated degree and betweenness centralisation, the explanation for this, I believe, is that Sheffield, though it had the same number of support personnel as Liverpool, had fewer dedicated support personnel. Many of the support personnel I identified were musicians who occasionally took up an often limited support role. Much of the work of organisation was centred upon one man: the 'mysterious'[7] Marcus Featherby. This does not seem to have hampered the Sheffield world, and it suggests that a successful world may thrive with only a relatively small number of dedicated organisers. But it also explains why Sheffield was more centralised.

To test this idea I removed Featherby from the Sheffield network and remeasured the relevant properties. The network fragments into eight components (although the biggest of these contains 73 per cent of all nodes). Degree centralisation drops from 46.10 to 16.3. And betweenness centralisation drops from 57.55 to 4.49 (closeness centralisation cannot be measured when a network has more than one component). Featherby made a big difference and was the source of Sheffield's centralisation.

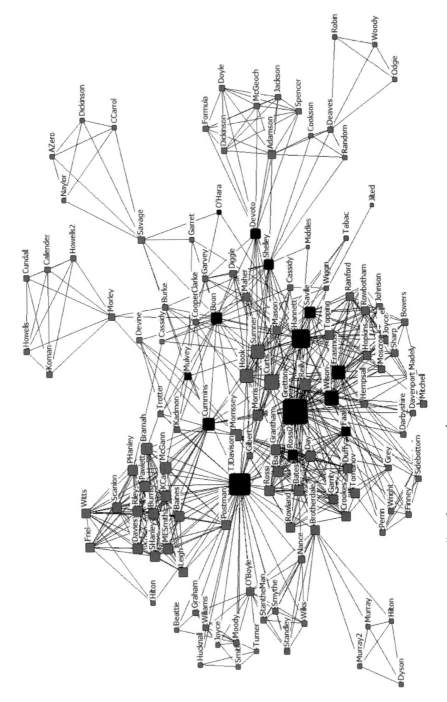

Figure 3.1 The degree centrality of support personnel.

City sounds and taste-makers

The central position of support personnel equips them to act as 'taste-makers', exerting a disproportionate influence upon the styles, musical and visual, practised within a world – assuming, of course, that they have strong ideas in this respect and seek to influence. Although the notion that a city has a particular 'sound' is problematic (Cohen 2007), specific styles and innovations can attach to particular cities and this can be explained, in some part, through the influence of central 'taste-makers'. There was a notable electronic emphasis in the Sheffield post-punk world, for example, evidenced most obviously in the work of Cabaret Voltaire, The Human League, Clock DVA and Vice Versa but also clear in other bands such as They Must be Russians. And one reason for this was the influence of Cabaret Voltaire, whose three members' degree scores are beaten only by Marcus Featherby. Much of the influence of Cabaret Voltaire may have come from their early live performances but not only from there. Martin Ware, for example, describes the formative effect of first hearing Kraftwerk, on a tape put together by Richard Kirk (Cabaret Voltaire) at a birthday party at the house of Chris Watson's (Cabaret Voltaire) girlfriend, Maggie:

> The speakers were pumping out Trans-Europe Express by Kraftwerk. It was a formative night of my life. It was the first time I'd heard them ... as exciting as any live gig that I'd ever been to and it really made me want to write actual tunes. All thanks to Chris and Richard and Mal.
>
> (Lilleker 2005, 41)

Furthermore, because many bands used Cabaret Voltaire's studio, usually also drawing upon the band's expertise, they were inevitably more 'vulnerable' to the influence of the band.

Liverpool too had its synth pioneers, in the form of Orchestral Manoeuvres in the Dark, but its 'sound', insofar as a city can be pinned down to a sound, is usually described as 'psychedelic' and the taste-makers for this sound, according to Strachan (2010, 127), were '[Eric's owner] Roger Eagle and Probe Records staff', a view echoed independently by two former Probe staff members:

> A lot of people's musical tastes were encapsulated by Probe; they would come in and find out about people they didn't know about.... If you knew somebody and they came in, you'd say 'Have you heard this?'
>
> (Norman Killon in Strachan 2010, 136)

> Every weirdo and no-gooder in the city would gravitate there on Saturday. Geoff ... is the second most important man in the history of Liverpool music. That's after Brian Epstein. He loved the album Forever Changes by Love and he never stopped playing it to people. All the young kids who would come into the shop looking for punk or the Velvet Underground – he would never miss the opportunity to play them that record. That or Captain Beefheart.
>
> (Connor 2013, 25)

These observations are echoed by Julian Cope, who first came across many of the underground psychedelic bands who influenced his early sound either at Probe or through Roger Eagle:

> Probe records was becoming more a scene focal point ... [Probe owner] Geoff Davies was the coolest. Another person I had to know.... Roger Eagle had played a compilation ...
>
> (Cope 1994, 25)

Interestingly, Davies does not have a particularly high degree ranking in the Liverpool network (Eagle does[8]) but this is probably because his influence operated in informal relations with Probe customers, which I did not record in my survey.

Core and periphery

Earlier in the chapter I pointed to the existence of a distinction in both the Liverpool and Sheffield worlds between an elevated inner core of participants and everybody else. We find a similar picture in Manchester, particularly in relation to those involved in Factory Records. They were not uniformly popular: 'We used to call them Fat Tory Records. The way they dominated the city felt very elitist' (Liz Naylor, cited in Nice 2010, 97).

Such distinctions often both reflect and reinforce a distinction within a network between a relatively dense 'core' of nodes and a 'periphery' who are much less densely tied to one another and also to the core but who typically have a greater density of ties to the core than to one another. As a final stage of analysis in this chapter I elected to test for this using UCINET's categorical core–periphery routine, an algorithm which identifies the best approximation of a core–periphery structure possible in any given network. My data, as noted earlier, arguably only captures the 'inner circle' of each of the worlds analysed; those faces influential enough to have left a trace in the archive. Nevertheless, the order of each network is big enough for me to hypothesise that some such distinction will exist within each of the networks. And in each of our networks the UCINET algorithm found clear and strong evidence for this (see Table 3.4).

The similarity between the three networks is, as with the more basic measures, striking. The core represents, in each case, about one-quarter of all nodes.

Table 3.4 Core–periphery density matrix

	Liverpool		Manchester		Sheffield	
	Core (28%)	*Periphery*	*Core (22%)*	*Periphery*	*Core (28%)*	*Periphery*
Core	0.52	0.082	0.5	0.07	0.35	0.07
Periphery	0.07	0.043	0.07	0.06	0.07	0.04

The Sheffield core is less dense, at 35 per cent, than either Liverpool or Manchester, which are 49 per cent and 50 per cent respectively, but the internal density of the peripheries and of core–periphery ties is, in each case, more or less identical. Each network manifests a clear core–periphery structure. Liverpool's core–periphery structure in visualised in Figure 3.2; the core are coloured black and the periphery grey.

Conclusions

Music worlds, whether local, national, international or virtual, are always, among other things, networks. This chapter has focused upon the 'inner circle' of key participants within three city-based post-punk worlds as they took shape between 1976 and 1980, seeking out similarities and differences between them. There are some differences. In particular Sheffield had fewer dedicated support personnel and this affected the shape of its network, making it more centralised. However, notwithstanding some differences, and allowing for the fact that data gathering in each case has been constrained by the information available in archives and secondary sources, what is very striking about the analyses reported in this chapter is the broad similarity of the networks. Density and average degree are very similar across all three, as are path lengths and clustering. Each involves a similar number of actors and forms a single component. Each has a marked core–periphery structure and involves a sub-set of support personnel who enjoy an elevated (degree and betweenness) centrality.

Network properties reflect the processes whereby networks are formed. They are consequences (mostly unintended) of the inter-activities of the actors involved in a network and of the constraints upon such interaction, albeit consequences which then act back upon those actors, in the form of new, emergent opportunities and constraints. Where network structures are similar, it follows, we may assume, that it is because of similarities in this generative interaction: its organisation, opportunities and constraints. I have begun to speculate about the explanation of certain of the commonalities that we find across my three networks in this chapter, and about certain of the differences. I have suggested that it is their possession of scarce resources, for example, which elevates the centrality of support personnel, and I have suggested that it is the smaller number of dedicated support personnel in Sheffield which accounts for its greater centralisation. I have only scratched at the surface of the mechanisms at work here, however. Much work remains to be done to establish both whether the properties I have found, which are important because they shape interactivity within a music world, are common to other (particularly local) music worlds and what might explain them.

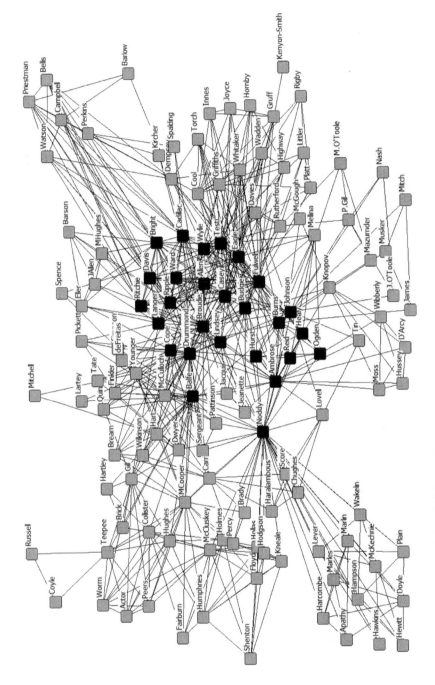

Figure 3.2 Core and periphery in Liverpool.

Notes

1 My title is taken from a song of the same name by The Fall, released as a single on Rough Trade in 1980.
2 Music worlds is a concept which I have adapted from Howard Becker's (1974, 1982) account of 'art worlds'. For further discussion of my take on this concept see Crossley (2011, 2015), Bottero and Crossley (2011), Crossley and Bottero (forthcoming).
3 The most important exception was Malcolm McLaren who was working in the US in early 1975, with The New York Dolls. McLaren participated briefly in New York's punk world during this period and later brokered its relation with the London punk world.
4 An early 'mover-and-shaker' who sang with Big in Japan and later formed both Pink Military and Pink Industry.
5 Manchester was very quick off the blocks in relation to the formation of a punk world, partly on account of the early Pistols gigs at the Free Trade Hall, promoted by Pete Shelley, Howard Devoto and Richard Boon. A number of pioneers from both Liverpool and Sheffield mention that, in the very early days, the Electric Circus was *their* closest punk venue.
6 Zine writers are complicated. If we tie them to all others with whom they 'work', and include interviewing as working, then one would expect that many will have ties to a large number of artists, making them very central. As journalists it is their job to make contact with and interview people. I did not have access to information on who my zine writers and journalists interviewed, however (most zines are not archived comprehensively). I only included other ties which they had. For this reason it seemed inappropriate to include them as support personnel for purposes of this test.
7 Mysterious because he appeared 'from nowhere' in Sheffield in the late 1970s, with a number of conflicting and exotic back stories; disappeared again, no less mysteriously, during the 1989s; and appears to have gone under different aliases both before and after his time in Sheffield.
8 He is ranked fifth, with a score almost three standard deviations above the mean.

Discography

Cabaret Voltaire (1979) 'Nag, Nag, Nag', Rough Trade.
Various (1972) *Nuggets*, Elektra.

References

Anderson, N. (2009) *Take it to the Limit*, Sheffield, ACM Retro.
Becker, H. (1974) Art as Collective Action, *American Sociological Review* 39(6), 767–76.
Becker, H. (1982) *Art Worlds*, Berkeley, University of California Press.
Blumer, H. (1969) Collective Behaviour, in McClung-Lee, A. (ed.), *Principles of Sociology*, New York, Barnes and Noble 166–222.
Borgatti, S.P., Everett, M.G. and Freeman, L.C. (2002) *UCINET for Windows: Software for Social Network Analysis*, Harvard, MA, Analytic Technologies.
Bott, E. (1957) *Family and Social Network*, London, Tavistock.
Bottero, W. and Crossley, N. (2011) Worlds, Fields and Networks, *Cultural Sociology* 5(1), 99–119.
Burt, R. (2005) *Brokerage and Closure*, Oxford, Oxford University Press.
Byrne, D. (2012) *How Music Works*, Edinburgh, Canongate.

Casey, J. (1993) Interview by Lin Sangster, www.appelstein.com/cif/jaynecasey.html (accessed 28 June 2013).

Cohen, S. (2007) *Decline, Renewal and the City in Popular Music Culture*, Aldershot, Ashgate.

Coleman, J. (1988) Free Riders and Zealots: The Role of Social Networks, *Sociological Theory* 6(1), 52–7.

Coleman, J. (1990) *Foundations of Social Theory*, Cambridge, MA, Belknap.

Connor, B. (2013) Untitled, *The Guide* (weekend arts supplement to *The Guardian* newspaper) 21 September, p. 25.

Cooper, M. (1982) *Liverpool Explodes*, London, Sidgwick and Jackson.

Cope, J. (1994) *Head-On/Repossessed*, London, Element.

Crossley, N. (2008) Pretty Connected: The Social Network of the Early UK Punk Movement, *Theory, Culture and Society* 25(6), 89–116.

Crossley, N. (2009) The Man Whose Web Expanded: Network Dynamics in Manchester's Post-Punk Music Scene 1976–1980, *Poetics* 37(1), 24–49.

Crossley, N. (2011) *Towards Relational Sociology*, London, Routledge.

Crossley, N. (2015) *Networks of Sound, Style and Subversion: The Punk and Post-Punk Worlds of Liverpool, London, Manchester and Sheffield 1975–1980*, Manchester, Manchester University Press.

Crossley, N. and Bottero, W. (forthcoming) Music Worlds and Internal Goods, *Cultural Sociology*.

Feld, S. (1981) The Focused Organisation of Social Ties, *American Journal of Sociology* 86, 1015–35.

Feld, S. (1982) Social Structural Determinants of Similarity among Associates, *American Sociological Review* 47, 797–801.

Fish, M. (2002) *Industrial Evolution*, London, SAF Publishing.

Florek, J. and Whelan, P. (2009), *Liverpool Eric's*, Runcorn, Feedback Press.

Gildart, K. (2013) The Antithesis of Humankind, *Cultural and Social History* 10(1), 129–49.

Lee, C.P. (2002) *Shake, Rattle and Rain*, Ottery St Mary, Hardinge Simpole.

Lilleker, M. (2005) *Beats Working for a Living*, Sheffield, Juma.

Milroy, L. (1987) *Language and Social Networks*, Oxford, Blackwell.

Nice, R. (2010) *Shadowplayers*, London, Aurum.

Nolan, D. (2006) *The Gig that Changed the World: I Swear I Was There*, Church Stretton, Independent Music Press.

Reynolds, S. (1990) New Pop and Its Aftermath, in Frith, S. and Goodwin, A. (eds), *On Record*, London, Routledge 466–71.

Reynolds, S. (2005) *Rip It Up*, London, Faber and Faber.

Reynolds, S. (2009) *Totally Wired*, London, Faber and Faber.

Savage, J. (2011) We Have Lift Off! *Mojo* (September), 52–61.

Simmel, G. (1955) *Conflict and the Web of Group Affiliations*, New York, Free Press.

Small, C. (1998) *Musicking*, Middletown, CT, Wesleyan University Press.

Strachan, R. (2010) Liverpool's 1970s Bohemia, in Leonard, M. and Strachan, R. (eds), *The Beat Goes On*, Liverpool, Liverpool University Press, 124–42.

Tarde, G. (2000) *Social Laws*, New York, Batoche Books.

4 Symbolic versus commercial success among British female composers

Siobhan McAndrew and Martin Everett

Why are there so few women composers? The question provokes eternal interest among researchers, musicians and the general public alike. In 2011, music critic Fiona Maddocks noted that '[c]lassical music, however much it has changed for the better, remains a predominantly male haven'. She went on to ask whether this was due to 'Prejudice? Misogyny? Lack of habit or confidence or education?' before concluding that it was 'all these things' (Maddocks 2011). She also noted that the emblematic BBC Promenade Concerts herald annual soul-searching: 'When the new season is announced next month the cry will go up, as it does each year as surely as the huntsman's tally-ho: "Where are the women composers?"' (Maddocks 2011). In 2012, a mere 14 per cent of the members of the Performing Rights Society for Music Foundation – the section for composers, songwriters and music publishers – were female (Andrew 2012).

Practising composers periodically offer answers. Composer Amy Beth Kirsten recently suggested that women are now well represented among composers and that the label 'woman composer' should be retired as 'highly insulting' (Kirsten 2012). Belinda Reynolds reported of her own experience that, while few women may be found studying composition,

> in school I thrived. Even though all my teachers (save one guest) were male, they never singled me out for being a woman.... Yes, I have encountered stereotypical sexism and discrimination from time to time. But that's true for most professions, and I have not found it to be unduly more so in music.
>
> (Reynolds 2007)

However, the historical experience of women composers is generally thought to be one of exclusion from access to greatness, both through lack of access to the years of learning required, and discrimination in professional life (Tick and Tsou n.d.). Some commentators additionally suggest that women may have different preferences regarding artistic careers, being less inclined to pursue them with the intensity with which male artists do (Piirto 1991; Reis 1999). Others suggest that neurological and hormonal differences between men and women generate higher variability in creative ability for men – the controversial 'more prodigies, more idiots' thesis (Pinker and Spelke 2005, summarised in Baer and Kaufman 2008, 21).

Here, we add to the extant knowledge on how gender affects musical composition as follows. We review the relevant literature, and then explore how the social networks of female composers differ from those of male composers on a number of key measures. We then examine how connectedness, measured by degree centrality, affects composers' output, using both a measure of symbolic success and a measure of commercial success. We finish with a number of conclusions regarding the career paths chosen by British female composers in the twentieth century.

The gender gap in composition: biological, psychological and social accounts

Because we are concerned with the question of female under-representation in a prestige field – and one which additionally confers prestige on wider society – it is important to review, even if briefly, the range of accounts of why under-representation might occur and evidence used in these accounts. As sociologists, our tendency is to point to differential socialisation or differences in structural location between men and women, rather than physiological differences. Women are thought to be socialised to be 'agreeable' and risk-averse. They may well have been encouraged away from years of hard musical study from childhood, not least because of the expense. They may have been encouraged to be less single-minded and obsessive than required to compose successfully. Structural location theories highlight the importance of differential family and employment contexts. Women tend to be primary carers of children and elderly relatives; they also participate less in the labour force, and participate then in distinctively female roles. In that case, caring responsibilities may have drawn women away from composing just at the point where years of serious training begin to pay off, disrupting their careers and their establishment of a reputation, and delaying careers in a profession where being 'young and gifted' has publicity value. Given the ferocity of competition, and the fact that talent is not directly observable, males have often an advantage over women taking career breaks in having an unbroken record of sustained achievement from the earliest career stages. This factor has not been constant over time: the contraceptive pill, which was made more widely available in Britain from 1961, allowed women to choose not to have children, or to time childbearing so as to minimise career damage. In turn, fertility control encouraged women to invest more in their human capital in the first place (Bailey 2006, 297).

We should also consider at least some of the evidence for biological correlates of musical talent and whether there are important differences between the sexes in this regard. Crude biological accounts are controversial; Larry Summers's speech in 2005, explaining female under-representation in science as partly due to 'issues of intrinsic aptitude', caused such disquiet that it played a role in his resignation a year later, having lost the support of much of the faculty (Finder *et al.* 2006). With regard to composition, however, his analysis is not unique. Journalist and cultural critic Fiona Maddocks has asked, for all the many good, even excellent women composers, why has there not yet been a great one? Where is the possessed, wild-eyed, crackpot female answer to Beethoven, who battled on through deafness, loneliness, financial worry and disease to create timeless masterpieces?... The answer, and I run for cover even raising the matter, may lie in biology or even psychopathology.

(Maddocks 2011)

Camille Paglia, in more hyperbolic vein, summarised likewise when she said 'there is no female Mozart because there is no female Jack the Ripper'. She likens historic male achievement in music, maths and philosophy to male dominance of murder rates, with both rooted in a 'perversion of male intelligence' (1990, 247). *Oxford Music Online* (as of April 2011) suggests that 505 notable British composers were born over the century from 1870, on average about five a year. Only the most outstanding composers are likely to achieve notability, never mind make a living. If there are sex differences which are only perceptible at this extreme tail of the distribution, this could account for the lower representation of women. As Maddocks implied, the question is controversial, even emotive. We feel instinctively that great talent is almost sacred and that different social groups should have access to greatness. In the wake of the Summers affair, Pinker wrote that the broader question of whether psychological differences exist between men and women is approaching taboo, understandably so because women have been held back by bogus claims of essential differences; he reported alarm that the taboo clashed with the values of free inquiry. Nevertheless, given that there has been a good deal of research by psychologists into hormonal, neurological and personality differences between the sexes associated with differences in musical talent and creativity, it is worth reviewing them briefly here.

Some have raised the question of whether differences in brains relating to the ability to 'systemise' might be associated with musical ability. Happé and Vital have reviewed the aspects of autism which relate to talent and the development of special skills, suggesting that weaker 'mentalising' (associated with empathy) allows greater originality since people with this trait are less likely to conform automatically with preconceived wisdom, to experience self-consciousness or to expend mental resources on social concerns (Happé and Vital 2009, 1370). The executive dysfunction associated with autism spectrum disorders, due to an impaired ability to switch attention, makes task completion more difficult but enables immersion. Finally, preoccupation with detail and 'restricted and repetitive behaviours and interests' from an early age confer an advantage when developing talents. It has also been established that those with autistic spectrum conditions are more likely to be male than female. To the extent that such traits are associated with musical aptitude, a gender gap in composition might well arise.

Spatial ability has also been hypothesised as a correlate of musical ability, with testosterone thought to influence development in this ability during the pre-natal period (Hassler *et al.* 1990, 35). In a study of 23 contemporary male composers and 14 female composers, Hassler *et al.* found that composers differed from instrumentalists as well as from non-musicians in testosterone: composers of both sexes tend to be more androgynous than musicians or non-musicians, with male composers having lower levels of testosterone than both male instrumentalists and male non-musicians, and female composers higher levels (Hassler *et al.* 1990, 39). More recently, Borniger *et al.* have found that testosterone is associated with musical aptitude for female students, but not male students; they reiterate that the relationship is probably mediated by spatial ability (Borniger *et al.* 2013, 9).

Hassler *et al.* (1990), in their study of 37 contemporary composers, noted that most of their subjects began composing in their teens, by which time they were able to play at least one musical instrument competently. Over half had begun to play an instrument before the age of ten, and the majority had grown up in a musical family. Borniger *et al.* note that musical aptitude is a complex trait, with testosterone probably only

> a small part of a poorly understood system of biological and environmental stimuli that contribute to musical aptitude. Parental, social, cultural and economic factors play important roles in exposure to music and musical training. [However, it] is also possible that hormones may play a role in modulating musical aptitude, and that these effects may vary by gender.
>
> (Borniger *et al.* 2013, 9)

Hassler (1991) however emphasises that composition ability is associated with testosterone levels that minimise sex differences.

Sociologists might put forward a number of explanations for the under-representation of female composers. First, the existing contributions of female composers are neglected because talent and achievement tend to be idealised with a heroic narrative often employed: composer Nicola LeFanu has described this as the 'Master Musician' taboo (LeFanu 1987). The narrative behind artistic works and the creator's image matters for how they are perceived by other music actors and the public, regardless of the intrinsic quality of the work; male composers accordingly have an advantage because they look like people's preconceptions of what a composer looks like. Male composers also find it easier to build the 'right' career narrative without career breaks in their late twenties and thirties. A number also draw on the skilled support of spouses and partners; female composers appear less able to draw on such a resource. The encouragement of mentors and peers can also be critical for artists; however, prospective mentors may prefer to encourage those who 'look like them' – the phenomenon of homosocial reproduction (Kanter 1977). Accordingly, there is a continuing gender gap in classical music composition simply because there always has been; such biases on the part of individuals can be unconscious but nevertheless extremely powerful.

Some criminologists and sociologists employ Power Control Theory to explain gender gaps in a variety of phenomena, including delinquency and religiosity, as arising due to differences in risk preferences (Hagan *et al.* 1985). In brief, the theory predicts that in more patriarchal families, where mothers work within the home, daughters are the subject of more authoritarian social control than sons and accordingly are less encouraged to take risks. Originally developed to explain the gender gap in juvenile criminality, Grasmick *et al.* (1996) argued for it to be extended to explain gender differences in risky pro-social behaviours among adults, such as entrepreneurship, or the choice to pursue a risky occupation. How this might explain the gender gap in composition is unclear. Earning a living as a composer is difficult and risky, and most practising composers earn a living from teaching or other activities (Benjamin 2009). Women able to rely on the income provided by a husband or partner may have had something of an advantage: during the years when women were less likely to work outside the home, composition – like literary writing – was perceived as decorous and could be pursued flexibly from home. Intense study in childhood was arguably more likely to be fostered in authoritarian families; and after such a childhood the choice to continue such study at a conservatoire was arguably a 'safe' one compared with the challenge of choosing an unfamiliar field of study and subsequent profession.

Socialisation, the pressure of social norms and homophily may also explain why male composers are more successful at forging the 'right' connections. Women may be expected to be less instrumental and to pursue relationships for more intrinsic reasons, so that their attempts at networking are less favourably received. Homophily is also an important force. That social similarity predicts a social tie between two individuals is one of the longest-established findings in social network studies (McPherson *et al.* 2001, 416, citing Bott 1928). Homophily is known to make communication simpler, lower risk through improving predictability of behaviour, and enhance trust (Kegen 2013, 64). In creative worlds, it is often the case that 'nobody knows' whether an artistic product or an emerging artist will succeed or not (Caves 2000, 3). Such uncertainty is very difficult to quantify and insure against, and accordingly people cling to the familiar. They also cooperate and share information and other resources in an attempt to pool risks and diversify opportunities.

It has already been established that centrality is associated with greater success as a composer, with networks providing these protective and enabling functions (McAndrew and Everett forthcoming). If a social world is dominated by one sex or the other, a finding of strong homophily would suggest that the minority sex will find it more difficult to forge connections and access resource flows such as information or cooperation opportunities (Kegen 2013, 63). In the wider literature, it is known that men tend to have more sex homophilous networks than women, especially in contexts where they are a strong majority, or where connections are status-loaded and concerned with advice, demonstration of respect and mentoring (McPherson *et al.* 2001, 423–4). In particular, it has been found that '[a]cross many cultures and work settings, both men and women use men as network routes to accomplish tasks and to connect to information in more distant domains' (McPherson *et al.* 2001, 424). Kegen's recent study of academic science networks in Germany found that women exhibited heterophily in some contexts, while men were homophilous. Her overall conclusion was that homophily 'minorly' affected involvement in science networks and that lower representation might be due to choices or constraints operating 'upstream', for example at graduate school level (Kegen 2013). Composition increasingly involves years of serious study, with many composers based in academic music departments; it also requires a similar capacity for abstract thought. We might well expect similar patterns to exist with respect to composers.

Having reviewed a range of explanations for the gender gap, we should be very clear. There is apparently weak evidence for some sex differences in some traits. However, there is no precise formula whereby these and other traits combine to predict musical talent and creativity exactly. Neither should it follow that discriminatory practices are justifiable, whether explicit, tacit or unconscious. Society should be relatively unconcerned if many women choose to avoid a career which is difficult and where there is no shortage of candidates. However, it should be very concerned if highly qualified women suffer career failure because agents, programmers, educators and the general public hold lazy preconceptions of what a working composer and a 'brilliant career' should look like.

Data and methods

In this chapter, we use quantitative analysis, including network analysis, to examine the composition success of female composers. We look first at the position of female composers in the wider network of British composers. In previous work, we have suggested that network connections are critical for achieving greater success in having works performed at the annual BBC Proms, perhaps because networks mediate innate talent (McAndrew and Everett forthcoming). In other words, networks and connections act as the pathway whereby raw talent achieves success. We also suggested that female composers were not less likely to succeed, at least in terms of having more works performed at the Proms. Instead, their lower overall representation appeared to be largely down to cohort effects: being born in the late Victorian period predicted greater success, and women of that generation found it difficult to access music education and pursue professional careers. It is also possible that, for later generations, exclusionary norms and practices operate at an earlier point in life. The composers in our dataset typically benefited from several years of serious training, and so the women in our dataset had generally cleared the hurdle of winning a place at university or a conservatoire.

The data do not allow us to examine discrimination acting to deter women from studying composition in the first place, but they do allow us to look more deeply at how male and female network positions differ. We draw on the network and attribute data sourced from *Oxford Music Online*, and described in more detail in McAndrew and Everett (forthcoming). To summarise, individual biographical entries for composers born from 1870, and either primarily educated or primarily active in Britain, were coded for data analysis. A network connection between two composers was identified where a face-to-face relation-ship existed, for example as family members, friends, colleagues, teacher and student, or mentor and mentee. Women comprise 68 of the population of 505, or 13.5 per cent, a percentage which changes surprisingly little over each ten-year birth cohort, as illustrated in Figure 4.1.

We can also examine the extent to which being female matters for different types of composition output, to see if women tend to have different types of careers. For this, we use both a 'symbolic' measure of success relating to esteem of the music world, and a 'commercial' measure of success, namely the number of recordings on which each composer is featured in the Amazon classical music catalogue (November 2013).

Our first task is to examine where women are situated in the wider network of composers. Figure 4.2 below illustrates the position of women, with female com-posers identified by black nodes and labelled by name. It is apparent that women are apparently well dispersed throughout the network; they do not appear to sit in a particular female cluster, nor feature only on the periphery of the network.

One way in which we can measure the differential connectedness of female composers is via network centrality measures. In our earlier work, we ranked composers in terms of their degree centrality, eigenvector centrality, and betweenness centrality, measures described in more detail in the introduction to this volume. In terms of degree centrality, we list the top-ranked women in Table 4.1.

How does this list compare with that for male composers? In our earlier paper, we noted that no female composer featured in the top 20 positions for degree centrality or betweenness centrality, although four captured a top 20 place when ranked by eigenvector centrality (McAndrew and Everett forthcom-ing). Among the full set of 505 composers, Elisabeth Lutyens and Imogen Holst rank thirtieth in terms of degree centrality, with the same score as Oliver

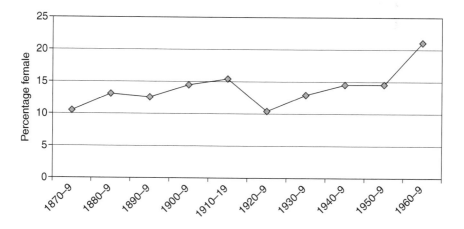

Figure 4.1 Percentage of each ten-year birth composer cohort that is female (source: *Oxford Music Online*).

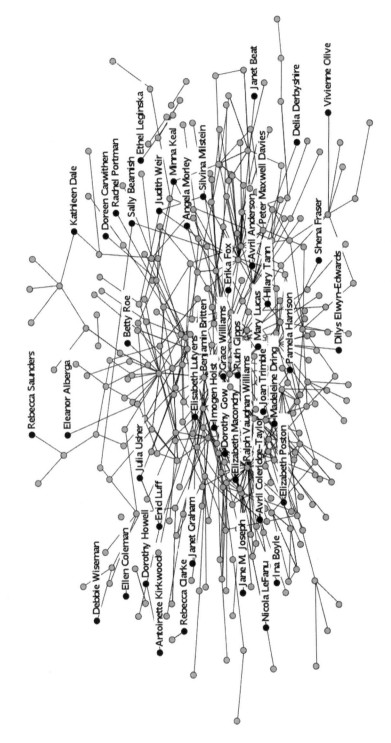

Figure 4.2 Female composers in the main component of the 1870–1969 British composers' network.

Table 4.1 Most central female composers

Name	Degree centrality
1 = Imogen Holst, Elisabeth Lutyens	1.389
3 = Elizabeth Maconchy, Grace Williams	1.190
5 = Dorothy Gow	0.992
6 = Madeleine Dring	0.794
7 = Avril Anderson, Avril Coleridge-Taylor, Ruth Gipps, Minna Keal, Mary Lucas, Enid Luff, Joan Trimble, Judith Weir	0.595

Source: *Oxford Music Online* and authors' analysis.

Knussen, Cornelius Cardew and Peter Warlock. Holst is well known to music historians through her work as an amanuensis for Benjamin Britten and as an animateur, or community music organiser; she was also the only child of Gustav Holst. Lutyens's high ranking is perhaps surprising because she typically presented herself as a musical outsider. By the 1940s, when her career was well established, she was attracting criticism for her promotion of contemporary music and early adoption of serialism; musicologist Rhiannon Mathias described her as having 'publicly backed the wrong Viennese horses ... [and] banished to a position well outside the boundaries of the British musical mainstream' (Mathias 2012, 75). In terms of eigenvector centrality, Grace Williams, Elizabeth Maconchy, Dorothy Gow and Ruth Gipps are the four ranking among the top 20 of all composers. Williams, Maconchy and Gow, who were close friends throughout their lives, each have connections to R.O. Morris and Gordon Jacob, leading teachers of composition, as well as Vaughan Williams. Gipps was a pianist, conductor and composer who, when facing difficulties in being selected to work as a conductor, set up her own orchestra, which she ran for almost 30 years. She was known for her energy, 'firebrand personal style and prickly character' (Halstead 2006: ix). The relatively high eigenvector centrality scores suggest that women may tend to be less connected overall, but perhaps quite strategic in terms of the connections they do forge: they may well aim to be connected to the highly connected. A number of male composers also aimed to recognise talent without regard to gender. Alain Frogley, drawing on the research of Jennifer Doctor, cites 'the extraordinary lengths to which Vaughan Williams went to support other composers both young and old ... especially remarkable ... was his unflagging support for female pupils such as Elizabeth Maconchy and Grace Williams' (Frogley 2003, 251).

To examine how female and male positions differed, we conduct the following analyses. First, we test for average differences between female and male composers in connectedness, measured by degree, eigenvector and betweenness centrality. Second, we examine how patterns of connection differ between men and women with regard to sex homophily – whether men are more likely to connect to men, and women to women.

We first look at whether there are differences between male and female composers in average degree centrality, eigenvector centrality and betweenness centrality. As reported in Table 4.2, male composers have a larger number of connections (degree centrality) at the 10 per cent level of significance. They are also more likely to fall along the paths linking other composers (betweenness centrality), and therefore are more able to act as a broker or control information flow, although differences are shy of the conventional levels of significance. There is no difference between male and female composers in their eigenvector centrality, namely the extent to which they are connected to the highly connected. This might be interpreted positively: female composers, constrained in the extent to which they can forge connections (for example, because they have shorter careers due to caring responsibilities) perhaps ensure that the connections they do forge are to the influential. However, this result could also be due to female composers having studied with leading teachers of composition; and the failure to translate promise as students into lasting careers would then be of concern.

Second, we examine sex homophily. We can look at the percentage of ties which are to network members of the same sex and test whether there is a significant difference between male and female patterns of selection. For those composers identifying ties to others, 94 per cent of the ties of male composers are to other male composers, while only 21 per cent of female ties are to other female composers. This apparent difference in tendency to homophily is significant at the 0.1 per cent level of significance. The E–I index provides a further measure of homophily: for each group it gives the number of ties external to the group minus the number of ties that are internal to the group, divided by the total number of ties (Borgatti et al. 2012, 274). This value can range from 1 to –1, with the index positive when a group is outward-looking, and negative when a group is inward-looking. Table 4.3 confirms that the E–I index for female composers indicates heterophily and that for males indicates homophily; and that the indices are significantly different, again at the 0.1 per cent level. Borgatti et al. emphasise, however, that these measures fail to take account of relative group size and the ties not chosen. It might be that female composers link to males simply because there are so few other female composers with whom they can connect. The Yule's Q measure of association, however, takes account of

Table 4.2 Comparison of female and male centrality

	Average male score	Average female score	Test of differences: two-tailed test
Freeman centrality	0.447	0.286	$p=0.075$
Eigenvector centrality	0.018	0.018	$p=0.967$
Betweenness centrality	0.320	0.112	$p=0.188$
N	437	68	

Source: *Oxford Music Online* and authors' analysis.

Note
Statistical significance is computed by UCINET using permutation trials with 10,000 per run. The centrality values for each individual in the network are not independent of those of other composers, and so randomisation is employed for significance testing.

Table 4.3 Comparison of male composers' and female composers' homophily

	Percent homophily (%)	E–I Index	Yule's Q	N
Male composers	94.0 (N=297)	−0.880 (297)	0.772	297
Female composers	20.6 (N=43)	0.589 (43)	−0.424	43
Test of differences (df=338)	21.909 (p=0.000)	t=−21.909 (p=0.000)	t=12.490 (p=0.000)	

Source: *Oxford Music Online* and authors' analysis.

relative group size (Borgatti *et al.* 2012, 272–3). In this case, we still find that female composers exhibit heterophily and male composers homophily. Male composers have fairly plentiful opportunities to form connections with other male composers with access to resources, while female composers must connect with male composers to achieve the same access – an example of induced heterophily (Ibarra 1992). It is known that information and influence spreads more readily where links are homophilous (Valente 2010, 178); in fields where information flow is critical for progression, then, simply being a member of a salient minority will impede progress to an extent.

We can now move on to explore how gender, centrality and success are associated. It is worth giving some detail on how we created our measures of success. First, we count the number of works each composer has ever had featured in the Proms. The BBC Proms, running since 1895 and supported by the BBC since 1927, is arguably the world's most significant classical music festival. It was intended by its founder, Robert Newman, 'to train the public by easy stages ... until I have created a public for classical and modern music' (Wood 1938, 92). This Victorian mission is now interpreted as a commitment to make canonic works, new commissions, underappreciated works (particularly British works) and other serious music accessible to a wide audience: about 100 concerts are performed over eight weeks in the Albert Hall, a venue seating over 5,000, and broadcast live on television and the radio. Programming decisions are formally made by the Proms Director, but its current Director stresses that decision-making is collaborative:

> it is a team effort ... [t]he Proms is a focus for the whole music industry and suggestions come in from all over the place – from my own colleagues on the Proms team and Radio 3, from BBC performance groups, from publishers, from the artists themselves, from people who want to visit with their own orchestras.
>
> (Dickson 2013)

He has also stated that while the festival is international, 'it is also a British institution run by a British institution and it is important to feature British artists and British music – but they are placed in an international context' (Tilden 2011:

online). In sum, the works are selected by a small but apparently open elite group of the Proms Director and those connected to the Proms, to stage concerts and provide an experience which the market would not.

The count of works is drawn from the 1890–2011 seasons, using the BBC Radio 3 searchable online database available at www.bbc.co.uk/proms/archive.[1] As we discuss elsewhere (McAndrew and Everett forthcoming), this measure has issues: songs are given equal weight with symphonies, and popular works performed repeatedly count as heavily as a single work performed once. However, it is arguable that having a large number of works performed once indicates artistic success, and some composers might prefer it to having written a single hit song performed annually. Furthermore, while the Proms are not necessarily representative of concert life in general, the measure is attractive in that it reflects the decisions of an elite group of music providers and performers, and their esteem for composers.

We provide a further perspective by creating a second measure of success: a count of the number of records on which each composer has featured as listed in the Amazon's classical music catalogue. Again, there are issues with this measure. In this case, having a three-minute track featured on an album is given the same weight as a single opera recording, while multiple recordings of the same work are counted separately. In this case, the count is more likely to reflect the popularity of works since more popular works are more likely to be rerecorded. A secondary difficulty is that the Amazon catalogue search tool is not restrictive so that entries for those who recorded as performing musicians or conductors as well as composers had to be disambiguated one-by-one, introducing scope for error. Finally, works are continually added to the catalogue in real time, which means that composers searched for later are slightly more likely to have a larger number of recordings identified. Despite their issues, we consider that the measures have their uses as reflecting 'symbolic' success on the one hand and 'commercial' success on the other, and that they compare well with economist F.M. Scherer's measure of composition productivity based on column inches in the Schwann Opus reference guide to recorded classical music (Scherer 2003, 7). Furthermore, the Pearson correlation coefficient between the Proms and Amazon measures is 0.72 ($p = 0.000$) providing some reassurance that they both relate to composer output.

In Table 4.4, we list the top ten female and male composers ranked by each measure. As an exploratory step, in Table 4.5 we compare the means for males and females on each count: male composers appear to be more successful, albeit at only the 10 per cent level of significance.

To probe further whether the pram in the hall was the enemy of good art (Connolly 2008, 116), we did attempt to identify whether female composers were married or had a life partner, and the number of children they had. Where we could identify marital status, 39 had at least one life partner while ten had none. Where we could identify whether they had any children, 16 were childfree while 19 had at least one. There were no significant differences between those who were partnered and not, and those who were childfree and not, in terms of

Table 4.4 Highest ranking female and male composers in terms of works ever performed at the Proms and recordings listed on the Amazon classical music catalogue

	Female composers		*Male composers*	
	Number of works ever performed at the Proms	*Number of recordings listed on Amazon*	*Number of works ever performed at the Proms*	*Number of recordings listed on Amazon*
1	Teresa Clotilde del Riego 38	Rebecca Clarke 40	Benjamin Britten 94	Benjamin Britten 1,108
2	Thea Musgrave 20	Elizabeth Maconchy 28	Ralph Vaughan Williams 71	Ralph Vaughan Williams 860
3	Judith Weir 17	Thea Musgrave 28	Hermann Lohr 58	William Walton 464
4	Elizabeth Maconchy 13	Judith Weir 25	William Walton 52	Gustav Holst 435
5	Elisabeth Lutyens 11	Elisabeth Lutyens 17	Eric Coates 51	Herbert Howells 245
6	Alicia Adelaide Needham 10	Sally Beamish 14	Peter Maxwell Davies 50	Arnold Bax 193
7	Dorothy Howell 5	Elizabeth Poston 13	Montague F. Phillips 49	Malcolm Arnold 190
8	Ethel Barns 5	Madeleine Dring 12	Harrison Birtwistle 41	Frank Bridge 174
9	Priaulx Rainier 5	Rachel Portman 12	Arnold Bax 41	Michael Tippett 170
10	Grace Williams 4	Grace Williams 11	Michael Tippett 38	John Tavener 168

Table 4.5 Comparison of male and female composers' success

	Female mean	Male mean	Difference and standard error	Significance of difference (p-value)
Works ever featured in Proms	2.2	4.3	2.1 (1.2)	0.093
Recordings listed on Amazon	4.7	22.5	17.8 (9.5)	0.062

either the number of works performed at the Proms or recordings listed on Amazon. It may be that we have too few cases to run the test – due to the fact that marital status and number of children are not necessarily publicised, particularly for composers who are still active. It is also likely that those with children become more time-efficient and driven – and generally have few children in any case – so that the differences between the two groups are insignificant. It would be more helpful to test whether practising female composers are less likely to marry or have children than male composers or women working in other creative fields, to establish whether women with partners and families are particularly disadvantaged in the classical music field.

Review and discussion

How far does our exploratory analysis thus far chime with historians' and biographers' accounts? Here we follow Scherer in looking in detail at individual composer' careers 'to achieve depth of qualitative analysis along with quantitative breadth' (Scherer 2003, 9). From the *Oxford Music Online* biographies and the music history literature, we describe possible patterns here, although without strong claims to their generalisability.

In virtually all cases, these composers began studying music in early childhood with a great deal of parental encouragement; many were the children of professional or skilled amateur musicians. Phyllis Tate was unusual in being a self-taught ukelelist before studying music formally at the Royal Academy of Music at 17, having been discovered by Harry Farjeon (Fuller n.d.a). Grace Williams was more fortunate, 'born into a house filled with music'; her father founded and conducted the Romilly Boys' Choir which became renowned across Europe (Mathias 2012, 21–2). From a young age, she played violin with her family in chamber groups, and accompanied her father's choir in public performances. Ruth Gipps also benefited from very early immersion; she received a great deal of publicity as a child prodigy from the age of five, beginning her training very young with her mother, who had studied at the Frankfurt Conservatoire and went on to establish and run the Bexhill School of Music (Halstead 2006, 3–4). Having completed a piano concerto at 14, Gipps began five years' study at the Royal College of Music at the age of 16, immediately placed in the top grade for composition where she studied with R.O. Morris (Halstead 2006, 11).

Precocity of talent was not necessary for a successful career, however. Lutyens's family was not musical, although cultured and not actively discouraging. She appears to have begun serious study with Polyxena Fletcher at the age of 15; Mathias notes that, due to her mother's interest in theosophy, 'music had not always been [Lutyens's] central focus' and describes a period of disrupted study and mental ill-health in her late teens arising from her own following of the doctrine (Mathias 2012, 13–14). On entry to the Royal College of Music at the age of 20, she was not allowed to study composition with Ralph Vaughan Williams or John Ireland as the college's foremost teachers, and had to work hard to acquire a solid musical technique (Mathias 2012, 12, 15). At the extreme is the example of Minna Keal (1909–99), mother of socialist historian Raphael Samuel. She studied composition at the Royal Academy of Music during the 1920s, leaving early to contribute to household finances by working in the family business. She worked in manual occupations until returning to music by teaching during retirement, when she met the young composer Justin Connolly during his work as an examiner:

> Connolly encouraged Keal to start writing again. Still hesitant, she was given by her son composition lessons with Oliver Knussen, as a Christmas present in 1974 ... Connolly and Knussen persisted with their pupil and in 1982 Minna Keal began work on her Symphony ... when the Symphony was programmed at the BBC Proms in 1989, few could have guessed at its effect.... Despite appearing alongside the premiere of Taverner's cello masterpiece, it was widely noticed and acclaimed by the public and critics alike.
>
> (Bullamore 1999)

Marriage, even without children, could both help and hinder. A number of the most eminent – Grace Williams, Dorothy Gow, Imogen Holst and Elizabeth Poston among others – never married. For Rebecca Clarke, marriage arrived late; however, as feminist musicologist Sally Macarthur noted, she was nevertheless described primarily as 'wife of James Friskin' in her entry in the *Grove Dictionary of Music and Musicians*, even though he was scarcely better known and could have had little influence over her main body of work (Macarthur 2002, 91).

In some cases, a husband's income was very useful. Alicia Adelaide Needham, one of the earliest composers in our dataset, was given freedom to compose by her well-off husband, who actively supported her career, organising concerts and her earliest publications for her. She went on to write over 700 compositions, some of which were extremely popular in their day (Klein 2009, 1). Her career was one positive outcome from what her son's biographer described as 'a spectacularly disastrous Edwardian marriage' (Winchester 2008, 12). In other cases, husbands were themselves impecunious musicians or working in modestly paid professions. Roma notes that in the 1940s 'life for Lutyens was extremely difficult ... Neither her former nor her current husband made much money' (Roma 2005, 12).

In many cases partners provided critical moral support. The obituary for William LeFanu, husband of Elizabeth Maconchy and father of composer Nicola LeFanu, emphasised that he was 'devoted to his wife Elizabeth Maconchy and her career, delighting in her prolific musical achievements and sharing her admiration for Vaughan Williams, and was always at hand to assist her in every way' (Webster 1995). Some women asserted their need to work: Ruth Gipps refused to allow domestic life to intrude, writing that 'marriage could not in any way alter my attitude to my work; life without work would not be life' (Halstead 2006, 24).

Marriage to fellow musicians could also educate, widen horizons and enlarge opportunities. While Lutyens often claimed to have discovered serialism independently of the Second Viennese School from her own study of baroque music, her biographer and others have pointed out that her second husband, conductor and music administrator Edward Clark, was surely a critical influence. He had studied with Arnold Schoenberg in Berlin and knew Anton Webern and Ferruccio Busoni long before his relationship with Lutyens (Doctor 2004); accordingly, Tenant-Flowers concludes we should 'seriously question whether Lutyens's claim is entirely truthful' (Tenant-Flowers 1991, 68). As for Thea Musgrave, she was already well established when she spent some time in the US on a visiting fellowship, meeting and subsequently marrying American violist Peter Mark in 1971. She accordingly settled in the US, contributing to and benefiting from its rich musical life. Her husband's 35-year position as director of the Virginia Opera Society encouraged her to compose more works for opera from the 1970s, with the society giving a number of first performances of her works, including a work commissioned jointly by the Royal Opera House and Virginia Opera Society (Barnes 2002). Similarly, Sally Beamish's marriage to Scottish cellist Robert Irvine encouraged her to move from London to Scotland, where they both founded the Chamber Group of Scotland alongside composer James Mac-Millan. This move enabled her to focus on composition and her career as a composer subsequently flourished (Fuller n.d.b). Madeleine Dring and Freda Swain, among others, also composed works for instrumentalist husbands.

In other cases, marriage clearly diverted energies, even for this group of relatively successful women. Doreen Carwithen was a notable case; she won all the composition prizes at the Royal Academy of Music in the early 1940s, before being selected by J. Arthur Rank as an apprentice film composer in 1947 (Foreman, n.d.; Gray 2007, 293). She was to write scores for over 30 films, including the official film of Elizabeth II's coronation. She also continued to compose chamber and orchestral music. In 1961, she eloped with William Alwyn, her composition professor at the Royal Academy, becoming his secretary and amanuensis, and generally known as 'Mary Alwyn' as he preferred. She continued to prioritise his work until his death in 1985 before returning to her own. William Alwyn's biographer points out that as her teacher he had encouraged her to compose in the first place; but with her long break from composition and change of name, 'Doreen Carwithen in effect ceased to exist' (Wright 2008, 189). Indeed, 'Alwyn and Carwithen may be mirror images ... In trying to make sense of why Alwyn's reputation sidled into the margins of

British musical history, we should understand why Doreen Carwithen's reputation escaped its moorings' (Wright 2008, 3).

Children were more clearly a difficulty. Maconchy, eventually a mother of two, put it bluntly:

> [We] now have to do everything.... It is not impossible to write music if one has children, though difficult enough: but rearing them comes just at the time when one ought to be making a career, and it is almost impossible to combine the two.
>
> (Halstead 2006, 67)

Gipps took an eight-week break before the birth of her only child, only to find that she became 'a boring person'; a string of nannies was swiftly arranged until he was old enough to board at school (Halstead 2006, 68). Her biographer considered it 'clearly influential' that she had been brought up in a family where her mother was the main income-earner, showing that being a professional musician was not incompatible with having a family (Halstead 2006, 67). Sally Beamish began her composing career after winning an Arts Council bursary which allowed her to arrange part-time childcare: 'I booked a babysitter for 4 hours every morning. That was a good discipline. In fact I find it harder to be focused now that I have more time and I'm not paying anyone' (Thomas 2004). Film and opera composer Rachel Portman, who won an Oscar for the soundtrack for *Emma* in 1996, said in an interview of working full time with three children that 'I find ways of coping. They're very young [ages eight, five, and four] but I'm far more focused than I used to be. And I'm very rigorous about my work so [that] I have time for them' (Holleran 2003). Time is not the only casualty, however; children also need financial support. Lutyens's biographers highlight her need to earn an income given Clark's insecure career: 'Lutyens was forced to compose for film and radio to support her four children. The situation lasted over 20 years and seriously hindered her artistic development' (Payne and Calam n.d.). As stated above, we could only establish whether female composers had children in 35 cases, since many living and practising composers see no need to publicise their family life; of those 35, 16 had no children. It is plausible that children damage careers, and only the most focused and highly organised can continue composing with children. Nicola LeFanu, composer and daughter of Elizabeth Maconchy, clarified it thus in 1987:

> Most competitions, invaluable for their opportunities for professional performance and exposure, are for composers in their twenties and early thirties. This effectively excludes those women composers who choose to have their families at the most natural time. These women re-enter the profession in their late thirties or forties and find it almost impossible to gain a place other than on the periphery, since our society puts such value on the norm of early success.
>
> (LeFanu 1987, 7)

While it seems likely that some women composers made active choices to 'off-ramp' their careers for family reasons, examples of sex discrimination proliferate in the biographies, removing the possibility of choice for many. In her final year at the Royal College of Music, Maconchy was informed by the head of the college that she had won the prestigious Mendelssohn scholarship which would allow her to study abroad. It turned out he had been mistaken: the adjudication committee had changed their minds and awarded it to a male student instead. He justified this by saying 'anyway, if we'd given it to you, you'd have only got married and never written another note' (Mathias 2012, 28). Gipps faced enormous difficulties in working as an orchestral musician and conductor; for example, in 1955, on applying to the BBC, she was informed that 'it was impossible to give her the job, as a woman would not command respect from the male-dominated orchestra' (Halstead 2006, 47). Being denied opportunities to conduct hampered her composition; on founding her own orchestra, she gave first performances of her works which were often then taken up by other orchestras (Gray 2007, 57). In her early days, Elisabeth Lutyens occasionally published her works as A.E. Lutyens, while Rebecca Clarke published as 'Anthony Trent' for two decades, only admitting at age 90 that works published under a male name received more attention (Gray 2007, 52). As a music student, LeFanu believed that the discrimination experienced by her mother's generation was a thing of the past; by 1987 she had realised that while misogyny has largely disappeared, systemic discrimination remained. All the main musical institutions were run by men, while the 'new music' scene fostered composers fitting a particular – male – image of 'master musicians'; female composers still struggled to win commissions or feature on concert programmes at all, despite comprising about 15 per cent of the profession (LeFanu 1987).

Female composers have been mindful that such biases exist, with examples of collaborative effort to improve their hand. Following Vaughan Williams's and Gustav Holst's example, as students Maconchy and Williams began a life-long habit of mutual consultation and criticism in order to improve their work (Mathias 2012, 21). Lutyens, aware that she would face difficulties in getting her works performed, approached violinist Anne Macnaghten and conductor Iris Lemare in 1931 to organise concerts for young British composers; the Macnaghten–Lemare Concerts became an important platform for new music in the 1930s (Gray 2007, 53). Iris Lemare explained that 'our origin was strictly realistic, not altruistic. Three young women musicians found sex discrimination blocking all progress for them' (Roma 2005, 10).

The gender penalty in composition success

As a final step, we tested the effect of being a female rather than male composer, holding other characteristics constant, on our two measures of achievement: first, the number of works performed in the annual Proms concerts, and second, the number of recordings each composer has listed on Amazon in its classical music database. To illustrate achievement within the network, we provide two

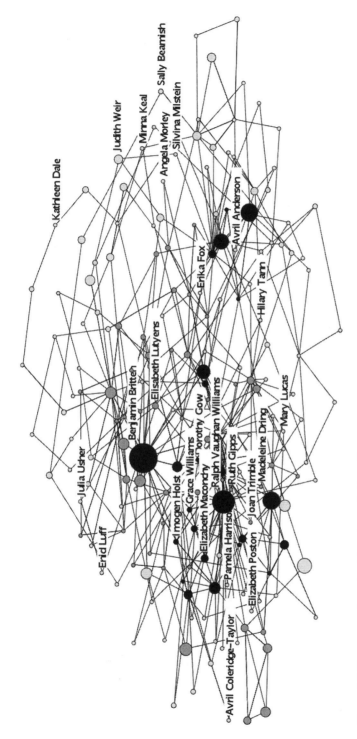

Figure 4.3 Two-core subgraph with nodes scaled by number of composers' works ever featured in the Proms.

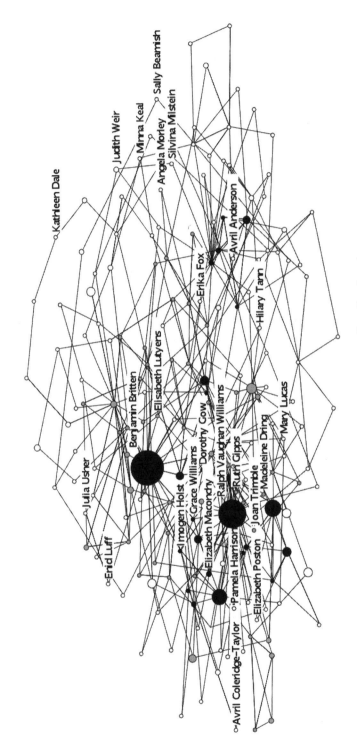

Figure 4.4 Two-core subgraph with nodes scaled by number of composers' recordings listed on Amazon.

visualisations here; for ease of display, we removed composers who were connected to only one other, leaving a graph of 190 (the two-core subgraph). Nodes in the first graph are scaled by the number of works ever featured by that composer in the Proms; and nodes in the second are scaled by the number of recordings on which each composer features on Amazon. Female composers are labelled; the location of Benjamin Britten and Ralph Vaughan Williams is also given for information. The graphs illustrate that there is considerably more inequality within composers in the number of recordings than in the number of works performed at the Proms.

We now move on to examine the drivers of success, using a range of predictors: birth cohort, nationality, professional role, network centrality, and sex. We use a multivariate multiple regression model with two dependent variables and the same explanatory variables, to examine both measures of success jointly, allowing the error terms to correlate.[2] The advantage of this approach is that we can see how the outcome variables are related once control variables have been included (through examining the correlation of residuals); and that we can test the effect of explanatory variables both across the two outcomes of interest, and taking both outcomes jointly.

As is typical for creative output (and talent markets more generally), our measures of composition success exhibit positive skew: this occurs because the creative process generates many outputs which do not succeed or which achieve very modest success, together with a small number of extreme values or 'hits'. Economist Sherwin Rosen has suggested two mechanisms: rewards may be more unequal than talent partly because audiences have most interest in, and are prepared to pay more for, the very best. Furthermore, 'joint consumption technologies' such as broadcasting and printing allow mass markets to be created which can be served by relatively few cultural producers (Rosen 1981). Others have suggested that audiences gain additional pleasure from experiencing cultural products that others experience so that preferential attachment effects drive 'hits' even where differences in quality are imperceptible *ex ante* (Adler 1985). The model employed is based on the conditional mean, which is not a good measure of central tendency for highly skewed measures. Therefore, because many composers feature no links to others, no recordings and no works in the Proms, we use an inverse hyperbolic sine rather than logarithmic transformation to deal with the 'zeroes'.[3]

The model results tell us the following. In the equation predicting success in the Proms, we find strong cohort effects, as we found in our earlier work (McAndrew and Everett forthcoming). Being an immigrant composer is associated with lower success, as is having more professional roles besides an identity as a composer (for example, as a teacher, conductor or performing musician). Centrality is significantly associated with success, while the squared term included to test for a nonlinear effect is shy of significance. Being female, as noted in our earlier work, has a negative effect, but is insignificant. The interaction term is also not significant: being a highly central female does not particularly damage female composers (which might happen if the highly central were more likely to work as enablers rather than on their own works) nor does it particularly advantage

Table 4.6 Results of the multivariate multiple regression models predicting success at the Proms and in having works recorded.

	Equation 1: Number of Works in Proms		Equation 2: Number of Recordings listed on Amazon	
Constant	1.646 (0.188) ***	0.000	2.380 (0.238)***	0.000
Born 1870–1889	–		–	
1890–1909	–0.546 (0.213)**	0.011	–0.269 (0.270)	0.319
1910–1929	–0.954 (0.147)***	0.000	–0.235 (0.186)	0.206
1930–1949	–0.905 (0.156)***	0.000	–0.174 (0.197)	0.377
1950–1969	–0.736 (0.185)***	0.000	–0.086 (0.233)	0.714
Scottish, Welsh or Irish	–0.141 (0.150)	0.348	–0.707 (0.189)***	0.000
Non-British origin	–0.510 (0.248)**	0.040	–0.785 (0.313)**	0.013
Professional roles	–0.172 (0.060)**	0.005	–0.032 (0.076)	0.679
Degree centrality	1.421 (0.300) ***	0.000	0.773 (0.380) **	0.042
Degree centrality squared	–0.016 (0.172)	0.925	0.320 (0.218)	0.142
Female	–0.171 (0.200)	0.392	–1.082 (0.253)***	0.000
Female*centrality	–0.375 (0.496)	0.450	0.675 (0.627)	0.282
N	505		505	
F	17.563		12.246	
Adjusted R^2	0.266		0.197	
Correlation of residuals	0.509***	0.000		
Breusch-Pagan test of independence: chi^2 (1) = 130.78 (p = 0.000)				

Notes
*p<0.1, **p<0.05, ***p<0.01. Base category is born in 1870–1889, English, and male in both models.

them (for example, if network connections assist women in a way which is distinctive to them).

The equation predicting success as a recording composer gives us another perspective on the correlates of musical success. In this case, the cohort effects are not significant. Being a Scottish, Welsh or Irish composer is associated with having fewer recordings – a finding which suggests that English (presumably metropolitan) composers are relatively more successful. That this 'Celtic penalty' is not found in the model for Proms success is interesting; Proms programmers may see it as their mission to represent composers from across the British Isles, or alternatively the quality recognised by Proms programmers fails to be recognised by commercial record producers. The term for immigrant composers is again negative and significant. In this case, having more professional roles has no significant effect. The contrast with the effect for Proms success is interesting; in this case it seems that conductors or performers use their reputation to record their own works which counterbalances any negative effect on their composition output from not pursuing it to the exclusion of other musical works. Alternatively, those working actively as conductors, performers or teachers may be more attuned to popular tastes. Centrality is again associated with success, and again there is no evidence for a nonlinear effect.

The effect of being a female rather than male composer is striking in this model: it appears that there is a significant gender penalty. The contrast with the effect of being female in the equation predicting Proms success is instructive. Because we have used a multivariate multiple regression model, we can test the effect of being female on both outcomes jointly: the null hypothesis is that the effect of being female is zero in both equations. We find that the effect of being female is negative taking both outcomes together: $F(2, 493) = 10.33$, $p < 0.000$. The large and highly significant negative effect of being female in the second equation is driving this result.

How can we interpret these findings? It depends. Proponents of the 'differential preferences' view of gender differences might argue that female composers channel their efforts into works of distinction, works which are recognised by the elite of the classical music world and featured in the programme of the world's largest classical music festival. Given the constraints faced by female composers in pursuing a professional career – for example, in gaining acceptance by agents and publishers, and in the film industry – they appear as a group to prioritise quality and thereby achieve a level of symbolic success similar to that of male composers. Their lower representation overall is likely caused by choices made and constraints experienced upstream. Alternatively, it could be argued that the lack of a gender penalty at the Proms may reflect the Proms' particular mission to educate tastes and reflect the diversity of British composing talent. If this representation does not translate into commissions, performances and recordings more broadly, then female composers will be less able than male composers to generate income streams, and we should question why.

We should qualify our findings as follows. We are aware that neither the measure of symbolic success nor that of commercial success is perfect; the models should be tested against other measures of composition output. However, in the absence of high-quality repertoire or recording sales data, these measures serve as useful proxies. Additional measures of success and esteem will allow the findings presented here to be tested further.

Conclusion

In this chapter, we set out to explore why women are under-represented in classical music composition. There is the obvious point that what sociologists call 'Matthew effects' predominate – the classical music canon was almost completely established in the eighteenth and nineteenth centuries, when women had almost no access to the profession. Even were women to dominate new music, concert programmes would show only a marginal improvement in the gender ratio. There are no female Mozarts or Beethovens primarily because of path dependence.

Second, the qualitative data drawn from biographies and interview sources suggest that female composers faced overt discrimination until quite recently. The norm that mothers are primary care-givers means that if they have children they are expected, or choose, to take on a good deal of work in the home just at the point when their professional life would benefit from sustained focus. A number of the composers in our dataset became highly time-efficient on parenthood whereas others avoided role conflict by not having children. Choice of life partner also had repercussions: some female composers prioritised their husband's work; others composed for partners who were instrumentalists; others still were influenced stylistically by their partner. For the group of women composers under consideration here, there is no obvious lack of giftedness but of recognition and access to opportunities. LeFanu was surely correct in arguing that institutional sexism causes additional constraints beyond those imposed by social strictures and family obligations.

Our quantitative data and network analysis add some further insights. A number of women clear the hurdle of having an identity as a professional composer, and those that do appear to be no less connected than male composers. Female composers are, however, different from men in their heterophily. In terms of success, the female composers in our dataset are no less successful than male composers in having their compositions featured in the BBC Proms; however, they are significantly less successful in terms of the number of recordings on which they feature. In other words, either the quality recognised by Proms programmers fails to be recognised by commercial record producers, for example because of lack of familiarity, risk aversion or a perception that there are no markets for their work (which may well be realistic). Alternatively, female composers may systematically compose fewer works, or fewer of the type of work which sells and is frequently rerecorded or included on compilation albums. More investigation into female composers' access to recorded music markets would be of interest.

What measures might help female composers while avoiding tokenism and quota-setting? The results and qualitative survey so far point to support following career breaks, fostering of connections and visibility via awards as areas where interventions could be useful. Funding is extremely tight and suggestions should be financially realistic. There are a number of salutary initiatives under way; for example, in 2010 the Performing Rights Society for Music Foundation established 'Women Make Music', a seed-funding scheme whereby female composers across all genres may apply for up to £5,000. Awards have been made to well-known composers and popular musicians alike, suggesting that these relatively small amounts are valuable even to the apparently successful. If career breaks cause problems, support for career re-entry could be provide through providing a short period of financial support via fellowships. Such schemes exist for science and engineering, for example via the Daphne Jackson Trust. Small grants to attend residential masterclasses on the Arvon Foundation model, where writers attend weekend or week-long retreats under the direction of an established writer, could be targeted at women returning to composition after a career break as well as other non-traditional applicants. Such courses provide space and time to work as well as the opportunity for contact with those active in the wider music world. Relatedly, an analogue of the Jerwood/Arvon mentoring scheme for writers could be targeted at emerging composers with non-traditional backgrounds, including women, and particularly those who have no current links to music colleges: winning a place on a mentorship scheme provides both connections and an award which can be used to strengthen or simplify a career narrative. Composition competitions open only to female composers – a music equivalent of the former Orange Prize for Fiction, now known as the Bailey's Women's Prize for Fiction – could similarly help winners build profile and signal their career intent. Targeted funding for festivals or festival streams promoting new female works – in similar vein to 2012's Women of the World Festival at the South Bank Centre in London – could also play an important role.

The story here is reassuring in many respects. For the women who do manage to break into the classical composition world, and who are represented in our dataset, there is little evidence that they are marginalised, at least in terms of their network position. The evidence for female heterophily shows that female composers have been successful at linking with influential male composers, even if they have not yet supplanted them. Female composers appear to enjoy symbolic success equal with men – again, conditional on being 'in the game' in the first place – even if they do not equally enjoy commercial success, and even if the number of female composer represented in the Proms is still small overall. Biographical evidence also reveals much initiative and resilience on the part of women composers developing their careers in the first half of the twentieth century. The challenge for the classical music world is to open up multiple entry and re-entry points into the profession, for composers who do not have the unbroken career path and record of apparent effortless success which appeals to marketers. Classical music needs more Minna Keals, preferably having their first symphonies performed well before their eighties.

There is scarcely a shortage of talent in the composition world, and so the need for such initiatives to diversify the pool may seem less than pressing. However, it is important to provide opportunities for recognition for both established and emerging composers who have different career paths, to encourage greater entry and more equitable access to a unique and totemic profession.

Notes

1 The data were extracted in April 2011. Easily extractable data on frequency of performances have only been added to the publicly accessible dataset since our data extraction; in further work we will enrich our dataset with this new information.
2 Simultaneous estimation of the two outcomes takes into account the covariance between them without imposing a causal ordering on the dependent variables. It also allows efficient estimates of model coefficients and standard errors.
3 The IHS of $x = \log(x + (x^2 + 1)^{1/2})$.

References

Adler, M. (1985) Stardom and Talent, *American Economic Review* 75(1), 208–12.
Andrew, K. (2012) 'Why There Are So Few Female Composers', *Guardian*, 8 February. Online, available at www.theguardian.com/commentisfree/2012/feb/08/why-so-few-female-composers? (accessed 3 December 2013).

Baer, J. and Kaufman, J.C. (2008) Gender Differences in Creativity, *Journal of Creative Behavior* 42, 75–105.

Bailey, M. (2006) More Power to the Pill: The Impact of Contraceptive Freedom on Women's Life Cycle Labor Supply, *Quarterly Journal of Economics* 121(1), 289–320.

Barnes, J. (2002) Thea Musgrave, *Oxford Music Online*. Online, available at www.oxford-musiconline.com/subscriber/article/grove/music/19399 (accessed 28 January 2014).

Benjamin, T. (2009) Economics of New Music, DPhil dissertation, University of Oxford.

Borgatti, S.P., Everett, M.G. and Johnson, J.C. (2012), *Analyzing Social Networks*, London, Sage Publications.

Borniger, J.C., Chaudhry, A. and Muehlenbein, M.P. (2013) Relationships among Musical Aptitude, Digit Ratio and Testosterone in Men and Women, *PLoS One*, E 8(3), e57637, 1–10.

Bott, H.M. (1928) Observation of Play Activities in a Nursery School, *Genetic Psychology Monographs* 4, 44–88.

Bullamore, T. (1999) Obituary: Minna Keal, *The Independent*, 16 November. Online, available at www.independent.co.uk/arts-entertainment/obituary-minna-keal-1126413.html.

Caves, R. (2000) *Creative Industries: Contracts between Art and Commerce*, Cambridge, MA, Harvard University Press.

Connolly, C. (2008) *Enemies of Promise*, Chicago, University of Chicago Press; first edition 1938.

Dickson, E.J. (2013) Roger Wright: Planning the Proms Requires a Cool Head and a Strong Hand, *Radio Times* 12 July. Online, available at www.radiotimes.com/news/2013–07–12/roger-wright-planning-the-proms-requires-a-cool-head-and-a-strong-hand (accessed 21 January 2014).

Doctor, J. (1998) Intersecting Circles: The Early Careers of Elizabeth Maconchy, Elisabeth Lutyens and Grace Williams, *Women and Music Journal* 2, 90–109.

Doctor, J. (2004) Clark, (Thomas) Edward (1888–1962), *Oxford Dictionary of National Biography*. Online, available at www.oxforddnb.com/view/article/40709 (accessed 30 January 2014).

Finder, A., Healy, P.D. and Zernike, K. (2006) President of Harvard Resigns, Ending Stormy 5-Year Tenure, *New York Times*, 22 February. Online, available at www.nytimes.com/2006/02/22/education/22harvard.html (accessed 22 January 2014).

Foreman, L. (n.d.) Doreen Carwithen, *Oxford Music Online*. Online, available at www.oxfordmusiconline.com/subscriber/article/grove/music/49089 (accessed 23 January 2014).

Frogley, A. (2003) Rewriting the Renaissance: History, Imperialism, and British Music since 1840, *Music and Letters* 84(2), 241–57.

Fuller, S. (n.d.a) Phyllis Tate, *Oxford Music Online*. Online, available at www.oxfordmusiconline.com/subscriber/article/grove/music/27549 (accessed 20 January 2014).

Fuller, S. (n.d.b) Sally Beamish, *Oxford Music Online*. Online, available at www.oxford-musiconline.com/subscriber/article/grove/music/45630 (accessed 21 January 2014).

Grasmick, H.G., Hagan, J., Blackwell, B.S. and Arneklev, B.J. (1996) Risk Preferences and Patriarchy: Extending Power-Control Theory, *Social Forces* 75, 177–99.

Gray, A. (2007) *The World of Women in Classical Music*, La Jolla, CA, WordWorld Publications)

Hagan, J., Gillis, A.R. and Simpson, J. (1985) The Class Structure of Gender and Delinquency: Toward a Power-Control Theory of Common Delinquent Behavior, *American Journal of Sociology* 90, 1151–78.

Halstead, J. (2006) *Ruth Gipps: Anti-Modernism, Nationalism and Difference in English Music*, London, Ashgate.

Happé, F. and Vital, P. (2009) What Aspects of Autism Predispose to Talent? *Philosophical Transactions of the Royal Society B* 364, 1369–75.

Hassler, M. (1991) Testosterone and Artistic Talents, *International Journal of Neuroscience* 56(1–4), 25–38.

Hassler, M., Nieschlag, E. and De La Motte, D. (1990) Creative Musical Talent, Cognitive Functioning, and Gender: Psychobiological Aspects, *Music Perception: An Interdisciplinary Journal* 8(1), 35–48.

Holleran, S. (2003) Interview: Rachel Portman, *Box Office Mojo*. Online, available at www.boxofficemojo.com/features/?id=1259&p=.htm (accessed 25 January 2014).

Howes, F. (1966) *The English Musical Renaissance*, New York, Stein and Day.

Ibarra, H. (1992) Homophily and Differential Returns: Sex Differences in Network Structure and Access in an Advertising Firm, *Administrative Science Quarterly* 37(3), 422–47.

Kanter, R.M. (1977) *Women and Men of the Corporation*, New York, Basic Books.

Kegen, N.V. (2013) Science Networks in Cutting-edge Research Institutions: Gender Homophily and Embeddedness in Formal and Informal Networks, *Procedia – Social and Behavioral Sciences* 79, 62–81.

Kirsten, A.B. (2012) The 'Woman Composer' is Dead, *New Music Box* [online magazine of New Music USA], 19 March. Online, available at www.newmusicbox.org/articles/the-woman-composer-is-dead/ (accessed 20 January 2014).

Klein, A. (2009) 'A Daughter of Music' – Alicia Adelaide Needham's Anglo-Irish Life and Music, paper presented at the Annual Conference of the Society for Musicology in Ireland and Royal Musical Association, Dublin, 9 June.

LeFanu, N. (1987) Master Musician: An Impregnable Taboo? Online, available at www.nicolalefanu.com/resources/MasterMusician1987.pdf (accessed 28 January 2014).

Macarthur, S. (2002) *Feminist Aesthetics in Music*, Westport, CT, Greenwood Press.

Maddocks, F. (2011) 'Women Composers: Notes from the Musical Margins, *Guardian*, 13 March. Online, available at www.theguardian.com/music/2011/mar/13/london-oriana-choir-women-composers (accessed 3 December 2013).

Mathias, R. (2012) *Lutyens, Maconchy, Williams and Twentieth-Century British Music: A Blest Trio of Sirens*, Farnham, Ashgate.

McAndrew, S. and Everett, M. (forthcoming) Music as Collective Invention: A Social Network Analysis of British Composers, *Cultural Sociology*.

McPherson, M., Smith-Lovin, L. and Cook, J. (2001) Birds of Feather: Homophily in Social Networks, *Annual Review of Sociology* 27, 415–44.

Reynolds, B. (2007) Woman Composer, *New Music Box* [online magazine of New Music USA], 19 February. Online, available at www.newmusicbox.org/articles/Woman-Composer/ (accessed 20 January 2014).

Paglia, C. (1990) *Sexual Personae: Art and Decadence from Nefertiti to Emily Dickinson*, New Haven, CT, Yale University Press.

Payne, A. and Calam, T. (n.d.) Elisabeth Lutyens, *Oxford Music Online*. Online, available at www.oxfordmusiconline.com/subscriber/article/grove/music/17227 (accessed 24 January 2014).

Piirto, Jane (1991) Why Are There So Few (Creative Women: Visual Artists, Mathematicians, Musicians)? *Roeper Review* 13(3), 142–7.

Pinker, S. (2005) Sex Ed, *New Republic* 14 February. Online, available at www.newrepublic.com/article/sex-ed (accessed 25 January 2014).

Pinker, S. and Spelke, E. (2005) The Science of Gender and Science. Pinker vs. Spelke: A Debate, Harvard University Mind, Brain and Behavior Inter-Faculty Initiative, 22 April.

Online, available at www.edge.org/events/the-science-of-gender-and-sciencepinker-vs-spelkea-debate (accessed 21 January 2014).

Reis, S.M. (1999) Women and Creativity, in Runco, M.A. and Pritzker, S.R. (eds), *Encyclopedia of Creativity*, vol. 2, Waltham, MA, Academic Press, 699–708.

Roma, C. (2005) *The Choral Music of Twentieth-Century Women Composers: Elisabeth Lutyens, Elizabeth Maconchy and Thea Musgrave*, Lanham, MD, Scarecrow Press).

Rosen, S. (1981) The Economics of Superstars, *American Economic Review* 71, 845–58.

Scherer, F.M. (2003) *Quarter Notes and Bank Notes: The Economics of Music Composition in the Eighteenth and Nineteenth Centuries*, Princeton, NJ, Princeton University Press.

Tenant-Flowers, S.J. (1991) A Study of Style and Techniques in the Music of Elisabeth Lutyens, PhD thesis, Durham University.

Thomas, C. (2004) Sally Beamish Interviewed by Christopher Thomas, *Music Web International*. Online, available at www.musicweb-international.com/classrev/2004/oct04/sally_beamish.htm (accessed 25 January 2014).

Tick, J. and Tsou, J. (n.d.) Women in Music, *Oxford Music Online*. Online, available at www.oxfordmusiconline.com/public/page/Women_in_music (accessed 21 January 2014).

Tilden, I. (2011) 'Proms Director Roger Wright Answers Your Questions, *Guardian* 11 July. Online, available at www.theguardian.com/music/2011/jul/11/classicalmusicandopera-proms-2011 (accessed 21 January 2014).

Valente, T.W. (2010) *Social Networks and Health: Models, Methods, and Applications*, Oxford, Oxford University Press.

Webster, A. (1995) Obituary: William LeFanu, *Independent* 7 April. Online, available at www.independent.co.uk/news/people/obituary-william-lefanu-1614569.html (accessed 22 January 2014).

Winchester, S. (2008) *Bomb, Book and Compass: Joseph Needham and the Great Secrets of China*, London, Viking.

Wood, H.J. (1938), *My Life of Music*, London, Victor Gollancz.

Wright, A. (2008) *The Innumerable Dance: The Life and Work of William Alwyn*, Woodbridge, Boydell and Brewer.

5 Music consumption

Networks and omnivorism

Paul Widdop

Unlike other chapters in this volume, which take up a position of examining network structure on music performing communities, here the chapter diverts away somewhat from this approach and investigates music consumption of everyday people. While retaining a network focused approach, this chapter seeks to determine how resources embedded in networks (social capital) facilitate and constrain music behaviour. We do this by examining how social networks impact upon cultural omnivorousness (Peterson 1992).

Cultural omnivorousness continues to attract our attention. In 2005 Richard Peterson published an article in *Poetics* reviewing the considerable literature showing the emergence of the cultural omnivore, since its discovery in 1992 (Peterson and Simkus 1992). It is now generally acknowledged that a shift has occurred in cultural consumption patterns of the middle and upper classes, essentially from Bourdieu's (1984) theoretical position. Where once the tastes and preferences of these groups were based around ridged rules of exclusion (Bourdieu 1984), now they are said to be structured on an openness to appreciate a variety of culture from the high and popular genres (Bennett *et al.* 2010). Even those scholars most aligned with Bourdieu, therefore by definition subtly positioned against the apparent omnivore–univore framework (as proposed by Peterson and Kern 1996) concede that findings suggest a growing omnivorous nature of consumption among those highest in social positions, but this does not rule out distinction through culture, just an alternative mechanism (Warde *et al.* 2008; Warde and Gayo-Cal 2009; Bennett *et al.* 2010; Savage and Gayo-Cal 2011).

The omnivorousness literature now spans much of Europe, Australia, North America and countries in South America and the Middle East (Alderson *et al.* 2007; Torche 2007; Van Rees *et al.* 1999; Van Eijck 2000; 2001). These studies have established that omnivorousness is related to high status (Chan and Goldthorpe 2005; 2007); class and education (Peterson and Simkus 1992; Peterson and Kern 1996; Sintas and Alvarez 2002, 2004; Chan and Goldthorpe 2007; Tampubolon 2008; Bryson 1996; Erickson 1996; Van Eijck 1999); gender and age (Erickson 1996; Van Eijck 2001; Sintas and Alvarez 2002; Warde and Gayo-Cal 2009; Widdop and Cutts 2013; Stichele and Laermans 2006; Van Eijck 2000); and place (Widdop and Cutts; 2012).

There remains a gap in the literature (as noted by Peterson 2005) between the relationship between consumption patterns and social networks in the rise of omnivorism. Yet studies by Erickson (1996) and Van Eijck (1999) claim that omnivores benefit from a broader and more diverse social network, where they can display knowledge gained from interaction with individuals in different social circles, which acts as a mechanism for reinforcing social approval within these circles. Therefore, omnivores benefit from resources embedded in networks, social capital. This is noted by Bonnie Erickson in her seminal study 'Culture, Class and Connections' (1996); she notes that 'the most powerful teacher of cultural variety is contact with people in many different locations'.

To date, social capital has been conceptualised and operationalised in several ways, most famously by Robert Putnam, Pierre Bourdieu and James Coleman (Lin 2001). In the Putnam tradition, social capital is conceptualised through interpersonal trust, norms of reciprocity and mutual aid and social involvement (Verhaeghe and Tampubolon 2012). For Putnam it is these elements that foster social cohesion and cooperation which result in benefits to individuals and communities through social capital. In contrast, Bourdieu's approach to social capital was conceptualised as the sum of the resources, actual or virtual, that accrue to an individual or a group by virtue of possessing a durable network of more or less institutionalised relationships of mutual acquaintance and recognition (Bourdieu, in Bourdieu and Wacquant 1992, 119). In short, a network resources approach (Verhaeghe and Tampubolon 2012) is a crucial element in determining levels of social capital. From a network resources approach, Nan Lin formulated a standardised measurement of social capital using a class-based position generator measure of networks. In this tradition emphasis is placed on an individual's position in the social structure and the diversity and homophily of an individual's network and strength of ties in the said network.

As this book demonstrates, networks and music are an active research field, yet studies on the subject of music and social capital tend to operationalise this capital in the Putnam tradition, concerned with social cohesion, civic engagement, trust and membership in voluntary organisations, measured against consumption patterns (Warde and Tampubolon 2008). In this chapter, while we control for social capital from Putnam's framework, we are interested in a network perspective, following the framework proposed by Nan Lin (2001; Lin and Erickson 2008). To that end, this chapter has fourfold aims. First, to establish if there are well-defined omnivorous–univorous patterns in music in England. Second, are these omnivorous–univorous patterns socially stratified (by education and class). Third, accounting for class and education, do social networks impact upon participation in music? Fourth, do types of ties in a network (friendship or family) influence how music is consumed? That is, are omnivorous behaviours more or less likely to be associated with larger diverse networks?

The position taken in this chapter is premised upon testing certain propositions in relation to music participation and networks. First an exploration of theories of consumption enables us to suggest that omnivores and univores can be found in the music field in England. Second, we explain how networks are important in this theory of consumption and how this allows us to explain music participation. This approach considers (1) whether strong network resources are positively related to music participation (or omnivorism), whereas weak network resources are negatively related to participation, and (2) whether diverse networks increase liberal consumption patterns (omnivorousness) as evidenced by the music participation data.

The omnivore–univore thesis

To put this research into context we must first take an in-depth overview of the omnivore thesis, as this is the position from which network effects will be explored. Up until the early 1990s, the path-breaking work of Pierre Bourdieu's 'Distinction' represented the most comprehensive theoretical understanding and explanation of the apparent interrelationship between cultural and social hierarchies (Bourdieu 1984). The existence of a homology in cultural stratification, that people belonging to the dominant classes affirmed their higher social status through the consumption of highbrow culture while those with lower social status preferred and consumed lowbrow culture, became the orthodoxy for 20 years or more. However, by the last decade of the twentieth century, scholars began to question whether Bourdieu's theory still reflected contemporary social reality (Lamont and Lareau 1988; Van Eijck 1999; Stichele and Laermans 2006). In a series of important articles, Peterson and his colleagues (Peterson 1992; Peterson and Kern 1996; Peterson and Simkus 1992) reformulated the relationship between status hierarchy and cultural taste. They noted that high-status groups had a broader cultural repertoire, appreciating more middlebrow and lowbrow activities than the orthodoxy suggested. These groups were labelled 'omnivores', and were measured against lower-status groups with much more restricted consumption patterns. The lower-status groups attached themselves only to mainstream or popular culture, and were, therefore, coined 'univores' (Peterson 2005; Peterson and Kern 1996; Peterson and Simkus 1992). Following this groundbreaking work, numerous scholars have sought to classify cultural preferences in a broadly similar way, with many supportive, although not exclusively so (Bryson 1996; Van Eijck 1999, 2001; Sintas and Alvarez 2002; Van Rees *et al.* 1999; Chan and Goldthorpe 2005).

A large body of scholars in this field have observed the existence of an omnivore group, and theorised that greater socio-cultural heterogeneity reflects the rise in social mobility over recent decades (Peterson 2005). The growth of the mass media, advancement in online technology, the development of the leisure industry and easier access to higher education have all been used as a mechanism for explaining growing omnivorousness (Peterson 2005; Stichele and Laermans 2006). Nonetheless, numerous empirical findings suggest that the omnivores are a relatively small group and that its socio-economic make-up does not purely reflect the relationship between economic class and patterns of consumption (Sullivan and Katz-Gerro 2007; Katz-Gerro 2006). Generally, studies have shown that higher education, higher income and higher occupational status are strongly associated with omnivorous cultural preferences (Van Eijck 2001; Sintas and Alvarez 2002). Other studies have demonstrated the effects of gender and age, but the findings are not universal. Whether gender is strongly associated with omnivorism depends upon the domain of activity selected for the analysis, as shown by the differentiated gender effects found in a number of studies (Van Eijck 2001; Sintas and Alvarez 2002; Warde and Gayo-Cal 2009). Similarly, age effects have been contested, with some scholars suggesting that younger age cohorts are more inclined to be omnivores (Widdop and Cutts 2012; Stichele and Laermans 2006; Van Eijck 2000), while others allude to a more middle-aged profile (Warde *et al.* 2007; Warde and Gayo-Cal 2009). In this chapter we therefore seek to address the following research questions (RQ):

> *RQ1: In the music field in England can distinctive lifestyle patterns be found that match the framework laid down in the omnivore–univore thesis?*
>
> *RQ2: Are these music consumption patterns or lifestyles socially stratified by class, education, age and gender as found in other studies of music and cultural domains?*

Social networks and cultural participation

Although limited, there have been studies that have shown that omnivores benefit from broader and more diverse social networks where they can display knowledge gained from interaction with individuals in different social circles which reinforces social approval within these circles (Lizardo 2006; Kane 2004; Warde and Tampubolon 2008; Relish 1997; and Erickson 1996). These studies all observe that network structure and an individual's position within that structure impact upon resources available to them for constructing cultural lifestyles. That is, it is somewhat of a mediating factor in their construction and socialisation of cultural preferences and consumption patterns.

Diversity in the network

Network homophily and heterophily are important concepts in network structure. Homophily works on the premise that people like people who are similar to themselves, birds of a feather flock together (Borgatti *et al.* 2013). Therefore a homophilous network consists of individuals who are similar in characteristics, such as social class, age, etc. In contrast network heterophily is indicative of a socially diverse mix of individuals in a network. Naturally these two network concepts impact upon forms of behaviour such as music consumption, but to date both concepts have been used to explain behaviour in cultural activities.

For Mark (1998) musical preferences are transmitted through homophilous network ties, similar people interact with each other and develop similar musical tastes. However, Erickson (1996), in a study of cultural preferences in the workplace, noted that people with varied connections (heterophily) knew more about different types of culture and developed omnivorous tastes that allowed them to respond in different social settings. For Erickson (1996) the most widely useful cultural resource was cultural variety and that cultural variety is closely linked to network variety. The greater the diversity of the network, the greater the exposure to different forms of culture, for which the individual must respond, stimulating omnivorous behaviour.

For Erickson (1996) personal networks are a major source of cultural resources and a more powerful source than class itself. High-status people will certainly have a greater level of cultural capital (through childhood socialisation and education), but this is not because of their class as such, but by being embedded in diverse class-based networks. Furthermore, Kane (2004) notes that omnivorous behaviours and diverse networks may indicate an underlying desire for cosmopolitanism. This is compounded by the fact that in all studies of this nature high levels of cultural consumption and diverse networks are associated with high status. To that end one would expect to find that analogous to omnivorous behaviour, low-status groups would be characterised by low participation rates and restricted networks. This leads us to the following research questions:

RQ3: Do omnivores have a greater propensity to have greater level of diversity in their networks?

RQ4: Do those with univore or inactive musical behaviours have less diverse and more homophilous networks?

Types of ties

While diverse networks might be the key to unlocking the growing omnivorous patterns found in different cultural fields across Western Europe and America, who is in this network might also be crucial. Music consumption is a social act; people may listen to music on their own but inevitably they interact, communicate and consume physical forms of music with family, friends and acquaintances. Therefore, as well as diverse networks, who you share music with socially will be important; the types of ties in your social networks will mediate consumption behaviours. For example sharing time with a diverse friendship network might be very different to having a diverse family network. This brings to the fore arguments relating to Mark Granovetter's Strength of Weak Ties Theory.

In Granovetter's (1973) seminal study in framing his Strength of Weak Ties Theory, he noted that new information flowing into a network was more likely to occur in more socially diverse networks, where weak ties are preferable to strong binding ties. While he was looking at the employment market, the same rationale can be applied to music consumption. The network structure of weak ties allows individuals to tap into a greater variety of music genres, which act as conduits for these music sources otherwise removed from the individual (Kane 2004; Granovetter 1973). Therefore, under this framework, individuals with omnivorous behaviour are more likely to have looser, less dense networks made up of more bridging types of contacts, where new information about music is more readily available and accessible. Therefore, we would expect omnivorousness would be more reliant on diverse friendship and acquaintance networks, measured against less musically active groups who have more bonding ties characteristic of dense family ties. The final research question then is:

RQ5: Are the types of ties in a diverse network important in classifying consumption behaviour?

Methods

Data

The analysis of music consumption in England uses data drawn from Wave 3 of the Taking Part Survey (TPS). The TPS surveyed adults via face-to-face interviews about their participation in music and other cultural activities, between July 2007 and June 2008. Households were drawn from the national postcode address file, and interviews were conducted with a randomly selected member of each household aged 16 or over. As part of the questionnaire design, questions on social capital and participation were only asked to a randomly taken sample of respondents. This sample consists of 12,991 respondents.

Music consumption

To assess music consumption, respondents were asked a series of questions relating to their music activities at live events in the last 12 months ('*Have you been to the following live music event in the last 12 months':* 1 = Yes, 0 = No). To my knowledge the Taking Part Survey is the only data source that captures this live event information, making it unique in that aspect.

The omnivore thesis rests on the assumption that consuming a variety of music cross-cuts the perceived link between cultural and social stratification. A total of nine musical genres from the data were used to represent six music consumption indicators in the model: classical music performance; opera performance; rock or pop concert; soul, R&B, and hip hop (an event that covers three genres: soul music; rhythm and blues, and hip hop or rap); folk and country (music event on folk music, and country and western); and finally jazz performance (see Table 5.1).

Table 5.1 Participation in music

	Percentage
Classical music	7.3
Opera	3.7
Rock and pop	17.2
Soul, R&B, and hip hop	4.7
Folk and country	4.4
Jazz	4.7

Individual characteristics

In the TPS, education is coded to the six official National Vocational Qualifications levels (England), ranging from degree level to no qualifications. It follows a near linear distribution so we treat it as a continuous variable. Following the National Statistics Socio-economic Classification, we distinguished between the salariat class (managerial and professional occupations), intermediate class (lower supervisory and technical occupations, and small employers and own account workers), and working class (semi-routine occupations, long-term unemployed, and people who have never worked). Along with social class and educational attainment, other variables include gender (female dummy variable), age (continuous) and age squared to mediate the curved relationship.

Social capital

Three elements of social capital are measured: neighbourhood trust, social participation and network resources. We dichotomised the neighbourhood trust variable (*'generally speaking, would you say that most people in your neighbourhoods can be trusted?'*) into a 'distrust' category, including the answers 'you can't be too careful' and 'it depends', and a 'trust' category. Social participation was measured by asking how often respondents meet up with friends (1), and with relatives outside the household (2). Response categories were 'never', 'less often than once a month', 'once or twice a month', 'once or twice a week', and 'most days'. These two variables were dichotomised into low participation (never or less often than once a month) and high participation (once or twice a month or more).

Social network resources are measured using the position generator method (Lin 2001; Van der Gaag 2005; Verhaeghe and Tampubolon 2012). This instrument asks people about their network members' occupational positions and considers these positions as good indicators of the network resources available (Verhaeghe and Tampubolon 2012). In this study, respondents were asked whether they know friends, relatives or acquaintances who hold any of the jobs from a list of 11 occupations. All 11 occupations are salient in British society and range from factory-worker to university/college lecturer (Verhaeghe and Tampubolon 2012). In this chapter, the approach to the position generator is to calculate the volume of network resources by counting the number of different occupations accessed by respondents. This measure is related to network size (Van der Gaag 2005; Verhaeghe and Tampubolon 2012). Furthermore, this is split into three variables, volume of network resources that are friends; volume of network resources that are family; and volume of network resources that are acquaintances. This is to account for different processes occurring as individuals invest in different types of network ties.

Analytic strategy

Consumption of one particular type of music genre does not happen in a social vacuum, it is part of the wider cultural make-up of an individual. Rather than examine musical items (genres) as discrete components, individuals should be grouped on observed patterns of consumption (Peterson and Kern 1996; Chan and Goldthorpe 2005; Sintas and Alvarez 2004; Van Eijck 1999). Here we assume that there are relatively well-defined types or clusters of music consumers who can be placed into lifestyle typologies based on their engagement in different musical events. This is executed through a latent class analysis (LCA) modelling approach. This type of model make is possible to identify different types of music consumers (for example omnivores, univores, etc).

The LCA identifies typology groups or clusters whose music consumption behaviour will be different depending on membership of these clusters. A path diagram of the model is presented in Figure 5.1, where the subscript u defines a categorical variable of interest (i.e. attending a rock or pop concert, a jazz performance, etc.), the circle encapsulating the C is an underlying latent class measure (can include 1, 2, 3 ... n classes). Thus the indicator variables are seen as arising from the unobserved latent class measure and are subject to measurement error. This is the measurement part of the model. The X variables influencing the latent class measure are independent control variables (i.e. social class, education). This second component adds structure to the model and allows

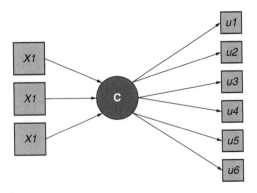

Figure 5.1 Path diagram – latent class analysis and Multiple Indicators and Multiple Causes (MIMIC) model.

investigation into the relationship between latent class clusters and a set of theoretically informed explanatory variables. In its simplest form, this model is a simultaneous method of latent class analysis and multinomial regression, or logistic regression when there are only two levels of the latent variable (two classes) (Widdop and Cutts 2013).

LCA usually assumes local independence and estimates two essential parameters, latent class probabilities (the probability of an individual being in a particular cluster) and conditional probabilities. Conditional probabilities are akin to factor loadings and are the probabilities of an individual in cluster t of the latent variable C, being in a particular level of the observed variable (Magidson and Vermunt 2004).

In a latent class model, the standard chi squared measurement (L^2) can be unreliable because of the number of sparse cells in the model. We therefore use an alternative measure to determine the goodness of fit, the most widely used and statistically robust is the Bayes Information Criterion (BIC), where a model with a lower BIC value is preferred over a model with a higher BIC value (Asparouhov and Muthen 2006; Widdop and Cutts 2013). In this study a three-class solution returned the lowest BIC and was therefore deemed the best model to use. That is, three cultural consumption groups were identified with each having different types of consumption behaviours.

Results

Profile of music clusters

In Table 5.2 the three latent class clusters are presented along with their estimated size and estimated conditional probability of consuming each of the six music forms given membership in a latent lifestyle cluster.

Cluster 1 was populated by 11 per cent of respondents and was distinguishable from its counterparts through its propensity to consume a wide range of musical forms, but extensive consumption of high art/musical forms. Derived

Table 5.2 Latent class probabilities

	Latent class 1	Latent class 2	Latent class 3
Relative size (%)	11	19	70
	Omnivores	*Univores*	*Inactives*
Classical music	0.52	0.04	0.01
Opera	0.28	0.02	0.00
Rock and pop	0.32	0.74	0.00
Soul, R&B, and hip hop	0.03	0.20	0.00
Folk and country	0.11	0.13	0.00
Jazz	0.22	0.06	0.01

from the conditional probabilities, this group attended events in classical music, opera, and jazz, the typically perceived high art forms, at a greater volume and range than any other latent class group. This cluster also had preferences that cross-cut the perceived hierarchy between more exclusive ('highbrow') and popular music as they have a high probability of attending events involving rock and pop, and folk and country and western music (when measured against averages in Table 5.1). We have labelled this group 'omnivores' because individual members had a breadth of music consumption, which closely matches that identified in other scholarly work (Van Eijck and Lievens 2008; Peterson 2005; Peterson and Kern 1996). However, they have an appearance of being highbrow omnivores, as they do distance themselves from soul, R & B and hip hop, and much more likely to be high consumers of high-class musical forms than the more popularised forms.

Cluster 2, to which 19 per cent of the population were classified, are consumers of popular forms of music. They are the group most likely to attend events of rock and pop; soul, R&B and hip hop; and folk and country and western music. We labelled this group 'univores' as popular forms of music are a key classifier of this group. They match Peterson and Kern's (1996) definition of a univore. Members of this cluster did not readily consume exclusive musical forms that are perhaps indicators of privileged lifestyles.

While Cluster 1 and 2 show the classic structure of Peterson's omnivore–univore framework they account for 30 per cent of the survey population. The largest populated cluster is Cluster 3, exemplars of a non-active group, who consume very little in the music field. They account for 70 per cent of the population and we label this group the 'inactives'. The size of this group and the fact they are non-consumers indicate that in reality the music field, in terms of consumption outside of the home, is relatively small.

Characteristics of clusters

To determine the constitution of the groups the different clusters were simultaneously regressed against each other and the key findings are reported in Table 5.3. The findings provide an initial insight into the socio-economic make-up of each music cluster showing that a variety of stratification variables play a significant role in determining the latent clusters.

Socio-demographic characteristics

The next step is to determine who constitutes membership of the clusters. Table 5.3 presents the regression coefficients of membership for each music cluster by education, class, age, gender, size of networks, social capital, and social participation. The findings provide an insight into the socio-economic make-up of each music cluster, also illustrating that social capital and networks play a significant role in determining latent class membership. We start by looking at the socio-demographics.

Table 5.3 Results of latent class multinomial regression (reference category in brackets)

	Uni vs. (Omni)		Ina vs. (Omni)		Ina vs. (Uni)	
	b	*odds*	*b*	*odds*	*b*	*odds*
Education	**−0.684**	**0.50**	**−1.015**	**0.36**	**−0.331**	**0.72**
Lower middle	**−0.363**	**0.70**	**−0.517**	**0.60**	**−0.154**	**0.86**
Salariat class	**−0.698**	**0.50**	**−1.001**	**0.37**	**−0.303**	**0.74**
Age	**−0.156**	**0.86**	**−0.211**	**0.81**	**−0.055**	**0.95**
Age sq.	0	1.00	0.001	1.00	0.001	1.00
Female	**−0.847**	**0.43**	**−0.66**	**0.52**	**0.187**	**1.21**
Ethnic group: non-white	**−0.635**	**0.53**	**0.889**	**2.43**	**1.524**	**4.59**
Volume of family networks	**0.12**	**1.13**	−0.003	1.00	**−0.123**	**0.88**
Volume of friends network	−0.09	0.91	**−0.156**	**0.86**	**−0.157**	**0.85**
Volume of acquaintances	0.013	1.01	**−0.088**	**0.92**	**−0.102**	**0.90**
Trust	**−0.204**	**0.82**	**−0.381**	**0.68**	**−0.177**	**0.84**
Socialise with relatives	**0.466**	**1.59**	**0.381**	**1.46**	−0.085	0.92
Socialise with friends	−0.233	0.79	**−0.922**	**0.40**	**−0.689**	**0.50**

Note
Figures in bold are significant to 95%.

When measured against the 'univores' and 'inactives', the 'omnivores' have a greater likelihood of being from the highly educated section of society, with a greater propensity to be highly educated and from the salariat classes. Clearly education and class play a significant role in differentiating these music classes. However, it is evident that gender, age and ethnic group are also salient measures, with females much more prevalent in the 'omnivores', as are younger age cohorts, while non-white ethnic groups are twice as likely to be 'inactive' as opposed to 'omnivores'.

Class and education are significant between 'univores' and the 'inactives', with the former having a greater propensity to have a higher level of education and be drawn from higher social classes. Age and gender are both drivers between these two groups, with 'univores' being more associated with young age cohorts and males.

The role of social capital and network resources

Table 5.3 shows that social capital matters for an individual's consumption patterns, after controlling for socio-economic factors. People who are trusting and socialise with friends or relatives are more likely to attend musical performances. The findings with respect to the network resources show that having a diverse network is associated with being active in the music field. Being active in music is much more complex than simply basing it on theoretical assumptions of class and education, it is fundamentally a social act; the level to which you engage in music and the genres you attach to are somewhat dependent upon the networks you are embedded in and position in the social structure.

When compared against the 'inactives', both 'omnivores' and 'univores' were significantly more likely to be trusting. They were also significantly more likely to socialise with friends. Indeed, 'omnivores' were 1.5 times and 'univores' 1.2 times more likely to report trusting fellow citizens than 'inactives'. Furthermore, 'omnivores' and 'univores' were both twice as likely to report socialising with friends than the 'inactives'. However, there are some interesting subplots in the results that indicate that types of networks and how people socialise impact upon membership of latent clusters. Those who are classified 'inactive', are likely to meet up and socialise with family to a far greater extent than 'omnivores', so too are 'univores'. While we can't test the concept here, this is indicative of bonding social capital, with family networks clearly important for the two less active clusters.

This leads us on to exploring network resources among the three clusters. Network diversity clearly shares an association with membership of latent groups and their musical patterns. Diverse friendship networks are significant for 'omnivores', who are much more likely to have a larger diverse group of friends than 'univores' and 'inactives', whereas it is a diverse family network that is characteristic of 'univores'. This is an important distinction: the type of networks individuals are embedded in impacts upon their leisure and cultural habits. A strong family network indicates ties that bind, in other words strong bonding capital. It is this type of capital that might constrain cultural lifestyles. Alternatively, a large diverse friendship network actually mediates omnivorous behaviours.

Discussion and conclusion

The first aim of the study was to examine music participation and its association with the omnivore–univore thesis (RQ1). Results identify two sets of lifestyle groups comparable to that of the omnivore and univore laid out by Richard Peterson's theory. The omnivore group attends events in a range of different types of music, but are much more aligned to highbrow forms. In contrast the univore group attends musical events most associated with the popularised forms; they are quite consistent with the theoretical framework. However, as found in other studies (Widdop and Cutts 2013; Alderson *et al*; 2007; Torche 2007; Tampubolon 2008; and Stichele and Laermans 2006), we show evidence of a large proportion of the population who abstain from participation. The defining feature of this group is not primarily strong preference for a limited number of items, but rather, strong disengagement with physical forms of live music (Tampubolon 2008). The dichotomy between omnivore and univore might now need to be addressed to encompass this phenomenon found here and elsewhere across different fields. However, we must treat this finding with caution; here we are only examining attendance at music events at locations outside the home. This may not be true in relation to taste or knowledge of music, or consumption in the home.

The second aim of the study focused on the socio-economic make-up of these identified music clusters (RQ2). Our findings suggest that the socio-economic make-up of the music clusters was largely analogous to that found in other cultural fields. The omnivore group was small in size and dominated by those from the higher social strata. It included many individuals who were highly educated, from a younger age cohort, female and white. The univores contained respondents who were male, mainly from the middle to lower social strata, and tended to have average education. Finally, the inactives were characterised by low social status and educational levels and were more likely to come from ethnic minority groups.

The third question sought to examine the extent to which consumption of music is mediated and constrained through networks (RQ3). Our evidence suggests that consuming physical forms of music is very much a social act; those who are embedded in diverse networks consume music to a much greater degree than those who are not. The more people you know in different locations of a network the more you consume, if people's attitudes, beliefs and expectations are socially constructed they will inevitably be tied up with others who occupy the same social world (Galster 2001). Music is socially learned and stimulated. Our evidence supports results found by Erickson (1996) that network variety is related to cultural variety.

Our final aim of the study was to examine the type of ties in a network and their influence on consumption (RQ4; RQ5). We noted that omnivores, being the most active group, would have a larger diverse friendship network than other groups, irrespective of class and education. The results supported this idea; individuals with omnivorous behaviour were more likely to have diverse friendship networks. Conversely the univores were more reliant on family networks as opposed to friendship networks. This finding suggests that both are reliant on networks but alternative mechanisms of social capital are in place. The univores are reliant on their social network of their family and socialising with them. The omnivores portray a socially mobile group with reliance on less dense and looser networks (less socialising with family), made up of friends in different locations of the social structure. The inactives have a much more restricted network, which reflects their latent music consumption.

While education and class remain important aspects of the omnivore–univore thesis, clearly consumption is mediated and constrained thorough networks. This evidence, along with that found by Erickson (1996); Kane (2004); and Lizardo (2006), shows that social networks and social capital play a much more significant role in cultural behaviour than the theoretical frameworks suggest. Further research is much needed.

References

Alderson, A.S., Junisbai, A. and Heacock, I. (2007) Social Status and Cultural Consumption in the United States, *Poetics* 35, 191–212.

Asparouhov, T. and Muthen, B. (2006) Robust Chi Square Difference Testing with Mean and Variance Adjusted Test Statistics, *Mplus Web Notes*, No. 10. Online, available at www.statmodel.com/download/webnotes/webnote10.pdf.

Bennett, T., Savage, M., Silva, E., Warde, A., Gayo-Cal, M. and Wright, D. (2009) *Culture, Class, Distinction*, London, Routledge.

Borgatti, S.P., Everett, M.G. and Johnson, J.C. (2013) *Analyzing Social Networks*, London, Sage Publications.

Bourdieu, P. (1984) *Distinction: A Social Critique of the Judgment of Taste*, London, Routledge.

Bourdieu, P. and Wacquant, L. (1992) *Réponses*, Paris, Seuil,

Bryson, B. (1996) Anything but Heavy Metal: Symbolic Exclusion and Musical Dislikes, *American Sociological Review* 61, 884–99.

Chan, T.W. and Goldthorpe, J.H. (2005) The Social Stratification of Theatre, Dance and Cinema Attendance. *Cultural Trends* 14, 193–212.

Chan, T.W. and Goldthorpe, J.H. (2007) Social Stratification and Cultural Consumption: Music in England, *European Sociological Review* 23(1), 1–19.

Erickson, B.H. (1996) Culture, Class and Connections? *American Journal of Sociology* 102(1), 217–51.

Galster, G. (2001) On the Nature of Neighbourhood, *Urban Studies* 38(12), 2111–24.

Granovetter, M.S. (1973) The Strength of Weak Ties, *American Journal of Sociology* 78, 1360–80.

Kane, D. (2004) A Network Approach to the Puzzle of Women's Cultural Participation, *Poetics* 32, 105–27.

Katz-Gerro, T. (2006) Comparative Evidence of Inequality in Cultural Preferences: Gender, Class, and Family Status, *Sociological Spectrum* 26, 63–83.

Lamont, M. and Lareau, A. (1988) Cultural Capital: Allusions, Gaps and Glissandos in Recent Theoretical Developments, *Sociological Theory* 6(2), 153–68.

Lin, N. (2001) *Social Capital: A Theory of Structure and Action*. Cambridge, Cambridge University Press.

Lin, N. and Erickson, B.H. (2008) Theory, Measurement, and the Research Enterprise on Social Capital, in Lin, N., and Erickson, B.H. (eds.), *Social Capital. An International Research Program*. Oxford, Oxford University Press, 1–26.

Lizardo, O. (2006) How Cultural Tastes Shape Personal Networks, *American Sociological Review* 71(5), 778–807.

Magidson, J. and Vermunt, J.K. (2004) Latent Class Models, in Kaplan, D. (ed.), *The Sage Handbook of Quantitative Methodology for the Social Sciences*, vol. 10. Thousand Oaks, CA, Sage, 175–98.

Mark, N.P. (1998) Birds of a Feather Sing Together. *Social Forces* 77, 453–85.

Peterson, R.A. (1992) Understanding Audience Segmentation: From Elite and Mass to Omnivore and Univore, *Poetics* 21(4), 243–58.

Peterson, R.A. (2005) Problems in Comparative Research: The Example of Omnivorousness, *Poetics* 33(5–6), 257–82.

Peterson, R.A. and Kern, R.M. (1996) Changing Highbrow Taste: From Snob to Omnivore, *American Sociological Review* 61(5), 900–9.

Peterson, R.A. and Simkus, A. (1992) How Musical Tastes Mark Occupational Status Groups, in Lamont, M. and Fournier, M. (eds), *Cultivating Differences*. Chicago, University of Chicago Press, 152–86.

Relish, M. (1997) It's Not All Education: Network Measures as Sources of Cultural Competency. *Poetics* 25, 121–39.

Savage, M. and Gayo-Cal, M. (2011) Unravelling the Omnivore: A Field Analysis of Contemporary Musical Taste in the United Kingdom, *Poetics* 39(5), 337–57.

Sintas, J.L. and Alvarez, E.G. (2002) Omnivores Show up Again: The Segmentation of

Cultural Consumers in Spanish Social Space. *European Sociological Review* 18, 353–68.

Sintas, J. and Alvarez, E.G. (2004) Omnivore versus Univore Consumption and its Symbolic Properties: Evidence from Spaniards' Performing Arts Attendance, *Poetics* 32(6), 463–84.

Stichele, A.V. and Laermans, R. (2006) Cultural Participation in Flanders: Testing the Cultural Omnivore Thesis with Population Data. *Poetics* 34, 45–64.

Sullivan, O. and Katz-Gerro, T. (2007) The Omnivore Thesis Revisited: Voracious Cultural Consumers, *European Sociological Review* 23(2), 123–37.

Tampubolon. G. (2008) Revisiting Omnivores in America circa 1990s: The Exclusiveness of Omnivores? *Poetics* 36, 243–64.

Torche, F. (2007) Social Status and Cultural Consumption: The Case of Reading in Chile, *Poetics* 35, 70–92.

Van Rees, K., Vermunt, J. and Verboord, M. (1999) Cultural Classifications under Discussion: Latent Class Analysis of Highbrow and Lowbrow Reading, *Poetics* 26, 349–65.

Van der Gaag, M.P.J. (2005) Measurement of Individual Social Capital, unpublished thesis, Rijksuniversiteit Groningen.

Van Eijck, K. (1999) Socialisation, Education, and Lifestyle: How Social Mobility Increases the Cultural Heterogeneity of Status Groups, *Poetics* 26, 309–28.

Van Eijck, K. (2000) Richard A. Peterson and the Culture of Consumption, *Poetics* 28(3), 207–24.

Van Eijck, K. (2001) Social Differentiation in Musical Taste Patterns, *Social Forces* 79(3), 1163–85.

Van Eijck, K. and Lievens, J. (2008) Cultural Omnivorousness as a Combination of Highbrow, Pop and Folk Elements: The Relation between Taste Patterns and Attitudes Concerning Social Integration. *Poetics* 36, 217–42.

Verhaeghe, P. and Tampubolon, G. (2012) Individual Social Capital, Neighbourhood Deprivation, and Self-Rated Health in England, *Social Science and Medicine* 75(2), 349–57.

Warde, A. and Gayo-Cal, M. (2009) The Anatomy of Cultural Omnivorousness: The Case of the United Kingdom, *Poetics* 37(2), 119–45.

Warde, A. and Tampubolon. G. (2008) Social Capital, Networks and Leisure Consumption. *Sociological Review* 50(2), 155–80.

Warde, A., Wright, D. and Gayo-Cal, M. (2007) Understanding Cultural Omnivorousness: or, The Myth of the Cultural Omnivore, *Cultural Sociology* 1(2), 143–64.

Warde, A., Wright, D. and Gayo-Cal, M. (2008) The Omnivorous Orientation in the UK, *Poetics* 36(2–3), 148–65.

Widdop, P.A. and Cutts, D. (2012) The Importance of Place: A Case Study of Museum Participation, *Cultural Trends* 21(1), 47–66.

Widdop, P.A. and Cutts, D. (2013) Social Stratification and Sports' Participation in England, *Leisure Sciences* 35(2), 107–28.

6   Between social worlds and local scenes

Patterns of collaboration in francophone rap music

Karim Hammou

J'suis qu'un belge j'devrais faire marrer leur fils Limite ils m'verraient bien en feat avec Manneken Pis C'est l'modèle pour leur faire brasser l'fric Et ma pochette devrait être moi une bière et un paquet d'frites.[1]

Scylla, 'BX Vibes', 2012

Music-making usually needs many different people to cooperate together (Becker 1982), and yet it displays very fluid forms of organisation. This paradox has led to a vast literature, improving our understanding of collective action in situations where people are not formally bound to each other through concepts such as field, world and scenes (Bottero and Crossley 2011). This chapter will show how social network analysis (SNA) may enhance the analysis of the two latter concepts.

According to Will Straw who introduced it in 1991, the notion of a 'local scene' describes 'a cultural space in which a range of musical practices coexist' in 'a distinctive relationship to historical time and geographical location' (Straw 1991, 373–5). The development of studies on specific musical scenes has helped to get over some of the difficulties raised by the subcultures approach. The subculture approach often reifies and homogenises cultural practices and aesthetics. It also favours the reception of music over its production (Guibert 2012, 97). By contrast, the notion of musical scene puts the stress on the close relations between musicians and audiences, and also on the manifoldness of commitment to musical practices 'clustered around a specific geographic focus' (Bennett and Peterson 2004, 6).

As it develops, the music scenes perspective draws near to another tradition, which focuses on 'social worlds'. Used in a loose sense for a long time, the notion of social world was first conceptualised by Tamotsu Shibutani. The development of a social world perspective is closely related to the assumption that through 'the development of rapid transportation and the media of mass communication, people who are geographically dispersed can communicate effectively.... Culture areas [may] overlap and [may] have lost their territorial bases' (Shibutani 1955, 566). Through this concept, Shibutani aimed to describe forms of grouping characterised by 'a culture area, the boundaries of which are set neither by territory nor by formal group membership but by the limits of effective communication' (*ibid.*). Then, identifying common communication channels is crucial to understanding any precise social world. Anselm Strauss (1992) deepens and popularises this concept of 'social world'. He especially underlines the role of actual institutions, sites and technologies in the making and continuity of any social world. Leisure studies offer several valuable examples of such loose yet effective sorts of grouping, and the role of the commodification processes in these organisations (Yoder 1997).

To contrast a social world perspective and a local scene perspective, two issues may be kept in mind. First, these concepts suggest a different approach towards locality. The notion of social world has been especially designed to cope with a kind of social organisation with boundaries which are not set by geography. A second issue has been debated to a greater extent, as we shall see, and relates to mass production and the industry. At first glance, the social world perspective raises the question of asymmetry in social participation through restricted communication channels and commodification, while the local scene perspective puts the stress on appropriations and connoisseurship in face-to-face social circles.

I do not wish to oppose theoretically these concepts. Both traditions look after the contradictory trend toward the one they highlight – dynamics of deterritorialisation in the case of musical scenes (Straw 1991, 374; Bennett 2004), processes of relocation in the case of social worlds (Strauss 1978; Clarke 1991). Moreover, Harris (2000) convincingly analyses the issue of commodification from a local scene perspective in the case of metal band Sepultura, through the concept of 'translocal scene'. My aim is rather to suggest ways to evaluate degrees of 'sceneness' and 'social worldness', to paraphrase Bennett and Peterson (2004, 12), through the empirical case of French-speaking rap music.

As Di Maggio (2011) underlines, SNA offers valuable tools to explore both the actual relationship between social groups or individuals, and also emic understanding of these relations. Thus, it provides empirical means to articulate culture and structure, two issues at the heart of the musical scene and social world perspectives. SNA especially offers two sets of tools. The first intends to cope with the cohesion of a group of actors and offers insight into its structural organisation. The second provides a sense of hierarchies and power relations among this group.

Both sets of tools require that we are explicit about what kind of 'nodes' and 'ties' are under scrutiny. The first step in using SNA should consist of clarifying the empirical facts shaped with SNA, in these study collaborations between rap artists in various francophone countries.

Using SNA to evaluate the 'sceneness' of musical practices

The development of francophone rap music across the world

Appropriation of rap music outside the United States of America began in the 1980s. By the end of the decade, several French-speaking cities across the world had a vivid local rap scene. This process of reterritorialisation and indigenisation (Bennett 2000) is well documented in the cases of Paris (Bocquet and Pierre-Adolphe 1997), Brussels (Lapiower 1997), Marseilles (Valnet 2013), Montreal (Chamberland 2002) and there are some tracks for smaller local rap scenes in Lausanne, Lyon and Bordeaux (Hammou 2012). This literature indicates similar issues found in other parts of the world (Mitchell 2001), notably the relation between authenticity and language (Pennycook 2007). The relocation of hip hop outside the US often leads to the use of French for a significant part of these local rap scenes, giving birth to francophone rap musics in several places across the world.

Negotiating their identities with a common US source, these francophone rap scenes had nevertheless little relation to one another, even when they belonged to the same country. There was no internet, of course, but also no TV programme, no national radio station playing local rap music, no widely distributed magazine promoting its artists, and almost no records, except for the Anglo-American ones. Until 1990, there were mostly local practices – local radio shows, small venues, informal meetings, etc. The few connections between these local scenes were thus slow and sparse – they relied on people's mobility rather than steady channels of communication.

The first francophone records of rap music exemplify this mechanism. Published in 1990, compilation albums like *Rapattitude* or *Brussels Rap Convention* reunited rap artists from the same city, Paris in the first case, Brussels in the second case. The same year, the first EP albums like *Concept* by the French band IAM from Marseilles, or *Le VIe Sens* by the Swiss band Sens Unik from Lausanne didn't include the participation of any rap artist from another city than their own.

All these records or tapes were published by small independent companies, and most of them were new local structures. Yet, come 1992, multinational music corporations and independent businessmen published new records which displayed a process of relocation of French-speaking rap music, transcending specific cities' scenes. In French compilations *Rapattitude 2* and *Nation Rap* or the Canadian compilation *Je rap en français*, artist and repertoire (A&R) men chose songs performed by rappers from different cities, initiating a logic of cooperation in tension with the 'local scenes' one.

These modes of experiencing and practising hip hop music differ significantly. Nevertheless, 'the scenes and industrial ways of making music depend on one another' (Bennett and Peterson 2004, 3). Local appropriations leaned on global and national cultural industries through the records and the video clips they produced and promoted. As soon as local labels contracted deals with big record companies and international distribution systems, the emerging hip hop scene of New York City became a mass product broadcast through international channels of communication and trade (Charnas 2010) coterminous with various social worlds. Yet the national or global commercialisation of rap music also requires local milieus to sustain the pool of wannabe rap stars, and produce the flavour of authenticity, especially since the marketing of rap as an art from coming from 'the street' has become a prominent feature in the US and French rap music industries (Forman 2002, Hammou 2012, 194).

The line between the way local scenes may be embedded in musical industries and the very process of exploitation fostered by multinational companies proves to be blurred. Does this embeddedness result from a negotiation, albeit an unequal one, between major companies and local avant-gardes benefiting from their involvement in emerging trends in popular music? Or is it rather a shift ruled by these global corporations in the context of late cultural capitalism, which aim at increasing labour flexibility, short-term projects and, after all, its control over the music market? Empirical cases studies suggest a more balanced view, where the status of both hypotheses may be unsettled.

The relation of musical practices toward locality appears to be less ambiguous. That's why it will be the connecting thread of this chapter.

A case study: collaborations among French-speaking rappers

The presence of cooperative links between people doesn't guarantee that these people share a common understanding of what they do, that they are part of the same 'reference group' (Shibutani 1955). As I move away from a precise qualitative knowledge of the relationships between the actors of specific records, I need to find a more univocal and nonetheless significant indicator. That's why I choose to observe collaborations between rap artists on their LP albums, also known as 'featurings'. I consider that featuring is not only a track of mutual acquaintance, but also a track of a minimal mutual recognition as a practitioner of rap music (Hammou 2009). The diversity of collaborations between rap artists doesn't boil down to featurings. But this kind of collaboration represents a strong tie with respect to artistic and professional issues. It is also both retrievable in the past years and interpretable, as the initiative of the collaboration is clear enough.

My empirical study will proceed in two steps, resting on two different kinds of data:

- an extensive exploration in the history of French rap music (1980–2004), with first-hand interviews, direct observations and a systematic inventory of rap albums ($n=388$)
- second-hand data on francophone rap acts during the same period of time in Canada ($n=107$), Belgium ($n=22$), Switzerland ($n=27$), Senegal, Mali, Algeria, Gabon and Cameroon ($n=30^2$). I also found traces from 30 more rap albums, most of them from Africa, but I was unable to collect enough information to take them into account in the analysis.

I will first analyse the relation between French local rap scenes, and then I will provide an exploratory study of the relations between local scenes in global francophone rap music.

Hypotheses

To explore the 'sceneness' or 'worldness' of French-speaking rap music, we need a set of indicators that contrast these type of organisations. As the channels of communication build reference groups which are not bound by a territory, a social world pattern should be all the more patent in that members of an organisation don't share a common geographic anchorage, but also that they don't show a clear preference for other members from the same locality, even in a diverse group. Yet, a certain kind of 'sceneness' may be also associated with a weak geographic homogeneity: the translocal scene organisation, by gathering different scenes through sparse relations, would display such a pattern. Nevertheless, a translocal scene would keep a strong tendency to privilege relations with homologous peers as regards geographic location.

The contrast between a translocal scene and a social world would become more marked if we pay attention to the structural properties of the organisation observed. We may expect a weak structural cohesion in the case of a translocal scene, as few brokers would reunite several cohesive local scenes. We may also expect a kind of polycentric structure, exhibiting a plurality of distinct sources of local innovations disseminating across the translocal scene. By contrast, a social world should possess a core–periphery structure, coterminous with the centrality pattern supported by common channels of communication. Finally, a local scene could equally be organised along a core–periphery model or along a more decentralised pattern.

To sum up, we can contrast three type of organisation (local scene, translocal scene, social world) through four continuous indicators. The structural cohesion may be analysed in SNA by following Moody and White (2003). The centre–periphery structure may be analysed by adding to this structural cohesion approach, using the k-core measure. By associating each node (each artistic unit) with a geographic attribute, we can also explore the degree of geographic homogeneity (how many nodes share a common anchorage in the network?) and the degree of geographic homophily (what proportion of the relations are tied with nodes from the same anchorage?).

The making of a social world of rap music in France (1990–2004)

A core–periphery structure of collaborations put to the test

Featurings between rap artists in France form a low-density network, built up from 216 artistic units and 408 ties. Nevertheless, this network only possesses one component, including 80 per cent of the artistic units studied. The 20 per cent remaining units don't form any alternative component – they are isolated nodes.

The main component displays a core–periphery structure, illustrated by the graphic representation of its different k-core (Seidman 1983; Everett and Borgatti 2000). There is a single 6-core at the heart of this network, and this

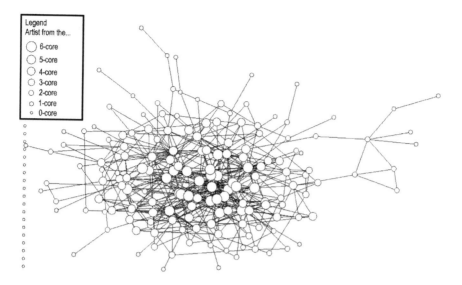

Figure 6.1 Collaborations between rap artists in France.

6-core is relatively large, gathering 40 artistic units among the 180 artistic units belonging to the main component. Less cohesive k-cores order around this 6-core, in concentric circles. There is no significant clustering pattern in this network. On the overall picture, we can underline that the main component of the network includes neither brokers nor structural holes except for its farthest periphery: some artistic units belonging to the 3-, 2- or 1-core of the component are the only paths to few pendant nodes.

Featurings on LP records are a very selective track of collaboration. It is unlikely that such a structure may emerge without any sort of informal collective organisation. However, we must verify if this common component is the result of two or more components artificially connected by the shift of a few artistic units between distinct sets of collaborations.

The durability of network ties is rarely taken into account by network analysts. My assumption is that featurings express a bond of mutual recognition that is neither everlasting nor just occasional. On average, French-speaking rap artists publish an album every two or three years. I will analyse featurings on successive and overlapping periods of two years. Year 1999, then, will stand for the collaborations on records published in 1998 and 1999. My aim is to avoid any artificial threshold that compartmentalised networks could drive.[3]

What is behind the single component that we can observe through the network analysis of featurings from 1990 to 2004? To answer this question, I will examine basic properties of the successive two-year networks of collaborations between rap artists: the number of components in each network, the number of nodes in the main component, the percentage of these nodes relatively to the sum of nodes in the overall network, and finally the size of the second largest component. This last indicator should provide a sense of the structural cohesion of each network.

Table 6.1 invalidates the hypothesis of several significant components artificially connected through the shift of few artistic units over the period 1990–2004. However, contrary to the overall network of featurings, here we can observe that there is not only one component at each period. From 1997, the main component reaches more than 75 per cent of the overall network, a size that places it far beyond the second largest component. This is also the period in which the number of artistic units involved in the network rises significantly, growing from 26 to 66.

The dynamic of a common informal organisation

From 1993 to 2004, there are always some small components in addition to the main component. Yet, they never include more than four artistic units. They are only chains of three or four nodes, or small cliques of three. In comparison with the main component, they appear to be outlying artistic units rather than rival coalitions of rappers. Actually, Table 6.1 suggests that collaborations in French-speaking rap music don't happen on the same basis at different moments of the period studied.

The situation depicted on the overall network of collaborations from 1990 to 2004 merges three distinct structural situations in French-speaking rap music. First, from 1990 to 1995, only a few artistic units publish an album. Moreover, they share on average fewer than two ties with each other. This weak cohesiveness is evidence for an absence of common organisation between French-speaking rap artists. Then, from 1995 to 1999, the number of artistic units involved in the network rises, and the number of their ties rises even more significantly. In 1999, there are three times more nodes and ten times more ties in the network than in 1995. Examining the degree density in the networks proves to be fruitful. Usually, a growth in the number of nodes implies a structural trend towards a decrease in the degree density (Faust 2006, 204): the larger the network, the harder the connection between each node. A counter-intuitive evolution of the degree density can be observed in this second period. In an expanding network of actors, degree density remains constant in 1997 and 1999, and even grows in 1998 (Hammou 2009). In 1995–9 a common body for French-speaking rap artists emerges, what we could name the birth of a '(French) rap game'. Since 2000, there is a third period characterised by the relative stability of the organisation, which sits in contrast to the more turbulent second period.

This dramatic shift in French rap music proceeds from three distinct social processes. The first process reflects the quantitative growth of the network. Record labels and rap crews, in other words marketing and artistic types of groupings, take advantage of the increasing appeal of rap music to promote new artists, especially through an intensive use of featurings. This process leads to the production of a wider network, which nevertheless doesn't explain the

Table 6.1 Movement of artistic units over the period 1990–2004

	1993	1994	1995	1996	1997	1998	1999	2000	2001	2002	2003	2004
Number of components in the network	3	3	5	4	2	3	3	6	5	3	2	6
Number of nodes in the main component	6	10	12	26	66	78	86	76	87	99	102	89
Percentage of the overall network	30	50	40	45	79	83	81	74	75	76	86	80

systematic linkage between these new groupings. A second significant process lies in how this growing network remains cohesive. Some artists act as middlemen, bridging parts of the network that would remain isolated without them. They occupy a structural hole in the overall network at one moment, similar to the role of the 'organiser of literature life' described by Björn-Olav Dozo (2010) in the case of the Belgian sub-field of literature. Yet, this role of middleman is only temporary, which bring us to the third process at work. Soon after one artist has bridged emerging groupings, other artists multiply the collaborations between those relatively remote parts of the network and strengthen its cohesion. Each structural hole in the network quickly loses its specific position, which demonstrates how different French rappers are able to work together – how they share a common perspective on their environment as far as rap music is concerned.

Paris, the French desert ... and Marseilles

The network of collaborations between French rap artists exhibits structural properties that are not consistent with the translocal scene hypothesis. However, the role of locality in this overall picture remains unclear. We could understand these empirical data as a social world organisation, just as well as a local scene one. SNA is useful to test these former rival hypotheses. A local scene organisation should exhibit strong cohesive cliques based on common anchorage, while a social world organisation doesn't imply any preferential ties between artists of the same geographical area.

The geographic scales that make sense for a majority of French rap artists are the neighbourhood, the city and, interestingly, the *département*.[4] There are 101 *départements*, referred to by a name and a number. The *département* number has been popularised by licence plates and postcode, and is often mentioned in French rap lyrics. *Département* offers an accurate level of geographic designation. It is meaningful for rap artists, sharp enough to distinguish different areas in the vast urban zone of Paris, and loose enough to bring together cities close to one another, in a country where a city's territory is usually very narrow.[5] Seventy-five per cent of French rap artists can be associated with a *département* through their self-identification in their lyrics or record booklets.

The networks of rap artists claiming a similar local anchorage contrast with one another. We can notice three distinct local configurations:

- some disconnected sets of nodes, which are consistent with the social world perspective assumption;
- some weakly cohesive structures, gathering some isolated nodes and few small components;
- some strongly cohesive local cliques, which display a kind of local scene structure at the level of *département*.

Almost each *département* outside the Paris region, Île-de-France, gathers together fewer than five artistic units. Most of them consist of a few isolated nodes. Discographic collaborations thus show no track of any local scene, even in the cases where such a scene is attested, if only at the level of hip hop as a pluridisciplinary cultural movement. For instance, the *département* of Rhône (code 69), with the major city of Lyon, include two unconnected artistic units. Only two rap bands from this region have been able to publish at least one long play rap recording from 1990 to 2004. However, many rap artists have been performing locally during this time (Aubert *et al.* 1998), and hip hop dance achieved international recognition at the beginning of the 2000s with hip hop companies like Pokemon Crew winning the Battle of the Year 2003 breakdance competition. There is one exception to this observation: Bouche-du-Rhône, the *département* of the city of Marseilles illustrated in Figure 6.2. The graph of local collaborations in this *département* gathers two isolated nodes and a strongly cohesive component of 11 nodes, spreading around a clique of four artistic units.

Other *départements* display a loose network gathering many isolated nodes and one or few small components with a low structural cohesion. This is the case of Hauts-de-Seine, a *département* to the west of Paris with major cities like Boulogne-Billancourt and Nanterre, as shown in Figure 6.3.

Here, the main component has a kind of chain form: the removal of only one node is enough to split the component. There are also many isolated nodes, more than in the single component, which suggests a weak local autonomy of rap musicians. This structure looks like the local structure of the other *départements* surrounding Paris, and Paris[6] itself. The only exception is the *département* of Val-de-Marne (94), with many isolated nodes, but also a strong cohesive quasi-clique.

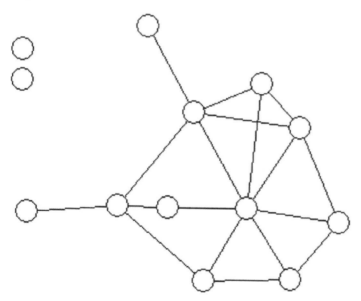

Figure 6.2 Collaborations between rappers from Bouches-du-Rhône (code 13).

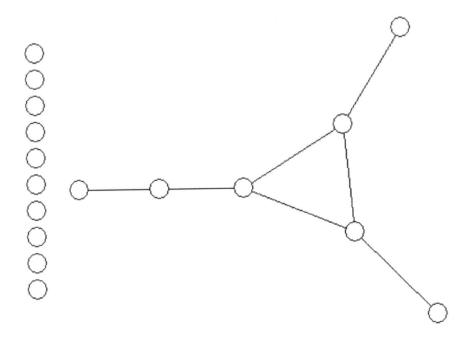

Figure 6.3 Collaborations between rappers from Hauts-de-Seine (code 92).

In each of these three cases, the status of locally isolated nodes is significant. In the *département* of Rhône (69), the two isolated nodes become part of the main component of the overall network of French rap collaborations. These artistic units have not recorded any rap song together on their LP acts, but do collaborate with rap artists of other geographic area. In the *département* of Hauts-de-Seine (92), most isolated nodes appear to be connected with other French rap artists if we consider the overall network. Only a minority of rap artists from Hauts-de-Seine shows a preference for collaborating with artists of the same geographic location. In the *département* of Bouches-du-Rhône (13), on the contrary, the two nodes remain isolated in the overall network of French rap collaborations. They are marginalised not only in the local network, but also in the national net of rap music. The cohesive quasi-clique of Bouches-du-Rhône, on the other hand, is tightly knit to the overall network: local and national integration go with one another in this area.

Grouped by the LP collaborations, French *départements*' 'sceneness' appears inconsistent outside the Paris region (like Bouches-du-Rhône), and weak in most *départements* surrounding Paris (like Hauts-de-Seine). Marseilles with its *département*, Bouches-du-Rhône, is the only area that shows a clear local scene structure in France. Yet, this local scene is embedded enough in the social world of French rap music to remain invisible in the overall network of collaborations. To a lesser extent, Val-de-Marne, to the south of Paris, combines a local scene structure which nevertheless fails to gather most of local rap artists connected. Thus, the French rap collaborations' network shows a strong 'worldness'. In the early 2000s, professional French rap music is almost coterminous with the local rap scene of Île-de-France, the region of Paris and its surrounding *départements*. Only Marseilles significantly complexifies this picture, and justifies a more accurate depiction of French rap music as a social world deeply marked by a centralist legacy. This result does not conflict with the presence of various local scenes as in Rhône, less reliant on the recording industries than on small venues and amateur practices gathering local artists and their fans. Yet, it supports the hypothesis of an asymmetry between various French local scenes and the social world of French rap music.

From structural cohesion to power relations in global francophone rap music

We could consider that this social world structure emerges from the kind of data gathered. Obviously, LP records are not the only way music happens, and this kind of music-making may blur local anchorages. Yet, it is a significant result that the most legitimate and gainful kind of popular music production in the 1990s moves away from a local or translocal scene organisation. It is all the more significant that rap music has been analysed as a type of cultural production with a strong local anchorage (Forman 2002), and that the lyrics of the French-speaking rappers support this view. Let's now explore a play of scales, considering the social world of French rap music itself as a local scene, indeed a Parisian-centred one, in the context of global hip hop. Does international francophone rap musics still display the same kind of organisational pattern, or does it come closer to what a translocal scene perspective would expect? In other words, does the social world of French rap music stand in relative isolation, or is it in tight connection with other rap scenes over the world?

Measuring asymmetries in the French-speaking rap music network

In France, the annual production of rap LP records has exceeded five titles since 1993. In other French-speaking countries, such a level was only reached at the end of the 1990s in Canada, and in the middle of the 2000s in Belgium and Switzerland. The development of rap acts and hence of featurings on LP records is thus concentrated in the early period of the 2000s, justifying their synchronic analysis. Nevertheless, in the network shaped by French-speaking rap artists' collaborations, France remains quantitatively predominant. More than 200 artistic units in the network are French, about 80 Canadian, and less than 20 Belgian or Swiss. There are also little more than 20 artistic units belonging to African countries, Senegal, Mali, Gabon and Algeria being the most significant. In each country, featurings play a significant role: from one-fifth to one-third of the rap songs feature different artists.

Except for some small two-node components, there is only one significant component in the network of collaborations between French-speaking rap artists.

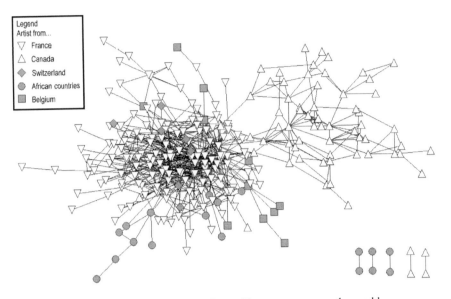

Figure 6.4 Collaborations between French-speaking rappers across the world.

Yet, this component doesn't look like the main component of Figure 6.1. Unlike the core–periphery structure of the collaborations between French rap artists; we observe here two sub-graphs loosely connected in the main component. On the left lies a large sub-graph with many grey nodes, corresponding to the French artists. Few other nodes are set at its periphery: these are African artists (indicated by circles), Belgian (by squares) and Swiss (by diamonds). On the right part of the main component, there is a subset of upright triangles, which stands for Canadian rap artists.

These observations suggest two results regarding the structure of French-speaking rap music across the world. First, some countries such as Belgium, Switzerland, Senegal and Algeria are subjected to the influence of the French (mainly Parisian) social world of rap, as far as LP records are concerned. They take part in a social world structure but stand at its periphery. Second, French-speaking rappers from Canada sustain very different relations with French rappers. The numerous ties between Canadian artists and the fewer ties with French rappers suggest a translocal scene structure between a strongly cohesive local scene of French-speaking Canadian rap and the social world of French rap. To clarify this overall approach, I will analyse each country's case in more detail. I will also give a closer look at the power-relation pattern between these countries through two additional indicators.

The ratio between indegree (inviting) and outdegree (being invited) can be interpreted as an evidence of appeal. If one can invite, and eventually pay to convince other artists to collaborate, one cannot be sure to receive an invitation in return. Actual invitations thus stand for public signs of respect, whether from equal peers, or from 'godfather' and 'heir' in rap music. A ratio between indegree and outdegree smaller than 1 (many invitations received and few invitations given) thus denotes the prestige of the local scene considered. If this ratio is bigger than 1, it shows that many invitations given are not associated with at least as many invitations received.

Another valuable indication consists of a systematisation of the kind of reasoning on local–global relationship used in the previous section. I describe three different patterns of relations between local and global settings, by focusing especially on locally isolated nodes. We can deepen this logic by measuring the proportion of collaborations tied with artists of the same geographic location. It gives an index of geographic homophily, or 'localism', going from 0 to 1 on the consistency of various spatial divisions. The closer to 1 this measure is, the stronger the sceneness is. Here, I will combine the level of *département* previously used in the case of France with the national level for other countries, due to the smaller number of French-speaking rap LP records outside France and the equally asymmetric French-speaking population in the different areas studied.

As we shall see, these two indicators don't correlate. Some subset of rap artists sharing a common local anchorage may be marginalised, yet independent, while another may experience both a significant centrality and a strong dependence toward the centre of the network.

The centre of the social world of French rap and its margins

The centre of the French social world of rap lies in Paris and its region, Île-de-France. This area hosts only 38 per cent of the artistic units involved in the network but is responsible for 60 per cent of the overall collaborative activity. Its cohesiveness is strong: Île-de-France as a whole displays a localism index of 0.91, yet each *département* of Île-de-France has a localism index lower than 0.4 except for Val-de-Marne (localism index of 0.73). If most *départements* of Île-de-France are closely dependent on one another, they possess various appeal. Some *départements* – Hauts-de-Seine, Paris inner city, Val-de-Marne – display a strong prestige, with an indegree/outdregree ratio lower than 1. The artists of other *départements* appear to invite more often than they are invited.

Départements outside Île-de-France, except Bouches-du-Rhône, and French-speaking countries outside France, except Canada, appear to suffer from a Parisian hegemony. The French capital experiences an exceptional concentration of artists, audiences and cultural structures which leads to its centrality in most systems of cultural and artistic production (Menger 1993). In the case of French rap music, this hegemony leans on the concentration of record companies, audiences and venues, three issues underlined by this Belgian rap artist:

> Rap music is not very strong in Belgium.... Rap music doesn't have enough place. First, there is no recording company labelled as 'rap'. There is no imprint, and also no money. So, without money, it's hard to develop any artist. That's what we have found in France: people get things moving. Rap

in Belgium it is just impossible, or you have to be an indie. But even as an indie, it's hard. You've got 60% Flemish-speakers in Belgium, 40% francophones. Among this 40%, half are older than 40, so not interested in rap music, so it's difficult, there isn't any audience. In France, we might have an audience. At the rate of 50 people each evening here, at the venue of Le Lavoir [Moderne, a Parisian venue], out of 60 million French-speaking people, we are already in touch with a small part of it![7]

Outside Île-de-France, only one geographical area possesses significant prestige: Bouches-du-Rhône, with the city of Marseilles. Its indegree/outdegree ratio is 0.67, which means that the artists from this area are much more often invited than they themselves invite. Bouches-du-Rhône also displays a strong autonomy. With a localism index of 0.67, artists from this area have recorded two-thirds of their featurings with artists from the same *département*. The rest of France appears as a more (Haute-Garonne, Alpes-Maritimes) or less (Bas-Rhin, Rhône, Seine-Maritime) prestigious periphery, nevertheless always highly dependent on artists outside their *département*, that is highly dependent on the French social world of rap and its centre.

In the French-speaking countries neighbouring France, the situation also varies. Switzerland appears to possess both low prestige and weak autonomy. Francophone rap artists from this country invite three times more than they are invited, and 75 per cent of their invitations are directed toward artists outside Switzerland (localism index of 0.26). On the contrary, Belgian artists display a significant autonomy, with a localism index of 0.56. If Belgium is not a very prestigious area in the French social world of rap, it has nevertheless a relatively balanced indegree/outdegree ratio of 1.41, much like Parisian *départements* such as Essonne (code 91), Seine–Saint-Denis (93) or Seine-et-Marne (77). Yet, there is also one local organisation which escapes the influence of the social world of French rap: the francophone rap scene of Canada.

The structural autonomy of French-speaking rap in Quebec

The first LP records of French-speaking rap music came out in Canada in the second half of the 1990s, with acts by artists such as KC LMNOP, Dubmatique, La Gamic or Rainmen. Most of them came from Montreal, and they chose to collaborate mostly with French rap artists: IAM and Fonky Family from Marseilles, Bouches-du-Rhône; Ménélik, Daddy Lord C, Rocca, Stomy Bugsy, 2 Bal and 2 Nèg from Paris and its neighbouring *départements*. At the end of the 1990s, these collaborations draw a picture of Canadian French-speaking rap music which was much like the Swiss one: a weak autonomy, and a low prestige. Indeed, although many French rap artists were invited by Canadian artists, French artists never invited any rapper from Canada on their LP records.

Yet, this organisation seemingly peripheral to the centre of the social world of French rap soon changed. Rap artists from the urban agglomeration of Quebec City (La Constellation, Yvon Krevé, Les Ambassadeurs…) seem to have given the crucial impulse, by featuring other local rap artists. This increase in the homophily of the collaborations goes hand in hand with a promotion of *joual*, one of the most widespread types of French slang from the region of Quebec, instead of standard French. A rapper from Limoilou, a central borough of Quebec City, expresses this evolution through his own career:

> At the beginning, we learnt to rap in English, we had to learn the language correctly. It was an anglophone culture, you listened at English music, you read English magazines. When we started to rap, it was inconceivable to do it in French. We didn't hear much yet, we didn't feel concerned. Stuff from France really didn't come to us. It touched some guys we knew, but for us, it was inconceivable, it had to be in English. When the feeling came, everybody started to switch, but with a French language from France, not *joual*, it was fake, it was strange. At some point, I though I had to switch also, for people to better understand what I had to say, but not with the French from France or that fake accent. After eight years of work in English, I had to learn everything again, how to perform in French so it feels good. It was akin a time in the wilderness, hard to do, but I did it. I began to work hard on it since the autumn of 2003, and I have only been ready since 2006, when we launched the LP record *Les Boss du Quartier*.[8]

In the middle of the 2000s, Canadian francophone rap music, whether from the agglomeration of Quebec City or Montreal, displayed a strong sceneness. This fact is reflected in its localism index of 0.93, which is very similar to the localism index of Île-de-France. Essentially directed towards their own local scene, Canadian francophone artists are invited almost as often as they invite, with an indegree/outdegree ratio of 1.07: the asymmetric collaboration pattern with France, from the late 1990s, soon turned into a negligible amount relative to the number of other collaborations between French-speaking Canadian rap artists.

From this time onward, the relation between the social world of French rap and the Canadian francophone rap scene displayed a kind of translocal scene structure. An asymmetry between these organisations remains patent. For instance, French rap artists organise venues in Canada, while the reverse is not true.[9] Yet, this situation does not weigh a lot in the everyday organisation of the Canadian francophone rap scene.

Conclusion

Musical practices are embedded in local dynamics, global trends and asymmetric transactions between various spatial levels. Behind this apparent play of scales lies the uneven reach of many different going concerns, some of which we label 'the music industries' while we name others 'small collectives … and volunteer labor' (Bennett and Peterson 2004, 5). Yet, there is not necessarily a difference in nature between these types of collective actions, and only a careful empirical investigation may settle the question. Social network analysis provides several valuable measures to determine whether precise musical activities such as francophone rap music organise along practices which are rather decentralised and firmly rooted in a precise area (local scenes), or are centralised and deterritorialised (social worlds). By evaluating degrees of 'sceneness' and 'worldness', I have demonstrated how seemingly contrasted sorts of groupings may blend and change over time. This approach of mixed organisational patterns needs to be deepened. Nevertheless, it speaks in favour of tools likely to grasp the numerous informal, blurred and shifting ways of doing (musical) things together.

Notes

1 'I'm just a Belgian I should make their son laugh loudly / They would even see me featuring Manneken Pis / That their scheme to make big money / And my record sleeve got to be me a beer and a cone of fries.'
2 Some francophone. On the whole, it has been difficult to listen to rap records from Africa. I found tracks of 30 more LP records from the countries mentioned above, and some rap acts had been recorded in Burkina-Faso, Benin, Ivory Coast and Togo, but I have been unable to take them into account.
3 I have also tested an overlapping period of three years. It produces similar results, although it turns out to be slightly less precise.
4 This administrative subdivision, larger than a municipality and smaller than the region or the state, was created after the French Revolution.
5 There are more than 36,000 municipalities in France, more than in the whole of the USA and about 20 times more than in the UK.
6 Paris inner city, with its two million inhabitants, is both a city and a *département* with code number 75.
7 James Deano, www.the-bip.com/wordpress/2007/10/24/james-deano-lave-le-rap-belge-en-famille/.
8 Webster, http://voixdefaits.blogspot.fr/2007/09/one-two-mike-check.html.
9 Just as American or British anglophone rap artists organise venues in France, while the reverse is only exceptional.

References

Aubert, A., Casimiro, de San Leandro, M. and Milliot, V. (1998), *Je texte termine*, La Camarillo, Paroles d'Aube.
Becker, H. (1982), *Art Worlds*, Berkeley, University of California Press.
Bennett, A. (2000), *Popular Music and Youth Culture. Music, Identity and Place*, Basingstoke, Palgrave Macmillan.
Bennett, A. (2004) Consolidating the Music Scenes Perspective, *Poetics* 32, 223–34.
Bennett, A. and Peterson, R. (2004) *Music Scenes: Local, Translocal and Virtual*, Nashville, TN, Vanderbilt University Press.
Bocquet, J.-L. and Pierre-Adolphe, P. (1997), *Rap ta France*, Paris, Flammarion.
Bottero, W. and Crossley, N. (2011) Worlds, Fields and Networks: Becker, Bourdieu and the Structures of Social Relations, *Cultural Sociology* 5(1), 99–119.
Chamberland, R. (2002) The Cultural Paradox of Rap Made in Quebec, in Durand, A.-P. (ed.), *Black, Blanc, Beur: Rap Music and Hip Hop Culture in the Francophone World*, Lanham, MD, Scarecrow Press, 106–23.

Charnas, D. (2010), *The Big Payback. The History of the Business of Hip Hop*, New York, New American Library.

Clarke, A. (1991) Social Worlds/Arenas Theory as Organizational Theory, in Maines, David R., *Social Organization and Social Process*, New York: Aldine De Gruyter, 119–57.

Di Maggio, P. (2011) Cultural Networks, in Scott, John and Carrington, Peter J. (eds.), *The SAGE Handbook of Social Network Analysis*, Thousand Oaks, CA, SAGE, 286–300.

Dozo, B.-O. (2010), *La vie littéraire à la toise. Études quantitatives des professions et des sociabilités des écrivains belges francophones (1918–1940)*, Brussels, Le Cri.

Everett, M. and Borgatti, S. (2000) Peripheries of Cohesive Subsets, *Social Networks* 21(4), 397–407.

Faust, K. (2006) Comparing Social Networks: Size, Density, and Local Structure, *Metodološki zvezki* 3(2), 185–216.

Forman, M. (2002), *The 'Hood Comes First: Race, Space and Place in Rap and Hip Hop*, Middletown, CT, Wesleyan University Press.

Guibert, G. (2012) La notion de scène locale. Pour une approche renouvelée de l'analyse des courants musicaux, in Dorin. S. (ed.), *Sound Factory: Musique et logiques de l'industrialisation*, Saffré, Seteun/Uqbar, 93–124.

Hammou, K.(2009), Dès raps en français au 'rap français', *Histoire et mesure* 24(1), online at http://histoiremesure.revues.org/3889.

Hammou, K. (2012), *Une histoire du rap en France*, Paris, La Découverte.

Harris, K. (2000), 'Roots'? The Relationship between the Global and the Local within the Extreme Metal Scene, *Popular Music* 19(1), 13–30.

Lapiower, A. (1997), *Total respect: la génération hip hop en Belgique*, Brussels, Éditions Fondation Jacques Gueux – Vie Ouvrière.

Menger, P.-M. (1993), L'hégémonie parisienne: Economie et politique de la gravitation artistique, *Annales. Economies, Sociétés, Civilisations* 48(6), 1565–600.

Mitchell, T. (2001) *Global Noise: Rap and Hip Hop outside the USA*, Middletown, CT, Wesleyan University Press.

Moody, J. and White, D. (2003) Structural Cohesion Embeddedness: A Hierarchical Concept of Social Groups, *American Sociological Review* 68(1), 103–27.

Pennycook, A. (2007) Language, Localization, and the Real: Hip Hop and the Global Spread of Authenticity, *Journal of Language, Identity and Education* 6(2), 101–15.

Seidman, S. (1983) Network Structure and Minimum Degree, *Social Networks* 5, 269–87.

Shibutani, T. (1955) Reference Groups as Perspectives, *American Journal of Sociology* 60(6), 562–9.

Strauss, A. (1978) A Social Worlds Perspective, in Denzin, Norman (ed.), *Studies in Symbolic Interaction*, vol. 1, Greenwich, CT, JAI Press, 119–28.

Strauss, A. (1992) *Continual Permutations of Action*, New York, Aldine Transaction.

Straw, W. (1991) Systems of Articulation, Logics of Change: Communities and Scenes in Popular Music, *Cultural Studies* 5(3), 368–88.

Valnet, J. (2013) *M.A.R.S. Histoires, et légendes du hip hop marseillais*, Marseilles, Wildproject.

Yoder, D. (1997), A Model for Commodity Intensive Serious Leisure, *Journal of Leisure Research* 29(4), 407–29.

7 Embracing difference in feminist music worlds

A Ladyfest case study

Susan O'Shea

Many authors argue that historically women have been alienated or marginalised from the means of musical production and public performance within the 'alternative' and 'indie' genres and assigned very specific roles within the music industry in general (Reynolds and Press 1995; Schilt 2003a, 2003b; Leonard 2007). Recent UK figures support those claims and show that fewer than 14 per cent of over 95,000 registered members in the music Performing Right Society (PRS, 2012) are women, highlighting that this exclusion, or omission, is not limited to alternative music genres alone. These figures include songwriters, publishers and performing musicians from classical music to jazz and everything in between. This low figure would suggest that, as well as being invisible in many areas of music creation, a large number of women are losing out economically by not tapping into various royalty streams and potential earnings from music. The numbers claiming royalties are likely to be much lower than the numbers of women actually taking part in music.

Two music movements which challenge the state of affairs, Riot Grrrl and Ladyfest, are discussed in this chapter within the context of what I call feminist music worlds. The idea of music worlds draws on the art worlds concept attributable to Becker (1974, 1982) and adapted in work by Crossley (2009, 2015), Bottero and Crossley (2011), and Crossley and Bottero (forthcoming). Little has been written on Ladyfest and Riot Grrrl, although more on the latter. While it is common to refer qualitatively to the networks of musicians, feminist activists, and organisers in much of this work and to discuss the importance of accepting differences, feminist cultural activists, music lovers and producers can sometimes appear elusive and cliquey. This chapter aims to bring a mixed-methods approach to bear on our hitherto qualitative understanding of the networks of Riot Grrrl and Ladyfest and to investigate the role of homophily in understanding why birds of a feather might flock together in feminist music worlds.

Riot Grrrl was born out of a desire to counter male dominance in the alternative and indie music scenes, in particular, the punk music scene. According to some it helped a new generation of young girls become feminists, find their voices, and fight for their rights (Rosenberg *et al.* 1998; Coulombe 1999). It originated in the United States in the early 1990s as a pre-internet underground feminist cultural revolution by and for girls. Bands like Bikini Kill spearheaded the movement from Olympia, Washington, and on the other side of the Atlantic, British band Huggy Bear paved the way.

The movement had a strong manifesto, it dealt with difficult issues such as abortion, rape and sexual harassment by providing a support structure (for those that could find out about it) through letter writing, sharing mix-tapes and 'zine' publications. Zines were small-scale self-produced low-quality prints, frequently in the style of a music fanzine, but with additional content. Riot Grrrl lay dormant for the best part of 20 years, although not extinct like some of its critics would suggest. It is currently experiencing renewed academic interest (Triggs 2004; Moore and Roberts 2009; Meltzer 2010; Downes 2012; Dunn and Farns-worth 2012; Pavlidis 2012; Payne 2012; Starr 2013) and non-academic interest with films (Anderson 2013), biographies (Marcus 2010) and retrospectives (Darms 2013) of the movement, while its imagery and ideology are being used by contemporary feminist groups such as the Russian protest art group Pussy Riot (see True 2012; Neu and Finch 2013).

Some argue that Riot Grrrl laid the foundations of the Ladyfest movement which was to follow (Schilt and Zobl 2008), while more recently others have argued against drawing direct connections (Dougher and Keenan 2012). Evidence presented in this chapter sides with the former opinion. Ladyfest originated in Olympia in 2000, one of the Riot Grrrl city strongholds. The moniker 'Lady-fest' acts as an umbrella term for a not-for-profit woman-centred music festival and a signifier for an expanding translocal, music and cultural feminist social movement. Primarily motivated by music, both the movement, as a process, and the festival, as one of the tangible outcomes, aim to create a safe space for women to take ownership of, and participate in, music, creative activities, polit-ical debate and gender-based activism. Between 2000 and 2010, there have been 263 Ladyfests forming a loosely bound translocal network in 34 countries world-wide with 32 separate events taking place in the UK alone during this period (Zobl 2013).[1] But who are the organisers and participants of these feminist music worlds and what impact do their relationships have on network structures? Do they really embrace difference or are activists more similar to each other than they think?

McPherson describes homophily as 'the principle that a contact between similar people occurs at a higher rate than among dissimilar people' (2001, 416). In sociology the concept of homophily has been in development since the early twentieth century (Simmel and Levine 1971). In social network terms, homoph-ily helps us predict the likelihood of a relationship existing or occurring between two people (also referred to as actors or nodes) based on a particular attribute. Homophily is closely related to social influence and social selection network the-ories. Social influence theory tends to look at how people influence each other's behaviour or attitudes, whereas social selection network theory looks at how par-ticular pairs of actors may be drawn to one another based on specific characteris-tics or attributes. Attributes can include a wide variety of variables such as attitudes towards feminism, music preference, gender, social class, education, occupation, ethnicity, age or sexuality.

Using participatory research methods, network and ethnographic data were gathered over time on the musicians and activists associated with three Ladyfest case study sites in Manchester, Oxford and London between 2009 and 2012. Ladyfest is often perceived by non-participants to be dominated by lesbians and closed to male participation. While it is evident that many Ladyfest participants aspire towards embracing diversity and difference and challenging heteronormative cultural practices, there has been no empirical evidence to date to support or refute those perceptions. For this reason, special attention is placed on relationship measures based on sexual preference to see if there is a stronger case for homophily or heterophily (preference for dissimilar others) within and between networks on this sometimes contentious attribute.

I begin by highlighting some empirical evidence that shows how women occupy disadvantaged positions in the music professions and the creative industries. This is followed by a brief biographical note that aims to help the reader understand how the personal and the political are interwoven in feminist music worlds. The following section discusses Riot Grrrl as a precursor to Ladyfest and the musical influence it has had on it. Riot Grrrl band networks are introduced to show how links between the movements are forged and how feminist music worlds are translocal in nature, tying cities and countries together. Focus then turns to exploring Ladyfest group homogeneity by examining demographic measures, in particular gender, age, ethnicity and sexuality measures. This is supplemented by qualitative data. Finally, the London Ladyfest case study is used to explore in detail the role of homophily in network structures and in particular whether sexuality has an influence on how organisers develop friendships over time.

The evidence

There are a growing number of blogs and websites that monitor gender progress in the creative and cultural industries, especially music (see for example, *Don't Dance Her Down Boys*, *The Girls Are* and *Drunken Werewolf*; all three are run by former Ladyfest organisers). These blogs are frequently run by volunteers, sometimes individuals, sometimes groups. They not only bring gender inequalities in the areas of cultural production to public attention, but also show how necessary it is to engage with this issue from a public perspective. Despite this, there is a paucity of quantitative data to back up many anecdotal claims about the inequalities women experience in the music and art worlds. While gender equality data are lacking for popular and alternative music participation and production across the spectrum of roles, some attempts have been made to conduct gender equality audits in other genres. For example, figures compiled by *Intermezzo2* reveal that there has been a small increase in the numbers of women performing at the BBC Proms in 2013. The figures show female composers numbered six out of 129 (4.6 per cent); conductors numbered four out of 74 (5.4 per cent) but with a proviso that two of those composers were gospel conductors appearing at the same Prom, not orchestral conductors, and a third was conducting a matinee concert. Marin Alsop took the title as the first woman to conduct the Last Night of the Proms, and the only other woman to lead an orchestra in 2013 at the Royal Albert Hall was Xian Zhang. The number of living composers who were female and had a work performed was four out of 26 (15.3 per cent), down significantly on 2012 figures but in keeping with previous years. Finally, on a slightly more positive note, female instrumental soloists represented 17 out of 52 (32.6 per cent) solo performers. However, this number is still far from ideal.

Inequalities persist not only in the performance field of music but also in the professional support and occupation arenas too. According to the most recent official UK statistics[3] generated by Creative Blueprint (2013) women are under-represented across a broad range of professions within the cultural and creative industries despite making up 41 per cent of the workforce numbered at 794,170. They are particularly under-represented in managerial and senior official positions, professional occupations and skilled trades, while vastly out-numbering their male counterparts in administration and secretarial roles, taking up 81 per cent of those occupations. In the music sector the representation of women is slightly lower when compared to the cultural industry total with women occupying 39 per cent of jobs within the area. However, there is even greater disparity across roles within the music sector. In the category covering the composition of musical works and music publishing only 28 per cent are women, with musical education being the only area where women outnumber men by 81 per cent to 19 per cent. There are some warnings attached to these figures due to the unreliability of the Standard Industrial Classification (SIC) codes for the creative sector on which they are based and should be treated as best available estimates. These limited statistics paint a picture of inequality in access to the means of cultural production and participation, especially in the music fields. At the heart of Riot Grrrl and Ladyfest ideologies are attempts to address these challenges by means of a revolutionary call to action; to encourage women and girls to take ownership of their own cultural and creative practices by participating in ways that make sense to them in their own locale while connecting them to wider international movements.

From the personal to the political

I first heard about Ladyfest in early 2005 through friends. I was surprised that I had never heard about it before, particularly when I learned about its deep-rooted connection with Riot Grrrl. My interests in music and feminism have been inter-linked long before I even knew what Riot Grrrl was all about. I subsequently heard that I am one of the lucky ones as I managed to see Huggy Bear in 1993 at The Village in Cork, part of the famed Sir Henry's club. I was intrigued by Huggy Bear, both their music and their distinctive approach to live performance. However, I was completely unaware at the time that they were an integral part of a feminist music movement.

My first direct experience of Ladyfest was as one of the organisers of Lady-fest Manchester 2008. I had moved from Ireland 18 months previously and was keen to get involved in the vibrant music scene in Manchester but without a network of like-minded people I was finding it a little difficult. My friends had just started planning Ladyfest Cork that year and they suggested I should try and organise one in Manchester. I was a little apprehensive at the thought of initiating a planning meeting on my own but as serendipity would have it a few weeks later I saw a poster on a lamppost asking people to come to a meeting and Ladyfest Manchester 2008 was born. The highlight for many of the festival organisers (including myself), and attendees, was having The Slits play their only UK gig as a reformed group with the original line-up intact (the other gig took place in Spain). A special mention should be given to Zoë Street Howe for her gentle words of encouragement while she was interviewing the band for her book *Typical Girls? The Story of The Slits* (2009). Ari-Up's support for Ladyfest was tangible with her boundless energy around the festival site. It was wonderful to see Viv Albertine back on stage after a very long hiatus. Albertine too has become a repeated supporter of Ladyfest, having played at numerous festivals and spoken about her experiences of gender-based discrimination, not only in music but in other art worlds, and how she learned to openly call herself an artist with pride and defiance at the age of 50. The main discussion panel explored feminism and the counter-culture, examining the role of gender in the creative and cultural industries. It was inspiring to hear, then Doctor, now Professor, Amelia Fletcher[4] speak on this topic, not only as a successful female musician who has been in many popular bands since the mid-1980s (Talulah Gosh, Heavenly, Marine Research, The Wedding Present, Hefner) and a working mother, but also as a prominent economist, now with an OBE (awarded 2014) for services to Competition and Consumer Economics. Fletcher's current band, Tender Trap, was just starting out around this time too, taking its first steps onto the gig circuit while solidifying the line-up. The other panellists of note included Sheila Rowbotham, Marion Leonard and Katherine M. Graham.

My first experience as a Ladyfest organiser (there have been many subsequently) was instrumental to the development of my friendship, feminist and music networks in the city. This led me to question if there are commonalities across different Ladyfest organising groups or if the impact Ladyfest has had on my personal networks was somehow unique.

Riot Grrrl networks at the root of Ladyfest

At the heart of social movements lie social relationships, and these relationships are often built over time, developing a kind of organisational memory and expectation that persist even when members come and go. Staggenborg suggests that as social movements rarely have clear beginnings and end points, as a result the 'notion of a social movement community allows us to conceive of movements as consisting of cultural groups and interactions as well as political movement organizations' (1998, 181). This is a useful point to consider when examining feminist music worlds. It is important to pay attention to the historical lineages, though arguably not a linear history, of feminist cultural activism and its attempts to challenge gender inequalities. These historical narratives are less about discrete chronological stages and more about blurry overlaps.

Movements 'can draw on the loose networks maintained by cultural groups and on resources provided by institutionalized elements of the community to generate visible collective action from time to time' (Staggenborg 1998, 200). Ladyfest as a movement emerges from its own particular history carrying forward previous social ties while at the same time developing new ones. As a translocal movement community, Ladyfest, and its predecessor and co-conspirator Riot Grrrl, continue to erupt into collective action that is frequently tied to other protest cycles or movements. Greiner and Sakdapolrak view trans-locality as having many interpretations 'revolving around notions of mobility, connectedness, networks, place, locality and locales, flows, travel, transfer and circulatory knowledge' (2013, 375). These distinct movements rooted in specific time periods can be seen within a broader context of networked feminist music worlds. This is important because fitting contemporary feminist cultural activism into neat time-specific periods perpetuates a popular discourse that all too quickly relegates feminist acts of cultural resistance during periods of seeming inactivity to, at best, the history books, and at worst something to be appropriated by capitalist structures and sold back in bite-sized watered-down versions to the very girls and women whom these Do-It-Yourself (DIY) activities are meant to empower (O'Shea 2012). However, this grand ideal of collective action and impetus to create new music and art worlds which counter mainstream conventions is not without its problems and critics.

Moore and Roberts (2009) point out in their article on DIY mobilisation, which includes a discussion on Riot Grrrl, that the junction between social movements and music is ripe for research. The Riot Grrrl movement materialised at a time when, according to Leonard (2007), women musicians such as Kim Gordon of Sonic Youth, Kim Deal of The Breeders and The Pixies and bands such as L7 and Babes in Toyland were becoming increasingly visible in the music media. But also it was a time when women's hard-earned rights to bodily autonomy and access to safe and timely abortions were under threat in America, with high-profile court cases being fought by world-weary feminists worn down by a media-fuelled feminist backlash. Riot Grrrl stepped up to challenge it. In many ways it filled a gap left by the second-wave women's movement of the 1960s and 1970s. It brought the personal back to the political because it was a movement created by young angry women with stories to share and a desire to change the cultural landscape.

In various art- and music-based movements the initial motivation for engaging in activism is women's lack of visibility in the art world and, where women are visible, a disagreement with the narrow roles they are frequently assigned, along with a desire to make all avenues of artistic production and participation available and accessible to all women. Exposing network connections between different feminist cultural movements in different time periods allows for a continuity of experiences and a chance for subsequent generations to learn from one another through dialogue, rather than perpetuating the perceived generational rifts so often referred to in literature on feminist waves and by those who purport that feminism has failed. In a way what Riot Grrrl managed to achieve, through the use of cultural signifiers such as zines, clothing styles, music as genre and writing on the body, was to develop what Becker calls 'a coherent and defensible aesthetic' (2008, 134). This aesthetic became the basis on which Riot Grrrl, and subsequently Ladyfest movement members, were, and still are, able to 'evaluate things in a reliable and dependable way' and to make 'regular patterns of cooperation possible' (Becker 2008, 134).

Musically, Riot Grrrls took their inspiration from women of the 1970s and 1980s punk scene. For example, Poly Styrene of X-Ray Spex, The Raincoats, Joan Jett, Patti Smith, Fifth Column and The Slits, many of whom have until recently been written out of rock history and are still neglected in contemporary music magazines. Perhaps surprisingly, Viv Albertine, despite her role as guitarist with The Slits, struggled with issues of self-esteem and the confidence to openly call herself an artist in the intervening time between the first incarnation of The Slits and their reunion in 2008. Albertine contributed to the discussion panel at the launch event for Ladyfest Ten (London) by saying:

> My name is Viv Albertine and I'm an artist. I'm 50 and I haven't ever dared say that before … if you want to be an artist it's a fight to the death basically and you have to decide what side you're on as a female artist. That's what we did in The Slits but there were four of us then and I'm on my own doing it and it's exactly the same fucking fight and I cannot believe it's the same fight 30 years later.
>
> (Viv Albertine, panel discussion, 2010)

The networks associated with Riot Grrrl have lasted well beyond the short period of initial activity in the early 1990s. The actors in the original Riot Grrrl network have played, and continue to play, important roles in Rock Camp and Ladyfest activities. For example, bands such as Bikini Kill, Bratmobile, Heavens to Betsy and Huggy Bear, often described at quintessential Riot Grrrl bands, have had a substantial influence on other Riot Grrrl associated bands.

Figure 7.1 shows a bipartite graph of an affiliation network consisting of bands and their relationships with cities. This two-mode matrix is made up of 118 bands (rows) and 43 cities (columns). We get a clearer picture of what is happening in the Riot Grrrl music scene when we break it down by location and the sociogram gives us a feel for the translocal nature of feminist music worlds. The dark squares represent cities and the small circles are bands associated with those cities. The larger squares represent the key cities most often associated with the development of Riot Grrrl, Ladyfest and Rock Camp activities. The triangles represent the four bands most often associated with Riot Grrrl: Bratmobile, Heavens to Betsy and Bikini Kill from the USA and Huggy Bear from the UK (Marcus 2010). Finally, the diamond shapes represent three additional bands, Pagan Holiday, Cadallaca and Partyline. These bands have been highlighted as the primary members of each band have participated in this research.

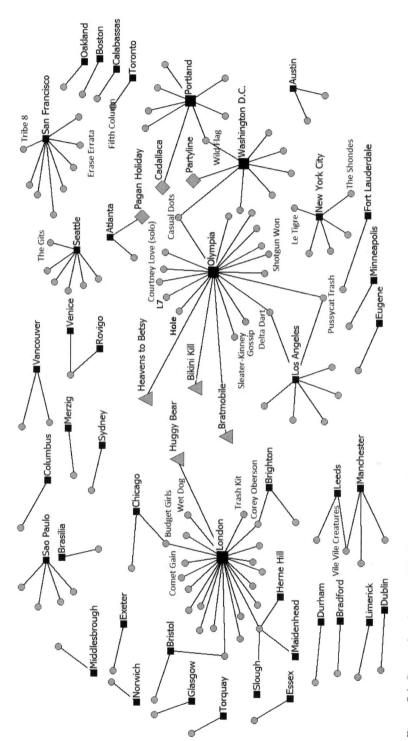

Figure 7.1 Connections between Riot Grrrl associated bands and cities.

Pagan Holiday's Stella Zine has engaged in extended personal email communication with me for other aspects of this research and she discussed her gender activism, involvement with Riot Grrrl, Rock Camp for Girls and Ladyfest. Both Cadallaca's Sarah Dougher and Partyline's Allison Wolfe participated by means of a video interview which they prepared for the launch of the Ladyfest Ten festival in London in 2010.

Some of the individuals connected with the bands mentioned in Figure 7.1 have influenced the development of Riot Grrrl chapters and music scenes in particular cities and countries predominantly in the UK and the USA, although this geographical profile is changing. For example, Allison Wolfe and her friend Molly Neuman, both members of the band Bratmobile, were associated with the beginnings of the Riot Grrrl movement. Wolfe then helped establish the first Ladyfest in Olympia, Washington, in 2000 and has since been involved with coaching and tutoring at Rock Camp for Girls. She currently lives in Los Angeles and is documenting an oral history of Riot Grrrl. This is a high-profile example, but one that is mirrored on many levels in relation to feminist music worlds. For example, Lisa Darms, one of the original Ladyfest Olympia 2000 organisers, has continued the Riot Grrrl spirit through her archival work at Fales Library and Special Collections at New York University, editing *The Riot Grrrl Collection* (2013) book. There are many more examples of creative collaborations that have come about from the ability of individuals to draw on the activism and support networks of feminist music worlds inspired by a punk DIY ethos. The cities highlighted in Figure 7.1 share links between all three movements and the cities represented by the largest light-shaded squares have been and continue to be some of the most active sites for counter-cultural creative activism.

Examining the two-mode network of Riot Grrrl associated bands in Figure 7.1 helps to understand not only how bands are connected in music worlds but how individuals inspire and connect across different time periods and cities. The importance of particular cities for the cultivation of feminist art and collaboration opportunities highlights the connection between cities, Rock Camp for Girls and Ladyfest even further. This point is applicable when looking at the importance not only of cities such as London and New York in terms of the diversity of opportunities and their economic position, but also cities such as Olympia (in Washington State), and Portland (in Oregon), despite the small population size of both these cities. Both Olympia and Portland are associated with wider punk music and artistic movements as well as being the site for the first Ladyfest festival and the first Rock Camp for Girls respectively. Washington, DC, another important hub tying both Olympia and Portland together, has a well-documented punk music scene dating back to the late 1970s.

Leonard's (2007) work on the discourses and representations of gender within popular music and the conceptualisation of Riot Grrrl as a network suggests that the importance of the Riot Grrrl network could be 'measured by the effect it has had on individuals' and that it 'opened debate concerning the participation of girls and women in creating and performing music' (p. 151). Leonard (2007) develops her networks thesis to discuss Ladyfest in similar ways drawing on notions of both Ladyfest and Riot Grrrl as facilitators for access to resources, a similar idea to that of Staggenborg (1998), mentioned earlier. The 'spatial dynamics of Ladyfest' can help 'explore emerging patterns of organisation and mediation within indie music-related networks' (Leonard 2007, 161). Moore and Roberts (2009) examine Riot Grrrl feminism as one of three social movements in the 1990s to spark their interest (including Rock against Racism in Britain in the late 1970s and the US hardcore scene of the 1980s). They claim that music and associated subcultural processes have functioned as mediums through which to organise, protest and agitate for social change. Claiming that these particular music examples are more important than being taste-makers or identity-formers, they suggest that a DIY ethic was central to transcending mere identity politics. They conclude by suggesting that the structures that grew from these collective movements 'were organized for action in a broader political context when the Right had gone on the offensive against the achievements of the movements for racial justice, peace, and sexual equality' and in doing so 'changed the cultural dynamics of the pre-existing anti-racist, peace, and feminist movements' (2009, 289).

On one level, Ladyfest remains the same from country to country, in that it is a women-focused arts and music festival with a feminist ethos which aims to highlight the inequality experienced by women at all levels in the creative indus-tries, and more broadly through its affiliations with particular charities. Yet on another level, exactly how this is put together and how the programme runs will have a very local feel. Likewise, different cities and different countries face diverse social challenges crossing the boundaries of class, culture, economics, disability, race and sexuality, all of which intersect with and are compounded by gender. This can influence the theme of a festival and how organisers might choose to deal with real-life issues in workshop sessions or panel discussions. In countries such as Ireland, Spain and Italy, where abortion is highly restricted, it is not unusual to find Ladyfest discussions focusing on the 'right to choose', improved freedom of information about reproductive rights, and in some cases providing a forum to help educate young women about sexual health. Similar themes have emerged in South American festivals too. While some Ladyfests take a strong overtly political stance, others may try to deal with issues more subtly by focusing on a celebration of the achievements of women or, as in many cases, a combination of the two.

Ladyfest is constantly evolving and changing yet still pays attention to its roots. It is very much a translocal festival network. Translocality as a concept fits well with Riot Grrrl and Ladyfest networks that are neither truly trans-national or international, nor parochial. They have a very real local feel and work within local contexts, yet draw and trade on cross-national and cross-city spaces and resources. Having looked at the historical roots of the Ladyfest movement, the question I examine next asks who participates in Ladyfest, who do we see, and what do we/they look like?

Through the looking glass – sounding reflections of ourselves

The greater the number of ties to other highly central actors (ego to alter) in a network, the greater the likelihood of increased network centrality for that individual. If, as Ibarra (1992) hypothesises, in interaction networks in organisational settings men tend to have more high-status ties characterised by homophily, could the same be said of queer-identified women in gender homophilous feminist music networks? Before looking at the question more closely we need to assess the data and some descriptive statistics that tell us more about the network participants and hint at the tendency for homophily in the networks.

The data

Surveys were administered to the three case-study sites by two modes, email or online, using Survey Gizmo: Ladyfest Oxford 2010 (email); Ladyfest Manchester (online), and Ladyfest Ten (online). Each survey contained demographic questions, the majority of which were asked across all three surveys. Oxford and Manchester information was sought for one time period only. Statistics are reported rounded to the nearest percentage. The survey response rates were as follows: Ladyfest Ten organisers, 60 per cent (once inactive mailing list members were discounted); Ladyfest Manchester, 40 per cent return generated from a ticket sales list (the festival sold out in advance); and Ladyfest Oxford returned six out of a possible eight surveys from the organising group. Respondents were encouraged to self-identify in a number of key areas. The open-ended categories included 'gender', 'sexuality', 'age' and the place they 'grew up'. Next I will briefly cover 'gender' 'age' and 'ethnicity' then focus more closely on 'sexuality'.

Gender

While men do participate in Ladyfest as both festival goers and organisers, there is a tendency towards gender homophily biased in favour of women. Gender homophily is unsurprisingly strongest for organisers, given the remit of the festival, with Ladyfest Ten being completely homophilous on gender. This is true for the most active core network and the peripheral network. Approximately 84 per cent of respondents across the three case-study sites identified as female and 14 per cent as male, only one study participant declined to nominate a gender and another chose to answer 'other' despite having the opportunity to self-identify in a free text box.

Age

The demographic data generated from the surveys let us build a picture of who participates in Ladyfest activities in the UK and give an indication of how homogenous a group Ladyfest participants might be and how this might affect homophily measures when examining the networks. Sixty per cent of respondents, a sizeable majority, were aged between 25 and 34. The results from this study indicate that the age bands and gender of participants attending and organising Ladyfest festivals reflect participation levels in other associated modes of participation such as on Facebook. For example, the age profile for 'fans' of the Ladyfest Ten Facebook page (www.facebook.com/pages/Ladyfest-Ten/ 298592715550) sees the highest number of participants in the 25 to 34 years age group with the 35 to 44 years group making up a sizeable proportion.

Ethnicity

Based on the UK Census ethnicity categories, the majority of respondents, 86 per cent in total, described themselves as belonging to one of three white categories (White British, White Irish and White Other). This figure is in keeping with the most recent UK Census data from 2011. According to a census briefing report by the Centre on Dynamics of Ethnicity (CoDE), while the number of people defining themselves ethnically as non-White has more than doubled in size from three million in 1991 to seven million in 2011, this non-White group remains a minority of the total population at 14 per cent (Jivraj 2012). Undoubtedly, there are problems within predominantly White feminist movements and real issues about equality of access to these movements for women from Black and Minority Ethnic groups (BME). However, it would appear from these case studies that women are participating in Ladyfest at rates that reflect the BME population in the UK. This goes some way to refute claims that Ladyfest is colour-blind, at least in a UK context. These figures may not represent the experience in the USA. However, it is important not to over-simplify this finding as, while some minorities may appear to be adequately represented in the Ladyfest movement, some voices and faces tend to represent feminist movements more than others and it is these often unintentional hierarchical roles that need addressing.

Sexuality

The question that had the greatest variation in discrete response categories was that of sexuality. There were 16 different free text responses, showing the variety along the sexuality spectrum and the importance of self-definition for those engaged in counter-cultural creative feminist activism. Additionally one respondent said they thought the question was not important and another replied 'other' despite having the opportunity to answer the question in their own words. The full list of responses is listed below:

1   Queer | Queer – Pan-sexual | Queer-Bisexual | Queer Lezzer
2   Lesbian | Gay Woman | Gay
3   Bisexual Gay | Bisexual (strong preference for women) | Bisexual

4   Mostly straight | Open minded-heterosexual | Heterosexual | Straight
5   Homosexual
6   Undecided | Not important | Other

The question was recoded, first into five broad categories that reflect the variety of responses and are closely linked to the first five groups above and displayed in Table 7.1. This was further collapsed into a binary variable 'non-heterosexual' and 'heterosexual'.

The results for 'sexuality' were examined across each case-study site. The differences in responses between Manchester, London and Oxford were statistically non-significant at the .05 level, suggesting that perhaps there is an element of homophily at work. It would appear that similar types of people tend to be attracted to Ladyfest festivals and associated feminist music worlds. The city in which the festival takes place does not appear to influence the degree of participation from sexual minority groups, although Manchester has a slightly higher percentage of respondents identifying as queer. Queer is not only used as a term for assuming a non-heterosexual sexual identity or a straight–queer rejection of heteronormativity, but also as a potent political identifier. Manchester has a long tradition of queer cultural activism and queer music which frequently sets itself in opposition to mainstream male gay culture in the city's Village area. The Village as a space is frequently sound-tracked by loud bubble-gum techno, hen-party chatter and festival tourism (see Hughes (2006) for more on this theme). Many Manchester-based queer activists perceive the area to have lost sight of its original remit associated with Pride, to be dominated by body-conscious consumerism, hostile to alternative lifestyles and pink-pound rejectionists, where aging bodies go unnoticed (Simpson 2013), while perpetuating the invisibility of lesbian lives and female-identified queers. One only needs to listen to any of the powerful punk-pop-feminist tracks of Ste McCabes (former Manchester resident, Ladyfest organiser and performer) to understand how charged these issues are.[5]

Ladyfest tends to attract participants and musicians who predominantly identify as non-heterosexual. Around 75 per cent of respondents fall into this

Table 7.1 Sexuality

	Frequency	Per cent	Valid per cent	Cumulative per cent
Valid				
Queer	20	26.0	26.0	26.0
Heterosexual	19	24.7	24.7	50.6
Bisexual	13	16.9	16.9	67.5
Lesbian/Gay	21	27.3	27.3	94.8
Undecided	1	1.3	1.3	96.1
Other	2	2.6	2.6	98.7
Missing	1	1.3	1.3	100.0
Total	77	100.0	100.0	

Source: Ladyfest survey data, Manchester, Oxford and London.

category. This was a surprising finding despite the association of Ladyfest with queer politics and its frequent alignment with the LGBTQ[6] movement for particular campaigns. However, it is a finding that may support popular public perceptions that feminism is for lesbian women only, although on closer examination we see that this is not an accurate assumption.

Ladyfest organising groups tend to discuss whether to even use the term feminism in case it conjures up these images and alienates people from joining the organising group or attending the festival, particularly as we are used to hearing the phrase 'I'm not a feminist, but…'. However, generally the feminist label remains attached to the movement and a central part of the festival's identity and as a way of reclaiming the term. As noted by one respondent 'as long as it stays feminist and stays artistic, I like that the model can be used however anyone wants it!' (Ladyfest Ten, survey respondent 2011).

London calling, behind the scenes

London, as the UK capital, is an ethnically diverse and cosmopolitan city. However, its size and high cost of living coupled with poor provision for disability access in venues and on public transport can make participation in cultural and music events difficult for many. It is a well-respected international music and artistic destination in the UK and internationally. There have been at least eight documented Ladyfest festivals in the city. Festivals took place in 2002, 2007, two in 2008, 2009 and two in 2010. The November 2010 festival was Ladyfest Ten and one of the case studies for this project, Ladyfest East, London, took place in April 2012. The Ladyfest Ten case study yielded the most fruitful network data, due in part to its size, the ability to engage in participatory research with the organisation right from the beginning and the mixed media that was used to plan, organise and promote the festival. Ladyfest Ten was designed to celebrate ten years of Ladyfest activism around the world and the organisers took a celebratory theme and an international slant to the festival, putting together a rich, and vibrant cross-platform music and arts festival.

The festival took place in the Highbury and Islington area of North London, chosen as it is well networked to various transport links with disability access. A number of community and music venues, including the local library, were used in this area along a straight stretch of road to house a variety of Ladyfest activities. Again, each of these venues had events on the ground floor for ease of access. However, the weekend the festival took place the London Underground network for this area was not working and the city experienced one of the worst weekends of heavy rainfall. This made the festival difficult for people to access, particularly those with mobility issues, and it greatly reduced the possibility of people coming along to the festival at the last minute. The main music venue was The Garage, a popular mid-sized venue, although large for a Ladyfest. It caters for well-known international touring bands. It was an ambitious sized venue to fill. Some of the organisers felt that, despite numbers being lower than anticipated, the feedback from the musicians who played in a well-equipped venue more than made up for the smaller than hoped for audience. The costs associated with this ambitious festival were high, particularly as there were a number of high profile international acts such as M.E.N (with former Le Tigre members JD Samson and Johanna Fateman) and Nicky Click. Poorer than expected advance ticket sales and the negative impact of the local transport and weather conditions meant the festival suffered financial difficulty. It required several post-festival fundraising activities in order to recoup some outstanding costs.

Network data

Ladyfest Ten had a defined network boundary and all the actors in the network were known before data collection began. A name roster, derived from a dedicated organiser's mailing list and online planning tool called NING, was used to generate network data. This was gathered at the same time as the main survey. Respondents were asked questions on how they perceived their relationships and activities with other organisers at the time of taking the survey (approximately six months after the festival) and at two other retrospective time points. These included the weekend the festival took place and the period before individuals became involved with the group. Demographic data was provided by 32 respondents who also represented most of the core actors within the network. The analysis was conducted in UCINET 6 (Borgatti *et al.* 2002). My knowledge of participants, their relationships and group activities, such as planning meetings and sub-group activities like fundraising, craft fairs, film nights, art exhibitions and club nights, provided a means of corroborating the nominations made by survey respondents. I am confident that the nominated relationship ties within the network to seemingly peripheral actors, are likely to be reciprocated by the non-respondents. However, most of the analysis is carried out on undirected ties avoiding issues pertaining to analyses of reciprocity. About six months into planning the festival, in order to streamline activities, those on the original Ladyfest email list were asked to join the NING social networking site to help with organising activities. Participants self-selected into this group and a few new members joined. There were 79 members of the NING group at its peak and this number represents active network members. The following analysis is conducted on the 79 nodes.

Network change over time

Longitudinal social networks have a tendency to follow one of four dynamic states: they can exhibit stability, shock or mutation or they evolve. In the case of Ladyfest Ten the networks underwent a period of evolution represented over three peak periods of activity. The first is at the point of network formation where network participants knew many other participants by name but did not rate a significant relationship with them. The second is around the weekend of the festival where the most intense activities and relationships are mapped.

The third is a period about six months after the festival, representing a stage of settling and allows us to assess the lasting impact of involvement in organising a Ladyfest on the relationships of participants.

In order to conduct an analysis of attribute-based network homophily that reflects a more meaningful relationship each time-point was dichotomised using the valued relation greater than or equal to 'acquaintance'. Analysis was then carried out on the stronger relationship ties, requiring actors to have some kind of contact with alters that is considered more consequential than just knowing someone to see or by name. There was a small downward adjustment in tie nominations between time two and time three. The latter period represents the enduring relationships between organisers approximately six months after their mutual reason for forming those ties is no longer a motive for them to stay in touch.

Figures 7.2 and 7.3 not only visually show how networks change over time but how the density of ties has increased threefold between the beginning of the festival planning period and several months after the event has taken place. This is in spite of only three new actor nominations occurring at the third time point.

The majority of ties in Figure 7.2 are at the level of acquaintance, whereas by Time 3 the majority of relations are based on friendship or close friendship ties. We can hypothesise from this that Ladyfest networks experience an evolutionary growth in density over time but that they also provide significant opportunities

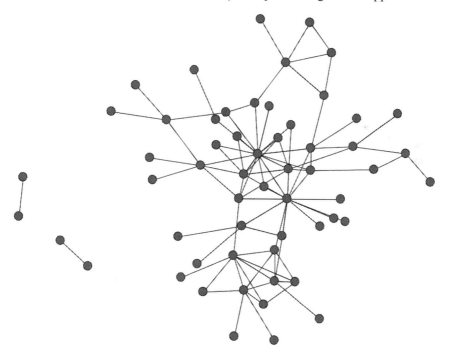

Figure 7.2 Time 1: strong relationships.

Note
Ladyfest Ten – 57 nominated nodes with 107 ties.

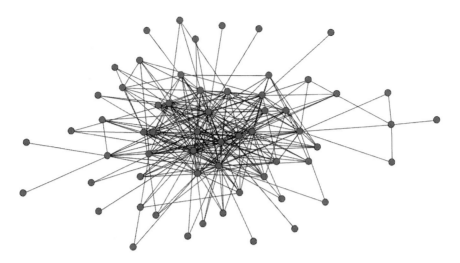

Figure 7.3 Time 3: strong relationships.

Note
Ladyfest Ten – 60 nominated nodes 374 ties.

for participants to form lasting friendship ties once the network dissolves. Next I briefly discuss average degree measures before coming back to homophily in greater detail by drawing on the idea of homophily based on sexual preference as mentioned earlier.

Average degree

Density measures are best represented in a comparative way, and help us understand how well connected a particular network is. In other words, 'density can be interpreted as the probability that a tie exists between any pair of randomly chosen nodes' (Borgatti *et al.* 2012, 150). While this is important to consider, we can see from Table 7.2 that although there has been an increase in density over the three time points, the increase is smaller than we might expect considering the evidence of enhanced network activity shown in Figure 7.3 and the relatively small size of the network. However, the average degree tells us a lot more as

Table 7.2 Average degree density

	Time 1	Time 2	Time 3
Density	0.034	0.108	0.106
No. of ties	107	422	374
Average degree	1.877	6.698	6.233

Source: Ladyfest Ten survey.

it 'represents the average number of ties that each node has' (Borgatti *et al.* 2012, 152).

This shows that, by the end of the festival, Ladyfest Ten organisers had increased their friendship ties from on average fewer than two to just over six. The difference in this respect between Time 2 and Time 3 is negligible, again showing that involvement with Ladyfest serves to increase sustainable relationships. This is important in the context of homophily as the following examples will show.

All together the same but different

Homophily, as we have seen, is not only an important sociological concept but it plays a central role in the development of social networks. Table 7.3 highlights the changes in homophily measures between the beginning of the festival planning period and after the festival, using attribute data on the whole network.

The E-I index is a measure of the external and internal ties of individual members of a particular group, for example those who share the same ethnicity, to members outside that group. If the index is −1 then all ties are internal to the group and if the index is +1 then all ties are external. On the other hand Yule's Q is a standard measure of association capable of controlling for the relative size of a category and of assessing the rate at which similar or different ties connect with one another in a whole network context. A value of 0 indicates no homophily with −1 representing perfect heterophily and +1 perfect homophily.[7]

Examining Table 7.3, the following E-I index attribute measures are moving in a positive direction, that is towards +1 even if still in the negative range, and are suggestive of a move from internal ties (homophily) to external ties (heterophily) between Time 1 and Time 3. These include education, ethnicity

Table 7.3 Whole network homophily

Attributes	Time 1		Time 3	
	E–I ind	Yule's Q	E–I ind	Yule's Q
Age	0.2121	−0.1473	−0.1278	0.2896
Education	−0.9091	0.1766	−0.3850	0.4659
Ethnicity	0.1212	0.0527	0.2932	−0.0043
White ethnicities	−0.6859	−1.0000	−0.3985	0.0439
White British	−0.0890	1.0000	0.0301	−0.0191
Festival area (from)	0.3508	1.0000	0.4812	−0.0166
Doing now (all options)	0.5079	1.0000	0.2857	0.1840
Work	0.0157	1.0000	−0.0150	0.0591
Student	−0.7487	−1.0000	−0.6090	0.1219
Social class proxy	−0.3226	0.0000	−0.3409	0.0584
Sexuality (6 items)	0.4974	1.0000	0.5865	−0.0037
Non-hetero/heterosexual	−0.1518	1.0000	−0.3534	0.1861

Source: Ladyfest Ten Survey.

(covering all ethnicity categories), White ethnicities, White British, festival area (where people feel they are from), student, and sexuality (broken down into the six categories highlighted in Table 7.1). For the same attributes the Yule's Q measure appears to suggest a similar pattern, in most cases moving from perfect homophily towards indicating heterophilous network relations. The social class proxy measure remains almost unchanged, while it appears people tend to form relationships more frequently with those of a similar age and education and if they identify as non-heterosexual.

These results may be tentatively interpreted as indicating that involvement with Ladyfest increases the opportunity of forming meaningful relationships with others from different geographical backgrounds and ethnicities, while sharing similar beliefs in things like feminism. Yet, involvement does not guarantee that some relationships are not hindered due to structural inequalities such as class. Caution is further advised about how these particular findings are interpreted with a proviso that they only pertain to an individual's network ties within this specific bounded feminist music world and not their networks in other areas of their lives.

Earlier in the chapter I posed the question whether queer-identified women in gender homophilous feminist music worlds might have similar homophily influenced high-status ties as men in interaction networks in organisational settings (Ibarra 1992). Table 7.4 highlights the density of tie strength based on sexuality. Queer has the highest density with almost 48 per cent of ties falling within the same group. The autocorrelation score is 0.445 explaining 45 per cent of the variance overall by ties based on sexuality.

When the dichotomous measure of sexuality is examined, 70 per cent of ties occur within the non-heterosexual category. From the evidence presented in this chapter it is clear that homophily is important in Ladyfest networks and, while there is support for the idea that strong ties are formed around sexual preferences, how meaningful that is and how important the conceptualisation of queer relationships are in this context is open to debate and in need of further investigation.

Embracing difference

Set against a wider background of gender inequality in music and the creative industries, I have attempted to show how two music movements, Riot Grrrl and Ladyfest, attempt to challenge these disparities. This chapter sought to move on

Table 7.4 Density of tie strength based on sexuality

	Queer	Heterosexual	Bisexual	Lesbian/Gay	Undecided	Other
Number	34	4	7	10	0	0
Density	0.472	0.056	0.350	0.238	0	0

Source: Ladyfest Ten Survey.

from a purely qualitative consideration of the networks of these feminist music worlds, by employing a mixed-methods social network approach to understanding why birds of a feather flock together.

The discussion on the Riot Grrrl band networks helped to provide an understanding of how, within music worlds, individuals as well as bands inspire and connect with other like-minded individuals across different spaces and places. Even a simple measure like playing in a band together can quickly reveal the complex and often dense networks behind seemingly unconnected feminist activists.

Next, three UK-based Ladyfest sites were introduced which highlighted the demographic characteristics of organisers and participants. Survey data revealed that 84 per cent of participants in these examples identified as female, they were mostly aged between 25 and 34, the majority were White, although the 14 per cent non-White minority is in keeping with recent Census statistics (Jivraj 2012), and almost 75 per cent identified as non-heterosexual.

Social network analysis techniques were used to discuss the organisational structure and evolution of Ladyfest Ten, a London based case-study. A longitudinal overview of strong ties revealed not only that networks change over time but that the density of ties increased significantly between the beginning of the festival planning period and several months after the event had taken place. This manifested as an increase in the average degree for participants' ego–alter ties, by four to over six, six months after the festival, showing how sustainable relationships are created and maintained as a result of involvement with Ladyfest. Whole network homophily measures suggested that involvement with Ladyfest increases the opportunity of forming meaningful relationships with others from different ethnic groups and places, and that there is a general tendency towards heterophily based on attribute ties as the network evolves. However, age, education, class and a non-heterosexual identity have a slight tendency to encourage more homophilous ties. This requires further investigation.

To conclude, it would appear that feminist music worlds not only aspire to embrace difference but do in fact embrace difference as revealed by the study of Riot Grrrl and Ladyfest networks. Feminist activists may outwardly appear to be a homogenous group with particular traits, but those traits are more complex and subtle than they first appear. Both homophily and heterophily have their role to play in network evolution, personal tie formation and friendship development over time. However, in these feminist music worlds we can safely say that birds of a feather rock together.

Notes

1 This is a reliable estimated figure. There is no formal record of Ladyfest activity and due to the often transient nature of online communications, blogs and websites and the difficulties and expense groups face with internet providers and server hosts, some information on previous Ladyfest festivals may be lost as websites shut down or perhaps festivals never took place, despite having an online presence. However, with the advent of the *Grassroots Feminism* web archive (www.grassrootsfeminism.net),

some of this lost information may be retrieved and at the very least there is now an online repository for future Ladyfest archives and other feminist media. There have been many more Ladyfest festivals since 2010.

2   http://intermezzo.typepad.com/intermezzo/2013/04/women-at-proms.html.

3   Creative and Cultural Skills (2010/2011) – Statistics generated from the Creative and Cultural Skills data generator resource: www.data-generator.org.uk (accessed 10 December 2012).

4   Fletcher's speech is available here: www.wearsthetrousers.com/2008/11/ladyfest-manchester-the-saturday-debate/.

5   www.ste-mccabe.co.uk/.

6   LGBTQ is usually shorthand for Lesbian, Gay, Bisexual, Transgendered and Queer. This is the most commonly used abbreviation of the longer, more inclusive but less memorable LGBTTTQQIAA (Lesbian, Gay, Bisexual, Transgender, Transsexual, Two-spirited, Queer, Questioning, Intersex, Asexual, Ally).

7   However, in this case as the numbers are low in many of the attribute categories and a small number have missing data, the strength of Yule's Q cannot be attributed to an exact figure but rather interpreted as reasonably good indicator of homophilous or heterophilous tendencies in the network. An advantage of the mixed-methods approach is that ethnographic data assist with interpretation and support these findings.

References

Anderson, S. (2013) *The Punk Singer*, video, USA, 80 minutes.

Becker, H.S. (1974) Art as Collective Action, *American Sociological Review* 39(6), 767–76.

Becker, H.S. (2008) *Art Worlds*, Berkeley, University of California Press.

Borgatti, S.P., Everett, M.G. and Freeman, L.C. (2002) *UCINET for Windows: Software for Social Network Analysis*, Harvard, MA, Analytic Technologies.

Borgatti, S.P., Everett, M.G. and Johnson, J.C. (2012) *Analyzing Social Networks*, London, Sage Publications.

Bottero, W. and Crossley, N. (2011) Worlds, Fields and Networks: Becker, Bourdieu and the Structures of Social Relations, *Cultural Sociology* 5(1), 99–119.

Coulombe, R.T. (1999) The Insatiable Banshee: Voracious Vocalizing … Riot Grrrl … and the Blues, in Barkin, E. and Hamessley, L. (eds), *Audible Traces: Gender, Identity, and Music*, Zürich, Carciofoli Verlagshaus, 257–72.

Crossley, N. (2009) The Man Whose Web Expanded: Network Dynamics in Manchester's Post/Punk Music Scene 1976–1980, *Poetics* 37(1), 24–49.

Crossley, N. (2015) *Networks of Sound, Style and Subversion: The Punk and Post-Punk Worlds of Liverpool, London, Manchester and Sheffield 1975–1980*, Manchester, Manchester University Press.

Crossley, N. and Bottero, W. (forthcoming) 'Music Worlds and Internal Goods', *Cultural Sociology*.

Darms, L. (ed.) (2013) *The Riot Grrrl Collection*, New York, Feminist Press at The City University of New York.

Dougher, S. and Keenan, E.K. (2012) Riot Grrrrl, Ladyfest and Rock Camps for Girls, in Downes, J. (ed.) *Women Make Noise: Girl Bands from the Motown to the Modern*, Twickenham, Supernova Books, 319.

Downes, J. (2012) The Expansion of Punk Rock: Riot Grrrl Challenges to Gender Power Relations in British Indie Music Subcultures, *Women's Studies* 41(2), 204–37.

Dunn, K. and Farnsworth, M.S. (2012) 'We Are the Revolution': Riot Grrrl Press, Girl

Empowerment, and DIY Self-Publishing, *Womens Studies – An Interdisciplinary Journal* 41(2), 136–57.

Greiner, C. and Sakdapolrak, P. (2013) Translocality: Concepts, Applications and Emerging Research Perspectives, *Geography Compass* 7(5), 373–84.

Hughes, H. (2006) Gay and Lesbian Festivals: Tourism in the Change from Politics to Party, in Picard, D. and Robinson, M. (eds), *Festivals, Tourism and Social Change*, Bristol, Channel View Publications, 238–54.

Ibarra, H. (1992) Homophily and Differential Returns – Sex-Differences in Network Structure and Access in an Advertising Firm, *Administrative Science Quarterly* 37(3), 422–47.

Leonard, M. (2007) *Gender in the Music Industry: Rock, Discourse, and Girl Power*, Aldershot, Ashgate.

Marcus, S. (2010) *Girls to the Front: The True Story of the Riot Grrrl Revolution*, New York, HarperPerennial.

McPherson, M., Smith-Lovin, L. and Cook, J.M. (2001) Birds of a Feather: Homophily in Social Networks, *Annual Review of Sociology* 27, 415–44.

Meltzer, M. (2010) *Girl Power: The Nineties Revolution in Music*, New York, Faber and Faber.

Moore, R. and Roberts, M. (2009) Do-It-Yourself Mobilization: Punk and Social Movements, *Mobilization* 14(3), 273–91.

Neu, E. and Finch, J. (eds.) (2013) *Let's Start a Pussy Riot*, London, Rough Trade.

O'Shea, S. (2012) Feminist Music Worlds: Riot Grrrl, Ladyfest and Rock Camp for Girls, *New Left Project*. Online, available at www.newleftproject.org/index.php/site/article_comments/feminist_music_worlds_riot_grrrl_ladyfest_and_rock_camp_for_girls (accessed 16 June 2013).

Pavlidis, A. (2012) From Riot Grrrls to Roller Derby? Exploring the Relations between Gender, Music and Sport, *Leisure Studies* 31(2), 165–76.

Payne, J.G. (2012) The Logics of Sisterhood: Intra-Feminist Debates in Swedish Feminist Zines, *European Journal of Women's Studies* 19(2), 187–202.

Prell, C. (2012) *Social Network Analysis: History, Theory and Methodology*, London, Sage.

PRS (2012) *Women Make Music* (press release). PRS for Music. Online, available at www.prsformusicfoundation.com/Funding/Women-Make-Music (accessed 10 August 2013).

Reynolds, S. and Press, J. (1995) *The Sex Revolts: Gender, Rebellion and Rock 'n' Roll*, Cambridge, MA, Harvard University Press.

Rosenberg, J., Garofalo, G. Bragin, L.H. *et al.* (1998) Riot Grrrl: Revolutions from Within, *Signs* 23(3), 809–41.

Schilt, K. (2003a) 'I'll Resist with Every Inch and Every Breath': Girls and Zine Making as a Form of Resistance, *Youth and Society* 35(1), 71–97.

Schilt, K. (2003b) 'A Little Too Ironic': The Appropriation and Packaging of Riot-Grrl Politics by Mainstream Female Musicians, *Popular Music and Society* 26(1), 5–16.

Schilt, K. and Zobl, E. (2008) Connecting the Dots: Riot Grrrls, Ladyfests, and the International Grrrl Zine Network, in Harris, A. (ed.), *Next Wave Cultures: Feminism, Subcultures, Activism,* London, Routledge, 171–92.

Simmel, G. and Levine, D.N. (1971) The Stranger (1908), in Levine, D.N. (ed.), *Georg Simmel on Individuality and Social Forms* (Kindle edition), Chicago, University of Chicago Press, 412.

Simpson, P. (2013) Alienation, Ambivalence, Agency: Middle-aged Gay Men and Ageism in Manchester's Gay Village, *Sexualities* 16(3–4), 283–99.

Staggenborg, S. (1998) Social Movement Communities and Cycles of Protest: The Emergence and Maintenance of a Local Women's Movement, *Social Problems* 45(2), 180–204.

Starr, C. (2013) Deploying Aesthetics: Riot Grrrl Feminists. Online, available at www.researchgate.net/publication/235677350_Deploying_Aesthetics_Riot_Grrrl_Feminists (accessed 20 September 2013), 1–15.

Street Howe, Z. (2009) *Typical Girls? The Story of The Slits,* London, Omnibus Press.

Triggs, T. (2004) 'Generation Terrorists': The Politics and Graphic Language of Punk and Riot Grrrl Fanzines in Britain 1976–2000, thesis, University of Reading.

True, E. (2012) ME and Pussy Riot: Everett True on Riot Grrrl, Russia and the Future of Music, *Overland* 209, 7–12.

Wasserman, S. and Faust, K. (1994) *Social Network Analysis: Methods and Applications*, Cambridge, Cambridge University Press.

Zobl, E. (2013) *Grassroots Feminism: Transnational Archives, Resources and Communities.* Online, available at www.grassrootsfeminism.net (accessed 24 November 2013).

8   The enabling qualities of Manchester's open mic network

Tim Edensor, Paul Hepburn and Nigel Richards

In this chapter, we investigate Manchester's open mic scene, a popular location for amateur music performance yet a scene that has been startlingly overlooked in social science research. We commence by giving a broad description of the scene, looking at the shape of a typical open mic night, the range of participants, the venues, the extent of the local scene and the much wider network to which it is connected. We then identify the conventions of the open mic night, its ethics and mores, and subsequently identify how the scene offers opportunities for a multitude of people with diverse objectives. We contend that this rather invisible social network is a particularly enabling realm, lacking boundaries of style, genre and musical competence and equally open to all who are prepared to perform irrespective of age, class, gender, sexuality and ethnicity. Accordingly, we argue that this provides a uniquely inclusionary space where participants are presented with a safe yet effective environment within which they may accrue social capital. The discussion is illustrated throughout with qualitative data gathered from 25 interviews with open mic performers and managers in Manchester, empirical observations accrued from numerous visits to open mic nights between May 2012 and May 2013, and the participant observation of Nigel Richards, a performer on the scene.

Overwhelmingly, open mic events take place in pubs, usually during midweek evenings, and constitute a boost for the ailing pub sector that is being superseded by other leisure and cultural attractions within the growing night-time economy (Chatterton and Hollands 2002). No performing fees are paid and, usually, no admission is charged, though performers might occasionally be rewarded with a free drink or two from the bar. Open mic nights are sometimes staged in the main bar of a venue, but more frequently in upstairs or downstairs rooms. In these settings, décor tends towards the rudimentary, and this minimalist environment is echoed in the provision of a basic sound system to facilitate the performance of amplified music. All such events are managed by organisers who deal with equipment technicalities, timetable the evening's rota of performances and ensure performers stick to the rules, and they take a greater or lesser role in introducing performers and acclaiming them following their act. Performers typically enrol on a sign-up sheet and are placed in the schedule according to a first-come, first-served basis, though at some venues, performers book their slot by phone or email. Crucially, as discussed below, there are few restrictions about who may participate in an open mic event. Most of the non-musicians at the events are friends or family of performers, though other unrelated drinkers attend the evening's entertainment.

The origins of the open mic scene are difficult to ascertain; performers express only vague ideas about when these events emerged, though they are generally estimated to have become prevalent over the last 20 years. There are no obvious pioneers or any cluster of interested parties who steadily consolidated a scene, as with the punk network discussed by Crossley (2008, 2009). However, the scene is no doubt connected to a host of antecedents, including the long-lasting folk clubs that offer a more circumscribed musical fare, informal jam sessions, the DIY ethos of the punk movement, and the more recent rise of media talent shows such as *The X Factor* and *The Voice*. It differs from these scenes, however, since it enforces no restrictions on musical skill, has no key figures who may pronounce on participants' musical ability, and revolves around no particular musical form or style.

The organisation and geography of the open mic network

It is salient to consider open mic culture as constituted through a network. As a kind of musical 'scene' (Straw 1997), it possesses shared conventions and ethics – though these are looser than most other scenes. However, it also extends beyond any identifiable geographical or cultural boundaries; indeed it is international in scale but also composed out of local constellations that become dense in particular urban settings such as Manchester.

Figure 8.1 illustrates the interconnectedness of these networks across different spatial dimensions. It maps the Facebook contacts of the author, a performer on the open mic scene. Facebook was, invariably, used by performers to communicate with each other and advertise gigs. NodeXL (http://nodexl.code-plex.com) was used to extract, analyse and visualise this network. Here we can see three distinct sub-networks: the grey nodes are family and friends; the dark nodes are open mic performers who are divided between those who are Manchester based – the large cluster in the middle – and those who form part of an international hand-made musicians network – the smaller cluster towards the left of the figure. This network map illustrates prominence in the network on the betweenness centrality measure. The bigger the node the more prominent it is on this measure and the more likely that person will play a bridging or brokering role in the network. The overall network itself is not very dense, that is, it is a loosely connected network which is good for the transmission of information (Granovetter 1982).

Notwithstanding these different geographies and interconnected networks our focus here is upon the Manchester-based performers. As Watson *et al.* contend, 'music is produced in many spaces, from the bedroom, garage or home studio ... to community and youth centres ... to street corners ... and clubs' (2009, 857). The open mic network contains a great number of dedicated

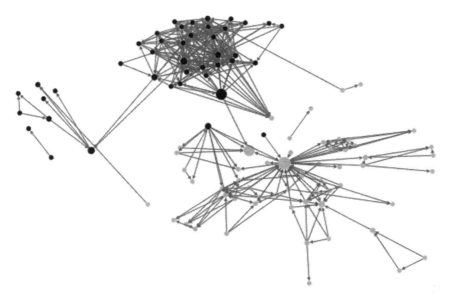

Figure 8.1 Facebook network of open mic performers
Note
Created with NodeXL (http://nodexl.codplex.com).

performance spaces in the form of pubs yet intersects with other musical spaces and scenes as well. Spatially, the network is constituted at various scales by a host of changing but also relatively durable pub venues. In the centre of Manchester, a compact network of pubs offers open mic sessions during weekdays, but these also exist more sparsely in the suburbs and smaller towns throughout Greater Manchester, and beyond, clustering once more in the cities of Sheffield, Leeds and Liverpool. There are no 'meccas' within the scene, though certain venues have acquired a reputation for being lively, possessing a good atmosphere or attracting a varied assortment of participants. To emphasise, the network of venues appears durable, with a critical mass of performance spaces, yet also shifting, with some locations closing down as new ones open. As Stephen says, open mic nights in Manchester are 'very much dependent on the goodwill of the landlord, and I think what happens quite often is, that the pub is a venue, and then it changes hands, and they say "I'm not having any of this"'. Equally, there are no key stars or presiding organisers, though there are signs that this may be changing with the emergence of 'curated' nights, as we discuss. Currently, however, regular participants and organisers keep the scene going through the consistent provision of space, performative participation and encouragement to others. The vibrancy of events is unpredictable as are the numbers turning up to play or spectate. For instance, Rosie claims that in Manchester

> it's a big scene but it's really hit and miss. One week I'll go to (a particular event) on Monday to play, and there'll be five people there, and then the next week I'll go there just to watch and there will be fifty people there having a pint.

The network is thus continuously emergent and variable, as well as durable but, as we have inferred, it is uneven across space, for instance, in terms of the density of a network in any one urban setting. Manchester possesses a particularly compact and stable network of venues and personnel and as such, provides a sense of community that is simultaneously networked and place-based. Many of our interviewees comment on this special quality. For instance, in referring to the particular virtues of its scale in comparison to London, Monica asserts that, in Manchester,

> you see people on the scene and get to know them a bit and make friendships as well ... Manchester has the right number of people to make it doable and I think London is just a bit too big. There are scenes in London but it's much harder to break into.

Will concurs:

> In London ... everyone is very segregated. So you might play open mics in your area but that's it and you don't get to know people so well ... Manchester is perfect because it is so small you can keep meeting the same sorts of people again and break into it. To start off fresh in London you're just kind of one in a million.

Martin articulates the sentiments of many on the scene, contending that 'there's so much going on really, it feels like a buzzing place to be and artistically, creatively, there is a lot of interesting stuff'. And Steve points out that 'a few people come over from other towns regularly to play ... apparently Manchester does have a good reputation for open mics outside of town,'

Certain key figures bestow a consistency over time to the Manchester open mic scene, with most interviewees drawing attention to organisers of particular nights. These people act to oil the wheels of the network, and play an important role in sharing knowledge about recent developments, good venues, interesting performers and various opportunities that may crop up. They also serve as shared reference points for participants that anchor a sense of belonging to this somewhat fluid scene, and other regular participants also provide a measure of consistency across the local network. Through multiple connections, these regular performers similarly share information, play together and support each other in a host of informal ways. As Richard discusses,

> a lot of it is to do with informal links.... The whole kind of scene is a bit underground. And that's why the networking thing, the whole informal relations thing is important, because otherwise people wouldn't know where to go or what's going on.

Tony further elaborates:

> as soon as I moved here and started playing it was the idea that every night led to another night … you suddenly established a network of people who you could not only play for but play with and … they weren't gigs per se but you got the experience and they always led to somebody who knows someone who knows somewhere for you to play, which is always good for a musician.

As Crossley insists, '(D)ifferent network configurations can have different effects and different positions in a network generate different opportunities and constraints for the actor(s) involved' (2009, 27). It is a key characteristic of the open mic scene that it is open to anybody who wishes to participate, and makes no demands on these participants other than that they are willing to perform according to the mores of the scene. This permits people to engage with the network with very different levels of involvement. Sheller and Urry contend that networks may be 'tightly coupled with complex, enduring, and predictable connections between peoples, objects, and technologies across multiple and distant spaces and times' (2006, 216) while at other times they may be intermittent, volatile and variable. In a more specific context, Watson *et al.* (2009) claim that urban musical networks may persist over time but that they may also merely endure as a brief burst of creativity before evaporating. Despite the rather loose ongoing formation of the open mic network, with its lack of hierarchy, privileged styles, transient and frequent participation, or perhaps because of these characteristics, it has proved remarkably durable, growing gradually since its emergence. These qualities also mean that, in contradistinction to the kind of network socialities depicted by Wittel (2001), the open mic network allows people to forge both ephemeral and lasting ties according to their dispositions, allowing for regular performance through which durable relationships are sustained as well as fleeting participation.

These various temporal modes of engagement mean that while some use it as a linear route through which to develop skills, record music and join with others to form bands, others participate in the scene according to a more circular rhythm, intermittently dropping in and out, or performing routinely without seeking any path towards personal or musical progress. Steve relates that before he became an organiser of open mic nights, he 'used to like to do at least two and used to average about four a week' and Rosie claims that she 'could go five times in a week'. Others, such as Krazy Horse, are even more embedded in the scene:

> I started about five years ago because I was retired … I decided to write my own songs … and I was amazed at the response from young lads coming up to me and shaking my hand and young girls coming up and kissing my cheek, I thought 'wow' so from then on I found out where all the other open mics were. There were loads, about 52 I've got in my book at the moment.

For others, participation may be an occasional pursuit or simply a one-off occurrence. For example, Richard plays 'once or twice a month' and Clare generally only performs once within a three- or six-month period. Because other routes for practising skills and making contacts are less easy to access, some participants perform across various venues several nights a week in pursuit of developing stagecraft and musical techniques and getting booked by promoters. Others belong to bands but like to play open mic nights to rehearse, try out new material or develop skills as a solo performer. Some participants are regular performers but lack any serious personal or musical goals, while others turn up with friends, play and may never return.

Accordingly, the scene chimes with Finnegan's (1989) 'hidden musicians' of Milton Keynes – hidden in that there is little awareness of the existence of such scenes in the world beyond. Finnegan depicts the numerous non-professional musicians who belong to particular musical scenes but shows how these scenes also overlap with other musical realms. As we will see, the open mic network also overlaps with more specialist scenes but is extremely liberal in allowing participants to pursue their own preferred styles and levels of commitment, take on different roles and seek varying outcomes.

This openness to diversity means that frequent surprises are apt to disrupt any sense of a normal evening. Anybody can show up. For instance, the connection of the Manchester scene to the larger international open mic network means that a fairly common occurrence is for performers from further afield, perhaps itinerant or travelling workers or open mic 'tourists' from other countries, to arrive at a venue and request to play. As open mic organiser Tony describes,

> I think we've had almost an act from every continent … you get a lot of touring people, who have gigs pulled elsewhere for whatever ridiculous reason, who might say 'we're in town and we've got all the stuff and we're free on a Tuesday'. I've had an act on from Australia, most places in Europe, Africa definitely, America … South America, yes, an awful lot, and we had a fantastic band from somewhere in Eastern Europe … a full on gypsy rock band.

The network is thus replete with consistencies as well as transient participation and unexpected occurrences, is both stable and fluid.

The ethics of the open mic night

Shared procedures and values that extend across the network foster the enabling environment identified above. Like other performative spaces, on open mic nights 'the space in which the performance takes place may function as a physical limit, providing a boundary within which values may be enacted through interpersonal behaviour between audience members, performers and other actors' (Atton 2012, 429). Such conventions are reiterated by performers and organisers during each open mic event, undergirding their prevalence across the whole network. But while the 'social relationships between the performers, audiences and other actors ... activate rules and norms in specific cultural settings' (ibid.), open mic nights differ from the scenes that Atton discusses in that they do not regulate the musical skill, style and performance instantiated by the reiterative conventions of fans and performers of particular genres or subcultures.

All the performers we spoke to held fast to a series of interconnected values, irrespective of their own abilities and styles. Foremost are the inclusive conventions that encourage wide participation. As Noel states, 'there are rules, like you can't be offensive to people or anything, you can't be racist on the microphone or anything else'. Furthermore, all participants are equal in terms of the time allotted to them, each usually allowed to perform three songs or musical pieces, or have a maximum of 15 minutes on stage. There is no audition or any necessary prior knowledge among organisers about musical ability and performers may play simply because they request to do so. It is not acceptable to violate these temporal constraints though, as we discuss, there are ways to access opportunities offered by other networks and people connected to the open mic scene.

Crucially, advanced musical skill is not a prerequisite. There is an atmosphere of support and encouragement for first-timers and those who lack advanced musical skill or confidence on stage, the antithesis of talent shows at which judges pronounce on the talent of the performer. Almost all levels of proficiency are tolerated and even the most mundane or haphazard efforts will be applauded by an audience willing to accept almost anyone who is willing to give it a go. The expression of equality between performers is paramount, as Tony insists: 'everyone should feel equal. It's like you have a guitar and you're playing, and talent aside there's clearly something we have in common.'

Thus, as Noel claims,

> as long as you're honest and open and want to get up and express yourself then ... you don't have to be good – it's a space to develop ... I think people understand that it's a space for people to come and fulfil themselves.

Will explains how 'the people that go to open mic nights are ... usually musicians. They understand how difficult it can be, they're respectful, they listen and they give positive feedback.' Carl points to the temporal structure of the scene in engendering this tolerant support, explaining that it provides 'practice in performing in front of people ... practising your songs without being judged ... 'cos if someone comes ... and they're not great ... two or three songs ... and they're done.' Rosie acknowledges the value of this for performers:

> it is a massive thing to stand up in front of people, it doesn't matter if you're good or bad at it, you're stood in front of people to show them something you love to do, and you have to show the performers that respect.

This assists inexperienced performers but also applies to musicians who may be out of practice, as Tom explains: 'nobody's going to say that was shit ... so it's a good place to start to re-establish confidence in my case.' If opinion is sought, advice tends to be constructive rather than trenchant appraisal. The imperative is to offer the opportunity to develop confidence in a supportive environment and the critical element of trust, facilitating the potential for performers to acquire social capital.

This openness means that there are usually performers from an array of gendered, ethnic, class and age backgrounds. For instance, Dave states that 'the age range is really fascinating, and goes from young people who say they're 18 but are probably only 16 right up to those in their 60s'. This welcome to anybody who wants to play is also based on acceptance of any particular form or style of music. Unlike other musical scenes, the open mic scene does not exclusively cater to fans of specialist musical subcultures (see Watson *et al.* 2009). There are no conventions such as those that prevail, for example, at a folk club, where powerful codes regulate the subject matter of lyrics, performative 'tradition', the instruments played and the premium placed on musical ability. As Dr Yad argues,

> open mic is more for the people than the folk club is, more open to everybody than the folk club which is more exclusive. It's not for all 'folk' anymore there's no electronic instruments and ... usually you just stand on the stage and project [your voice without amplification].

For Martin, this uncritical reception contrasts with the mores of the music industry:

> The kind of person who loves open mic is someone who feels they may be, in the music industry, judged for having not the right image or conventional talent needed to make it big. It's there as a non-judgemental platform.

So it is that performers at an open mic night might include – in addition to the prevalence of keening young male singer-songwriters with acoustic guitars – rappers, ska bands, a capella acts, synthesiser wizards, didgeridoo players, the inventive use of tape loops, as well as comedians, poets and burlesque acts. This quality of unexpectedness is relished, as Rosie elucidates:

> there was some guy doing stand-up jokes and stuff which was alright, and then he did a little acting bit from Dr Who or something, and then he started playing dubstep on a didgeridoo, and I was like 'what is going on?!'

More generally, Noel describes how

> At open mics you never know what's going to happen ... you don't know what you're gonna see. Like there was a guy playing the hurdy-gurdy the other day, and he was really well received. It's great when people you'd never have heard come out and play, and you see some fantastic things.

Despite these widely shared conventions, some participants attest that the ethics and conventions of the scene can be violated. Some express dissatisfaction with how certain performers are increasingly apt to be chosen by visiting promoters to perform at curated events, arguing that this mars the equality expected among participants and removes some of the best players from the scene. Dave contends that such practice 'does not seem "open" to me'. Alternatively, some complain that temporal constraints on performance can restrict opportunities to develop. Martin acknowledges that 'you can only do three songs as a band and you're only starting to get into it by the third song, starting to get a feel for what you're going to do'. In this sense, the organised curated engagements allow greater temporal scope for performers to develop.

Many grumble about performers who secure an early slot and then depart immediately after playing. Tom complains that an event can 'be full of players who go when they've done their set so if you are on last you can just be playing to the bar staff'. On occasions where friends come in numbers to support a particular act, this emptying out of the room can affect those performing next, as Richard explains: 'when one band finishes, the audience who came to see them … they leave … and then the next band have hardly got any audience. I think if you come, you should be there for the duration. It's awful.' Martin similarly contends that there should be a more prevalent 'etiquette about that. That you should stay and stick around for other performers … it's a bit rude to turn up and then just go.' And increasingly, some organisers offer opportunities to bypass the signing-up sheet by booking slots via social media, by texting or by Twitter message, and those who turn up early and find out that most or all of the performing slots have been taken by people who have booked remotely tend to express discontent.

The enabling capacities of the open mic scene

We now consider what kinds of outcomes for participants are enabled by this non-exclusive, non-judgemental, liberal and supportive environment. The scene provides a forum for various modes of engagement with different degrees of frequency of performance, seriousness and different goals. As Krazy Horse maintains, 'Some come for the experience, some come to try songs out, some come to meet other musicians, maybe get one or two jobs through it.' And Judith distinguishes between 'People wanting to get into the industry. Those who want a non-threatening stage to play on. Those who are first-timers and those who want to share their bedroom practice.' Clare highlights those more experienced performers, bands and paid musicians 'who like to "test" or showcase original material, as well as people who like to put a twist on covers'. Dave identifies those amateur musicians who

> take up music later in life, often to not a great standard of musicianship, but usually very keen. They do not expect to make it in the music biz … but are there for love of music. They may enjoy socializing with others, and maybe

having a drink... [as well as other] casual attendees, people just dropping in by chance, but who may offer to sing a song like they might at a drunken karaoke.

He also refers to 'people with personal problems or mental health issues, who are grateful for some chance to express themselves'. The open mic network thus makes possible movement towards certain financial or career-oriented objectives, but equally, performing may be an end in itself. Below, we identify the ways in which the scene offers a range of diverse opportunities for participants that testify to its loose culture and progressive tolerance of diverse forms of engagement, motivation and expression.

Most obviously, participants refer to the potential to develop musical proficiency and stagecraft, to collect advice, and compare ideas and skill. Audiences may access free and varied entertainment while the performers enjoy the opportunity to display their talents before a live audience. The lack of admission charge takes the pressure off the performers to deliver value for money, thereby opening the door to a variety of acts that might not otherwise be offered the chance. Aldredge rightly points to how 'open mic performers want input from fellow amateur musicians and the audience in the hope of facilitating their growth as musicians and performers' (2006, 112), and this may be the only opportunity that exists for non-professional performers to present their work in public. For, as Dr Yad relates, 'when I started when I was 17 or 18, in 1978, 1979, there was nothing like this. If you had a band you could get a pub gig, but there was nowhere to play other than that.'

The capacity to develop musical proficiency has a multitude of starting points, as Charlie relates,

> there are ... people that go straight from their bedroom to an open mic night with stuff that isn't ready to be taken to the stage, but then that doesn't really matter and then there are really, really good people who should be playing somewhere else.... There's a variety of levels.

In making no judgement on the former, he continues,

> [some] people don't have the material or the ability to do a full gig but they ... want to show their friends, get drunk and then play a few tunes and be told that they were awesome. It's fair enough though because where else would people play if they've just learnt an instrument or written a few songs.

As Tom maintains,

> There are a broad range of motivations. There are a lot of people like me who used to play and wanted to get back into it for something to do. Then there are those who are looking for a paid gig and they see it as a route to being spotted.

Several participants are clear in their aims and objectives. For instance, as Noel explains, 'I want to be a professional guitarist, you know getting paid for playing, it's the dream, but I'm stuck at the moment flapping round self-service. I work for Tesco part-time now and teach guitar the other half.' Within the scene, there are numerous, possibly apocryphal, stories about how big names emerged after playing at open mic event. Names such as Adele and Jake Bugg are cited, and it does not seem to require a great stretch of the imagination to envisage that such stars actually did practise their craft at open mic venues.

First-time performers can gain knowledge from old hands and student bands may compare their latest offerings with middle-aged rockers, in contradistinction to the often pervasive atmosphere of competition and the ruthless scramble for opportunities elsewhere in the music industry. For those seeking paid opportunities, there is the chance to make connections with other musicians, promoters, recording engineers and managers as part of a 'network sociality' (Wittel 2001). As Steve explains:

> I think it's the best way because so often you see people who go, 'I've got this song and I've been playing it for years in my bedroom and then soon as it gets to the second verse it all goes to pop', because they haven't figured out what the live dynamics are or how it would work on stage. And I've written songs which have gone completely wrong live and then I've figured out how to, y'know, fatten them up on stage. But if you mess up in front of a dozen, half a dozen people in open mic it's not the end of the world. In open mic you can take a chance; if it doesn't work then everyone has a laugh together.

He continues, pointing to how, in such a non-judgemental context, musical development might lead to outcomes that could not otherwise be accomplished:

> I think if you're musicians you naturally want to play in front of people ... well it's the best way for a young musician to start getting experience and to start ... working out how their songs work. But a player might ... also meet people who could ultimately get them gigs, so it's a foot in the door ... I think otherwise it would be very hard to meet any other musicians or promoters, because I do think there are several tiers within the music scene.

More broadly then, open mic performance provides a first testing-ground in developing music, and, according to Jane, is valuable in that 'one live performance is the equivalent of three practices in private'. As Noel remarks

> It's like football, if you haven't got games you can't perform well. So you know, you get up, you play on stage and it's better than playing in your bedroom, and you need stage time, and to be a professional you need to do the groundwork ... I was so unconfident in myself before I had started. Getting on stage and playing in front of people, getting feedback off people

saying 'oh you're great', you know. Every time someone comes over and says 'ah, I really enjoyed that', it makes my night you know, it makes me feel what I am doing is worthwhile, it makes me want to sit down and practise. It's an inspirational thing as an artist.

As Charlie details,

it can be a venue for experimentation. I won't just play something that I have no clue about but I might rehearse it for a week and then if I feel OK after two songs in then I might risk a new tune that I've not completely finished.

This opportunity to develop musical skills can pay off, according to Rosie:

I went back to Jersey at Christmas and I played a gig for the same guy I'd played for in the summer just before I left, and he said, 'Do you know what? You're completely different. You've identified your sound and you're a lot more confident.'

Open mic performance can also serve as a setting in which to develop technical skills, for as Martin says, 'you learn at open mics what works what doesn't work, and technologically for me, what I'm using in terms of loops and stuff, it was quite hard to do at first'.

Performers also develop stagecraft, as Steve expounds: 'I've become more confident on stage, I'm not singing to the floor anymore I'm acting out, playing out.' This can be challenging as well, for audiences are not always numerous or receptive, but this gives performers the flexibility and confidence to deal with various situations. Martin explains how 'random stuff will happen, like the memory goes, so you find ways to overcome those sorts of issues and you can only do that when you're in front of a group of people'. And Tom elaborates upon how open mic can be

like a nursery for musicians ... you have to deal with the blokes in the corner who are only there because they've just watched the football, but you have to keep going you have be able to do a decent gig ... open mic teaches you to adapt to an unpredictable environment.

For bands the open mic scene offers an opportunity to play together. As Monica reveals:

We've only just formed very recently ... we've just jammed with each other before ... but open mic is just good practice for learning to play live and getting feedback and confidence. We're all a bit shy. It's good as well because you are allowed to mess up, I mean I have played open mics where I've literally forgotten the words and stopped halfway through and people can be really nice and just say. 'It's alright, just start again', whereas at a gig you wouldn't be supported like that.

Similarly, with regard to her recently formed band, Jane discusses how, 'for us, because we've got a gig coming up in a few weeks' time … it's just about getting out and doing it live and just getting used to playing together'.

This chance to practise is also useful for those musicians who earn money in more formal musical contexts but like to test new material before playing in these settings. As Tony contends:

> I kind of think of it as a feeder into something bigger, as a launch pad … I've done it a couple of times where I've written something, and trying something new, different, radical, you don't just want to book yourself in for the biggest gig you can find, you need that platform, that experiment.

The open mic scene is, as Aldredge considers, 'a vital and flourishing setting in which amateur musicians learn, interpret, and negotiate musical roles, performances, and identities' (2006, 109), and these are extremely varied. But these negotiations need not, as Aldredge infers, be concerned with developing musical skill or advancing a career in music. For, as Watson *et al.* state, the practice of performing and producing music, 'in the first instance, involves small-scale creativity that often in itself has little instant economic value' (2009, 864). As we have already insisted, while some performers conceive the open mic scene as a step to greater things, for many participants the scene represents an occasional opportunity to play, for fun but with no overriding goal. As Mick says, 'You're not getting paid for them.… It's not for the money; it's got to be for the social.'

Tommy captures this disposition towards fun rather than any wider goal:

> I like an audience … I like singing. I like hearing my own voice. I sing everywhere. When I sing, people like listening to me sing. I have a good voice, and I make people laugh as well. I like to hear the audience laugh … I'm not a serious artsy bloke. I come here, I drink. I'm not an artist.

Mick underlines how he may have previously had bigger dreams but now simply enjoys playing:

> I mostly enjoy playing music, and the buzz you get from playing music. That's good. And I like playing with other people. But I think you have to realise, that it comes to a point, where I'm too old [to make it big]. I'm not even gonna pretend now.

Stephen considers that such an approach is widespread throughout the scene:

> I think most do it for the fun of it.… Not as many people are starry eyed these days. I think people are more realistic. I don't think many of them imagine themselves being on MTV any time soon.

Crucially, certain participants move back and forth between more formal musical scenes and the informality of open mic events. Carl reveals how his band's participation in the open mic scene has led to a blossoming of opportunity and achievement, but that this has been superseded by a continuing desire to play on after the momentum of the band's early success faded

> We've done quite well ... we sort of got to the stage, most weekends in London, 50 or 60 people coming ... we got one and a half thousand Facebook fans ... we went on a Euro tour last summer. Germany ... and up through Scandinavia. We won a few competitions. Sold a few thousand CDs and stuff... yeah, we did alright. But it's got too hard now.... People's lives go on. We did alright, but it just calmed down. We didn't get signed or anything. But I'll be always proud of what we did. I secretly hoped something would happen, and that ... someone would take it seriously. But then our cellist got fed up of the travelling and left. And ... we instantly knew we wouldn't be able to get anyone to replace her who would do all the travelling. So we just do it for fun now.

This is also the case for those musicians who previously scaled greater heights in their musical careers, who are drawn to open mic events where they can continue to play live music in front of a small audience.

We have identified many of the key motivations and opportunities for those who enter the open mic network to seek musical outcomes, revealing how the scene enables a medley of possibilities through its supportive, non-judgemental, non-hierarchical and loose organisation and the sustenance of distinct ethics and conventions. Yet the network also offers opportunities to foster the development of friendships and social skills.

From our interviews, it was clear that the scene served an important social function in providing a space for people who had been experiencing personal difficulties. These difficulties were apt to be ameliorated by performing on open mic nights, where confidence could be rebuilt and friendly people encountered. Jill, for instance, discussed how her confidence was low after a difficult divorce, but the open mic scene afforded a chance to rekindle much neglected musical skills and desires, culminating in regular appearances on the scene and the recording of a CD. Steve tells how his currently unemployed status is 'always a very big barrier to social engagement, which is important for all people ... so it's nice seeing an entire culture and scene built around people playing, and that's very helpful for people, that's very nice.'

For Holly, the scene proved to be an equally positive realm that offered entrepreneurial opportunities that allowed her to escape from her social situation:

> I was jobless and homeless and living in Manchester. I could have gone back home to St Helens but that wasn't an option. The music scene in Manchester was the first time in my life that I thought I could fit in. I went to loads of open mic nights, had no money. So I knew all these musicians and so someone said to me one night why don't you put a night on.

Noel similarly found this musical outlet vital:

> When I first started coming out I had only just split up with my girlfriend. I'd not been out playing for a long time and I was sat there depressed with my head on the table and I tried to get out, so that's what I did ... it filled a massive void in my life. They are a great service for ... people to come and express themselves and get out and play and pursue what they love.

In depicting the larger social capacities of the scene, Rosie celebrates how 'at open mics it's sort of like a little community and everyone's there to help each other out, speak to each other and give some tips about where to play'. This is supported by Steve who says, 'I've built the majority of my ... friendship base and musical or professional base.... As a player, I'll continue 'till forever 'cos I love meeting new players.' Martin alludes to the networked qualities of the open mic network, which offers opportunities for numerous connections:

> There is more scope for collaboration, more scope for people joining together and doing a one-off set you know ... and you've got at least 20 or 30 people in there who are all into music and interested in what you're doing. You build up contacts and network via that sort of route and find interesting people. Coming across interesting people who do interesting things and keeping in touch with them over the internet.

More specifically, Tom elaborates upon how he entered a network where a plethora of connections were possible:

> I've got my band – a slide guitar player, a percussion player and a guitar player – who I met through the OM nights at the folk club. So I have progressed and developed significantly as a musician. I have a whole new circle of friends and acquaintances I didn't have three years ago.

In addition to providing a space and occasion where musical and social skills might be developed and opportunities grasped, the open mic scene also offers a setting in which to develop management and organisational skills. Skills may be developed by the musicians as 'micro-entrepreneurs' in networking, recording and marketing, emphasising how, as McGregor and Gibson state, 'the diverse pathways to paid work in music necessitate flexibility and multiskilling' (2009, 278).

Equally pertinently, as we have discussed, each open mic event is arranged by somebody who books the location, provides sound equipment, and organises the running of the evening. Taking on this multi-faceted, often demanding role gives these organisers a grounding and training that they might not otherwise be able to gain, fostering the development of those who wish to work in the management and staging aspects of the entertainment field. Holly, an organiser of open mic events, has ambitious aims:

Hopefully, it can only get bigger and better for me.... One day I want to go into band management and then one day get my own label. I know someone who has a his own record label and I put bands his way ... he knows how hard it can be. I'm 20 years old and I've done this for 20 months and I don't want to stop now.

On the other hand, these management skills may serve more of a social function and provide other than remunerative forms of gratification as Tony implies:

I must admit money isn't the be all and end all ... the reason I do it is because I love it. I've been that 17 or 18 year old guitarist rocking up to a pub and asking, 'Can I play? Do you have any gigs on?' and being told, 'No, no room at the inn for the likes of you'. So I've put on acts that I know are probably not the most musically talented people in the world but I know that they'll have a fantastic time doing it and I know the audiences at open mic nights are the most welcoming and most friendly, because they know its the luck of the draw really and they aren't always going to see the best of the best.

In Manchester, the open mic scene has encouraged the development of revue-based events at which these managerial ambitions might be furthered. Organisers host and compère whole-day events and weekend festivals are arranged featuring contributions from open mic performers and other performance-based arts, encompassing live music, installation art, short film showings, poetry, theatre and even amateur burlesque performances. Such events fill a gap, fostering opportunities for people to develop events management expertise as well as musical skills.

In addition, some venues have developed curated nights at which a performer or band is given the opportunity to invite their own choice of associate performers for the evening. Such events perhaps point to the flexibility of the open mic format, in that those performing will be invited rather than being self-selected by just turning up on the night. While this deviates from the ideal that open mic performances should be accessible to all, it affords an opportunity for performers to progress, creating a step that bridges the gulf between amateur and semi-professional performance. As we have seen, some choose to perform at open mic evenings as a first step towards a professional career and the curated evenings, one-day events and weekend festivals provide another platform for them to move in that direction. As Nig attests:

I first started doing open mics in Johannesburg and when I came to Manchester I fell into performing at one almost by accident and, from there, it just mushroomed. Because I play a selection of home-made instruments it provided an opportunity to perform that I can't see would otherwise have been possible. Importantly, as a new person to the city it opened up opportunities to meet people, to work with other musicians and to develop friendships. More than this, meeting and playing regularly with other performers led to collaborations and, eventually to the forming of a fully fledged band, The open mics provided the opportunity for the members to meet, to perform, to share ideas and to eventually play together.

As we have discussed, the open mic scene intersects with other networks and thus offers possibilities for performing music and developing shared interests in other fields.

The networks stretch beyond the borders of the city or even the country in which the open mics take place. In my case, the making and playing of home-made instruments has led to me being a part of an international network of like-minded builders and performers. Although the open mics do not drive the manufacture of such instruments, the fact that they are there does encourage those involved by providing supportive venues in which to play. This has expanded further, with workshops being held at curated open mic events to show how the instruments are made. I think this illustrates how dynamic and widespread the open mic scene is.

Despite the emergence of these more organised and selective events, many performers who have moved on to paid professional employment or participate in the curated nights state that the camaraderie of the open mic scene entices them to try new material or to meet up with the other performers in this more relaxed social setting.

Conclusion

Social network theory and analysis are able to render visible and understandable otherwise invisible network effects illuminating 'structural relations usually opaque to lay actors, through delineating the ties between parts of social bodies' (Knox *et al.* 2006, 117). In the open mic scene in Manchester, participants look for both safety and effectiveness, seeking out a network to provide a trusted environment. Certain networks can become realms for like-minded people who exclude those with dissimilar characteristics (McPherson *et al.* 2001) or are typified by forms of connectedness between actors who foreground instrumental advancement (Burt 1992). In contrast to such networks, the open mic scene is not characterised by a shared musical or subcultural identity, but continuously reinstates the desirability of widening opportunities for musical participation irrespective of ability, musical style or objectives, and is inclusive with regard to age, sex and ethnicity. These liberal conventions and values are shared by a wide range of participants who share an enthusiasm for music and performance. Manchester's enabling, non-exclusive, fluid, open mic network suggests that the socialities that emerge and are fostered are not necessarily driven by instrumental goals (Wittel 2001). The reiterative ethics and the consistencies of the compact local network provide a stable realm in which participants may seek a range of goals with a greater or lesser degree of immersion.

The open mic network thus possesses resources that its actors, or even those outside the network, may draw upon to acquire social capital. It is thus an enabling network. In our understanding, social capital is enabled through a relational network (Bourdieu 1986) that provides a realm of shared collective interests and values for participants who share a disposition to create, maintain and develop the network. This can foster trust and reciprocity, but also provides opportunities for individuals to exploit social capital to achieve private objectives. Thus, participants in the open mic scene extract social capital in different ways, some using their 'investment in social relations with expected returns in the marketplace' (Lin 2001, 19). Bar owners seek profits by making their premises available for open mic nights and performers use events as a route towards a professional music career. However, others are inspired by non-economic motives, seeking a wider circle of friends and acquaintances, a chance to play music for an audience without any goals of economic advancement, or an opportunity to gain personal confidence following a difficult period. Moreover, as Putnam argues (2000), social capital may be produced that can be of benefit to a wider society as well as the network members; it becomes a public good. It may be that the open mic scene promotes social cohesion and inclusion, fostering creativity, contributing to the quality of urban life and adding to the ludic qualities of the city (Stevens 2007), besides providing a modest boost to the ailing pub economy.

Though the open mic scene may wax and wane according to the distribution of venues and the energies of participants, it does not seem susceptible to imminent disappearance; rather it will continually be recreated by legions of regular, transient and new participants. The scene in Manchester connects to the wider open mic network, and other networks, at various scales. As we have shown, some participants are contemporaneously active in several networks that may also influence social outcomes (Mische and White 1998; Rainie and Wellman 2012), for instance, moving in and out of the folk club circuit, the curated network and the home-made instruments network at various scales. Thus, because of its inclusive nature and multiple intersections beyond the scene, 'creativity finds newness in both space and time through the mixing, encounters and contacts between people and cultures, across multiple spatial scales' (Watson *et al.* 2009, 860).

Yet, as Watson *et al.* (2009) point out, certain cities act to influence these creative networks, possessing a cultural resonance, a critical mass of participants, numerous sites and multiple connections between participants, and as such, are key nodes in organising and disseminating styles and practices, and drawing in others from elsewhere. Manchester has a well-established reputation as a city in which distinctive forms of popular music are dynamically produced and enjoyed. Popular music is entangled with the city's identity imaginatively and in actuality, with strong linkages persisting between local record labels, night clubs, press, independent record stores, radio stations and venues (Milestone 2008; Halfacree and Kitchin 1996) that are in turn linked to wider music industry networks (Brown *et al.* 2000). Crossley (2009), who demonstrates how a critical mass of key actors forged and consolidated Manchester's influential punk and post-punk network, exemplifies the salience of these local networks. The compact, supportive, inclusive and dynamic qualities of the open mic scene in Manchester also testify to the importance of place, without diminishing the enabling qualities of wider (intersecting) networks.

References

Aldredge, M. (2006) Negotiating and Practicing Performance: An Ethnographic Study of a Musical Open Mic in Brooklyn, New York, *Symbolic Interaction* 29(1), 109–17.

Atton, C. (2012) Genre and the Cultural Politics of Territory: The Live Experience of Free Improvisation, *European Journal of Cultural Studies* 15(4), 427–41.

Bourdieu, P. (1986) The Forms of Capital, in Richardson, J. (ed.) *Handbook of Theory and Research for the Sociology of Education*, Westport, CT, Greenwood Press, 241–58.

Brown, A., O'Connor, J. and Cohen, S. (2000) Local Music Policies within a Global Music Industry: Cultural Quarters in Manchester and Sheffield, *Geoforum* 31, 437–51.

Burt, R. (1992) *Structural Holes: The Social Structure of Competition*, Cambridge, MA, Harvard University Press.

Chatterton, P. and Hollands, R. (2002) Theorising Urban Playscapes: Producing, Regulating and Consuming Youthful Nightlife City Spaces, *Urban Studies* 39, 95–116.

Crossley, N. (2008) Pretty Connected: The Social Network of the Early UK Punk Movement, *Theory, Culture and Society* 25(6), 89–116.

Crossley, N. (2009) The Man Whose Web Expanded: Network Dynamics in Manchester's Post/Punk Music Scene 1976–1980, *Poetics* 37, 24–49.

Finnegan, Ruth (1989) *The Hidden Musicians: Music Making in an English Town,* Cambridge: Cambridge University Press.

Granovetter, M. (1982) The Strength of Weak Ties: A Network Theory Revisited, in Marsden, P. and Linn, N. (eds), *Social Structure and Network Analysis,* Beverley Hills, CA, Sage, 105–30.

Halfacree, K. and Kitchin, R. (1996) 'Madchester Rave On': Placing the Fragments of Popular Music, *Area*, 28(1), 47–55.

Knox, H., Savage, M. and Harvey, P. (2006) Social Networks and Spatial Relations: Networks as Method, Metaphor and Form, *Economy and Society* 35(1), 113–40.

Lin, N. (2001) *Social Capital: A Theory of Social Structure and Action*, New York, Cambridge University Press.

McGregor, A. and Gibson, C. (2009) Musical Work in a University Town: The Shifting Spaces and Practices of DJs in Dunedin, *Asia Pacific Viewpoint* 50(3), 277–88.

McPherson, M., Smith-Lovin, L., and Cook, J. (2001) Birds of a Feather: Homophily in Social Networks, *Annual Review of Sociology* 27, 415–44.

Milestone, K. (2008) Urban Myths: Popular Culture, the City and Identity, *Geography Compass* 2(4), 1165–78.

Mische, A. and White, H. (1998) Between Conversation and Situation: Public Switching Dynamics across Network Domains, *Social Research*, 65(3), 695–724.

Putnam, R. (2000) *Bowling Alone: The Collapse and Revival of American Community*, New York: Simon and Schuster.

Rainie, L. and Wellman, B. (2012) *Networked: The New Social Operating System*, Cambridge, MA, MIT Press.

Sheller, M. and Urry, J. (2006) The New Mobilities Paradigm, *Environment and Planning A* 38, 207–26.

Stevens, Q. (2007) *The Ludic City: Exploring the Potential of Public Spaces*, London: Routledge.

Straw, W. (1997) Communities and Scenes in Popular Music, in Gelder, K. and Thornton, S. (eds), *The Subcultures Reader*, New York: Routledge, 494–505.

Watson, A., Hoyler, M. and Mager, C. (2009) Spaces and Networks of Musical Creativity in the City, *Geography Compass* 3(2), 856–78.

Wittel, A. (2001) Towards a Network Sociality, *Theory, Culture and Society* 18(6), 51–76.

9 Exploring music careers

Music graduates and early career trajectories in the UK

Roberta Comunian, Alessandra Faggian and Sarah Jewell

Music is a key sector of the cultural and creative industries as defined by the Department of Culture, Media and Sport (DCMS 1998). Overall, the music industry is very well researched both in relation to its economic–business dynamics in the private commercial sector (Lorenzen and Frederiksen 2005) and its cost characteristics as a public good within the arts economy literature (Frey 1994). Whether looking at the private commercial sector or the public, a key essential component of all socio- and economic analysis of the sector is related to the role of musicians and their creative work and careers (Bennett 2008; Hracs 2009). While this chapter does not adopt a network-based methodology, it is strongly related to other work in this book, as it explores the initial steps in music careers and music productions which are often at the base of future creative networks. Within this broader field of research, this chapter is specifically interested in exploring the dynamics and characteristics of early career musicians, specifically the ones who recently graduated with music degrees from UK universities. There has been a growing number of works on musicians' careers; most of them concentrate on specific patterns and aspects of music career structures of people who are already musicians. However less is known about the early steps of musicians, specifically in relation to how music careers start (Bennett 2007). While we acknowledge that many successful musicians are not university graduates, this chapter focuses on music graduates and their career perspectives, using data collected from the Higher Education Statistical Agency (HESA). Therefore, the chapter considers specifically the role played by a higher education degree in initiating and supporting the careers of aspiring musicians. Following earlier work (Comunian *et al.* 2010, 2011; Faggian *et al.* 2013) linking higher education degrees in creative subjects to career perspectives, this contribution aims to specifically explore the relationship between music graduates and their careers also in the broader framework of the creative economy.

Many authors highlight the importance of networks in artists' (Comunian 2012) and musicians' careers; it is therefore important to take a step back and reflect on when and where these network start and develop. The role played by education in starting and nurturing these networks needs to receive further exploration. The chapter is articulated as follows: the next section introduces the literature and previous research in the field. We then briefly describe the data and methodology used in this research. The following sections present the results from the short-term perspective of six months after graduation and explore the longitudinal data. Finally, we discuss the findings, conclude and present further possible future research avenues.

Music careers and music graduates

The literature on music careers is very extensive and acknowledges how music work fits within the broader characteristics of creative and cultural work (Banks 2007). In general, all these studies acknowledge that creative labour is character-ised by precarity, instability and low economic rewards (Gill and Pratt 2008; Gill 2002; Menger 1999). Further literature on music careers specifically considers also how this instability impacts musicians' work and life (Hracs 2009). The characteristics of this work are also intertwined with issues of self-identity and personal motivation as, for many, being a musician is not just a career choice but key to the perception of self and self-worth (Oakland *et al.* 2012). Others sources also highlight the collaborative nature of music work (Martin 2006) which is sometimes very informal but can also have strong organisational structures and patterns, for example in classical music (Faulkner 1973). Adding to an already complex balance of work, career and networks, technological changes are also having an impact on the music sector, as recent works emphasise (Hracs 2012).

Within this broader landscape of creative and music work, it is important to consider the role played by higher education and the delicate transition between training and work. This is very important and many authors consider training as part of the creative identity building. Oakley (2009) considers the role of higher education in shaping the attitude of artists towards work, wondering whether the attitude towards 'sacrificial labour' (i.e. accepting lower economic rewards and the emphasis on gratification coming from their practice) is in fact an acquired framework that is embedded in their training. Similarly, Juuti and Littleton (2010, 2012) reflect on how students form their identity entering academia and how after – in the transition from study to work – they redefine their possible identities and trajectories in relation to employment or career paths. The liter-ature also highlights how the networks developed within the higher education context determine and shape the career opportunities of recent graduates (Hearn and Bridgstock 2010).

In some of these studies there is also an emphasis on what role higher and further education institutions play in shaping the identity and employment oppor-tunities of music graduates. Bennett (2007), in respect to music graduates and their training, engages with the limited perspective of higher education towards the broader range of jobs and professions that can be undertaken by a music graduate: 'musicians require understanding of their diverse cultures and com-munities in order to provide services relevant to the community need' (Bennett 2007, 185). In this respect she specifically considers the new role that the cultural and creative industries can play: 'the wide range of activities within the cultural industries highlights the potential for suitably skilled musicians to diversify their roles' (Bennett 2007, 185). In the research Bennett (2007) also considers and questions what should be the role of higher education in reference to shaping careers in this field; reporting Aguilar (1998) she considers whether educational institutions 'should at all times take the responsibility for establishing a process of adjusting educational policies, goals and structures to the world in which future musician will work' (Aguilar 1998 quoted in Bennett 2007). Alongside the value and impact of higher education, it is important to also consider how the nature of music work and practice also shapes its employment patterns and the kind of opportunities that recent graduates can enjoy. In particular, Freakley and Neelands (2003) highlight the importance of networks for accessing different ranges of employment and opportunities: 'the notion of the artist as a micro-business in a network of trading relationships was completely unfamiliar to all but one of the participants' (p. 59).

These dynamics are hard to capture through statistical data but qualitative interviews can help uncover some of these network dynamics. Since the seminal work of Granovetter (1973) the literature on social capital has highlighted the importance of social ties for finding work opportunities in a range of fields and contexts (Erickson 2001). This literature is even more relevant for creative occupations, where career and opportunities are usually based around temporary projects (Cattani and Ferriani 2008; Tams and Arthur 2010) and where symbolic capital – as well as socio- and cultural capital – plays a pivotal role (Jones 2010, 2002).

However, these issues are not limited to music graduates. The broader creative graduates group has recently been the focus of further research (Ball *et al.* 2010; Comunian *et al.* 2011) and similar patterns emerge. Creative graduates are more likely to experience lower salaries and be in part-time or freelance occupations, and a lower percentage enter graduate occupations compared to other graduates (Comunian *et al.* 2011).

Therefore this chapter aims to focus on music graduates' career perspectives and consider their career opportunities after graduation, specifically linking these aspects with reference to the importance of networks to work in creative occupations.

Data and methodology

Our empirical analysis is mainly based on data collected by the HESA. However, in order to help understand the data and findings, a handful of qualitative interviews with recent music graduates in the UK were conducted between May and June 2013.[1]

In the UK, HESA collects student record data for all students annually, containing information on personal characteristics (such as age, gender, ethnicity), course characteristics (including subject studied as the four-digit JACS code,[2] mode of studying, i.e. full-time or part-time, institution attended, final grade achieved for finalists) and location of parental domicile (at unit postcode level). Within UK higher education the institution attended can be placed into several different groups: Russell Group universities (comprising 20 research intensive universities who receive the majority of research grant and contract income), other old universities, new universities (established as part of the abolition of the binary divide in 1992) and higher education/further education colleges. The Russell Group universities, followed by the other old universities, are generally considered to be more prestigious.

We link student record data to two further datasets:

1   Destination of Leavers from Higher Education Institutions (also known as DHLE). On behalf of HESA, all higher education institutions are required annually to collect data on the destinations of their graduates six months after graduation, via the DHLE survey, with a target response rate of 80 per cent for British domiciled full-time students. The DHLE provides information on graduate employment six months after graduation,[3] this includes not only the salary and location of their job, but also a brief description of their tasks and the SOC4 (standard occupational code) and SIC4 (standard industrial classification) codes of their occupation. We focus in particular on their ability to enter creative occupations. In this analysis, we utilise data for British domiciled students belonging to the 2004/5 graduate cohort. The student record sample consists of a total of 442,518 finalists, of which we have 313,800 valid DHLE returns (see Table 9.1). The sample includes both undergraduate and postgraduate students.

2   Longitudinal Destination of Leavers from Higher Education Institutions Survey (LDLHE). In November 2010 (up to 3.5 years after graduation) 224,590 of the 332,100 2006/7cohort of DLHE respondents were invited to undertake the LDLHE survey. In total 49,065 responses were received representing about 15 per cent of those responding to the original DLHE survey. Our sample excludes postgraduates and focuses on British domiciled first degree graduates and other undergraduate students, so we have a sample size of 34,229 students. Weights are provided to allow for the over-sampling of some groups and hence any descriptive statistics and regressions will be weighted using these weights. The LDLHE survey contains information on employment activity 3.5 years after graduation, similar to that of the DLHE survey, although the LDLHE is more detailed than the DLHE survey. In particular the LDLHE survey includes information on employment activity, employment since graduation, job characteristics, occupation, industry, location of employment, salary 3.5 years after graduation and questions relating to whether the degree/subject was important to the job. The LDLHE data is linked to their student record and DLHE return.

These two datasets are used to capture the career trajectory of music graduates. In the analysis, students are classified, according to the subject studied, at two different levels. First, we distinguish between creative and non-creative graduates.[4] Broadly speaking creative graduates include students in creative arts and design subjects (all JACS codes starting with W), creative media graduates (all JACS codes starting with P) and other creative graduates in subjects mainly linked to technologies-based creative subjects and architecture. We then separate out music graduates (JACS codes starting W3), so we have three categories: non-creative, other creative and music students.

Using a creative job approach as suggested by Higgs *et al.* (2008) we consider both creative careers within the creative industries and creative occupations in other non-creative industries. Our definition of a creative job is based on the initial DCMS definition based on four-digit SIC codes. However, we supplement this definition with the inclusion of other creative workers (based on occupations using four-digit SOC codes that are defined as creative) based in industries outside the creative industries as identified by DCMS (1998) (see also Comunian *et al.* 2010 for detailed SOC and SIC codes). Moreover, we also took on board some of the criticisms to the DCMS definition provided by a recent report by Higgs *et al.* (2008). We also divided creative jobs into specialised (creative occupations in creative industries), embedded (creative occupations in non-creative industries) and supportive (non-creative occupations in creative industries) jobs.

This chapter is also concerned with the careers undertaken by music graduates who do not stay in the music or creative occupations sector, therefore, an overall set of sector groups were created based on the occupation and industry with the creative sector superseding any other sector group (since there was some overlap). Careers categories are: (1) creative sector; (2) science, technology and engineering; (3) health and social welfare; (4) education; (5) financial, property and business; (6) public administration; (7) other.

A short-term perspective on music graduates

Data and sample

As Table 9.1 summarises, 51,697 students graduated in 2004/5 in other creative disciplines in the UK (corresponding to 11.7 per cent of the students graduating that year), with 5,299 music students (1.2 per cent). On average 71 per cent of students responded to the DLHE survey with slightly higher response rates for other creative (73 per cent) and music students (77 per cent).The LDLHE refers to a different cohort but the breakdown of the subject groups is very similar.

Table 9.1 Sample sizes

	Finalists		DLHE		LDLHE	
Non-creative	385,522	87.1	271,917	86.7	29,954	87.51
Other creative	51,697	11.7	37,831	12.1	3,822	11.17
Music	5,299	1.2	4,052	1.3	453	1.32
Total	442,518	100	313,800	100	34,229	100

Our analysis includes postgraduate (27.0 per cent), undergraduate (60.59 per cent) and other undergraduate (12.70 per cent), however, in the LDLHE data we only map undergraduates and other undergraduates data. If we look at the institutional typology breakdown (Table 9.2) to consider how music students are distributed across UK universities we can see that, compared to other creative students, they are strongly present in the Russell Group and other 'old' institutions and less present in new universities than other creative students. Faggian *et al.* (2013) argue that graduates from subjects with stronger presence in Russell Group universities can influence the salary and 'signalling potential' (Spence 1973) of these students in the labour market.

Two of the music graduates interviewed studied in a Russell Group university and highlighted the importance of the type of education and qualification an older university provides – more research and less performance based – compared to conservatoires

> the perception is you go to a reputable university and you get a research degree, it is very academic and on paper you have a good degree and a good university and that will open doors.
>
> (Sandra)

Destinations, employment and geography

Looking at the destination of students, six months after graduation, for the 2004/5 cohort (Table 9.3), using their DLHE survey responses, it is possible to

Table 9.2 Institution breakdown by subject

	Non-creative	*Creative*	*Music*
Russell Group	24.3	7.75	20.32
Other 'old'	27.68	13.41	19.82
New	39.5	57.62	32.61
Colleges	8.51	21.23	27.25
Total	100	100	100

Table 9.3 Destinations of 2004/5 DLHE respondents

	Non-creative	*Other creative*	*Music*
Full-time employment	55.93	48.29	34.4
Self-employed/freelance	1.46	6.3	11.65
Part-time/unpaid employment	7.86	11.41	12.27
Work and study	10.37	7.55	9.06
Further study only	12.51	10.02	22.01
Unemployed	4.72	7.92	4.91
Other	7.15	8.51	5.7

see that music students are less likely to be in full-time work and more likely to be in part-time work and particularly more likely to be self-employed/freelance than other students – although 22 per cent go onto further study which is more than double other creative students. Altogether it is also important to note that music students have a lower unemployment rate than other creative students.

As in previous research (Bennett and Stanberg 2006), the graduates interviewed were very aware of the challenges of work in the music sector and also of the importance of a portfolio career or a job to support living while pursuing a career in performance

> it is really hard to know what to do, the hardest thing, I haven't gone straight into freelancing I would have not survived this time last year, I did not know enough people, I had not done enough, moving to a new city ... I do not think many people can do it where you finish a degree and be a professional musician like that ... you have to build it up and do other things.
>
> (Maria)

> In my head I would love to do more performing, number two is developing the company and then teaching, at the moment is the other way around doing mostly teaching, secondly the company and thirdly gigging, so in the long term, I am trying to build the company so that the teaching can diminish.
>
> (Sandra)

In reference to the role played by further study, this seems very important for students (especially if they aim to become performers) as they understand their education as having to include a postgraduate qualification and potential life-long training. As the graduates interviewed reported, there is a general understanding that musician training will involve further qualifications

> so I hope to do a further postgraduate performance degree at a conservatoire ... I never saw that as being the end, I always had it in my mind that I would do either a postgraduate studies in performance or a Postgraduate Certificate in Education. I never saw that as being the end point.
>
> (Anna)

> I enrolled in a postgraduate diploma at the [conservatoire name] and half-way through the academic year I decided to transfer to the MA course as one year did not seem enough to do all I wanted to do.
>
> (Maria)

In the HESA survey, individuals (not all responded) are asked the name of the course and the subject they are studying. Based on this information, a professional subject of study is created (using the SOC code). For music students (Table 9.4), the most common occupational groups who take further study,

Table 9.4 Occupational subject of music graduates' further study

	Freq.	*%*
Teaching professionals	292	32.88
Musicians	406	45.72
Musicians	*136*	*15.32*
Composers, arrangers, conductors and musical directors	*64*	*7.21*
Musical instrument players	*206*	*23.2*
Actors/entertainers	54	6.08
Vocalists	48	5.41
Other	88	9.91
No. of obs.	*888*	*100*

33 per cent are on courses which are education related and 46 per cent are on music-related courses.

Looking more closely at the sectors of employment, we first consider whether music graduates enter creative jobs. Overall 42 per cent of other creative are in a creative job compared to 30 per cent of music students and only 9 per cent of non-creative graduates (Table 9.5). If we look specifically at creative sectors we find that only 21 per cent of music graduates find jobs in the music and performing arts sector. It is interesting to notice that the high concentration of music graduates in the music and performing arts group corresponds also to a high concentration of them in non-creative sectors, with in fact only 9 per cent entering the other creative sector.

Parkes and Jones (2011) consider a different motivation behind the choice of students towards a career in performance or a career in music education.

Table 9.5 Sector of employment by subject group

	Non-creative	*Other creative*	*Music*	*Total*
Creative	9.06	41.97	29.97	13.18
Advertising	1.81	3.59	1.62	2.01
Architecture and design	1.29	6.3	0.29	1.87
Design, designer fashion and crafts	0.53	12.42	0.85	1.94
Film, TV, radio and photography	0.53	5.7	3.16	1.17
Music and performing arts	0.74	5.22	21.29	1.5
Publishing	0.74	3.56	1.03	1.08
Software, computer games and electronic publishing	2.82	2.89	0.85	2.8
Libraries, museums and art galleries	0.6	2.28	0.92	0.8
Non-creative	90.95	58.03	70.00	86.83
Science, technology and engineering	10.34	4.68	2.71	9.58
Health and social welfare	24.81	3.82	4.07	22.1
Education	20.53	12.97	36.87	19.82
Financial, property and business	14.94	9.27	8.51	14.2
Public administration	5.79	2.85	2.24	5.4
Other	14.54	24.44	15.63	15.71

The graduate interviewed highlighted the difficulty of entering a career in music and tended to consider a broader career in the arts and other creative fields as a good alternative:

> having put all the efforts in, I was gigging regularly in several bands, there was enough work to sustain me throughout the summer, thankfully, which afford me the opportunity to look for jobs, I had 75 job applications during the period, 65 of them were related to arts and music in one way or another, the other 10 I would have been a chief salesman, bar-tender.
>
> (Mark)

Table 9.5 also includes a breakdown of the non-creative sectors with 37 per cent of music graduates in the education sector (which is a much larger proportion than other creative and non-creative graduates) and is the most popular sector for music graduates.

However, all of the interviewees highlighted the difficulty of translating their study into a profession (this of course links back to the issue of further training or retraining into a different field like education):

> there was very little in my degree, whereby I could say 'well, I have learned that, how can I apply that to the real world?' I think it was very much I am learning about music and I am in my own little music bubble, and then suddenly you leave university and you find there isn't a job for a music graduate, you need to find what your strength is and what the jobs available are, because I did not have a clue really of what I could do with my degree.
>
> (Mark)

If we look more closely at the type of creative jobs graduates get (Table 9.6), music students are more likely to be in supportive jobs than other graduates and less likely to be in specialised or embedded jobs than other creative graduates.

Three of the five graduates interviewed were currently working in a supportive role within the creative/music industry. This was considered a fulfilling career option (rather than being articulated as a failure to be a specialised creative).

Table 9.6 Creative job type

	Non-creative	Other creative	Music	Total
Specialised	2.28	21.74	16.65	4.74
Supportive	2.6	6.93	8.13	3.18
Embedded	4.17	13.29	5.22	5.26
Non-creative	90.95	58.03	70.00	86.83

I now work for a different agency in the city centre, I am doing the same role. I am an account executive, which is the person who liaises with the client and leads the creative team. I do not do the creative work myself but I organise it which is what I am good at.

(Laura)

Related to the role played in supportive roles (but also more broadly to music graduates who are working in other sectors), the students interviewed were able to articulate very well how the skills that they learned specifically in their music degree were valuable also in other areas of work:

the focus, to practice six to eight hours a day it takes some dedication, it is a mind-set, that practice takes a lot, there are a lot of tests along the way that push your buttons, it is managing the frustration of not being able to get it done straight away, the expectation of what is to come at the end, those skills were things I could take out into this role ... the performance aspect of it, helps you in meeting, showing venue, there is an air of confidence that is apparent.

(Maria)

Musicians are very good at working in a team, very motivated and disciplined ... our skills are more broadly applicable in life in most jobs, musicians have to be very organised with time and very efficient with your time ... the drive might initiate maybe earlier than university, but the punctuality for training and rehearsal is definitely trained in and expected ... the idea of efficiency comes at that high level of study.

(Sandra)

It is important to also consider the geography of study (linked to course provision; Comunian and Faggian 2011) in music and creative disciplines but also the region where graduates get their first employment. As Table 9.7 shows, other creative jobs followed by music graduates are more likely to be in London with music graduates more likely to be in the south-east than other graduates. London is the most frequent region for creative jobs with 33 per cent of all creative jobs in London and 41 per cent of creative jobs taken by music graduates in London.

As shown in Table 9.7 it is worth mentioning here that the largest proportion of music students are based in London and this is a greater proportion than other students especially non-creative. Other popular regions include the south-east and the north-west and Yorkshire and Humberside – which are common across all graduates. The importance of London emerged also in the interviews as one of the graduate highlighted and this will be discussed further in the chapter:

I am a Londoner, I commuted during my degree, it was silly to leave London to study music because London is the European capital of music.

(Sandra)

Table 9.7 Region of study and employment for creative jobs

	Region of study				Region of creative employment			
	Non-creative	Other creative	Music	Total	Non-creative	Other creative	Music	Total
North-east	4.7	3.44	2.94	4.53	3.45	2.57	2.33	3.1
North-west	10.79	9.79	10.62	10.67	8.66	8.86	10.71	8.78
Yorkshire and Humberside	9.13	8.96	9.66	9.12	6.44	6.42	3.11	6.36
East Midlands	7.82	9.79	2.98	7.99	4.79	4.66	2.64	4.69
West Midlands	8.13	6.44	6.53	7.91	5.92	5.51	5.75	5.76
East of England	5.1	3.17	5.06	4.87	6.56	5.16	5.9	6.02
London	14.93	21.61	27.25	15.86	30.71	35.6	40.99	32.77
South-east	14	13.3	14.53	13.93	13.89	11.11	10.87	12.79
South-west	6.68	9.49	6.3	7	7.08	7.66	5.43	7.26
Wales	5.97	5.93	5.11	5.95	3.19	3.68	3.73	3.39
Scotland	10.02	6.73	7.7	9.61	6.96	6.92	7.92	6.96
Northern Ireland	2.73	1.34	1.3	2.55	2.34	1.85	0.62	2.12
Total	100	100	100	100	100	100	100	100

A graduate from the a university in the north of England considered also the advantage of students based in London:

> in London where the industry is based, it is a lot London centered, there is a lot more opportunities if a record label sees you, an agency, they can pick you up from an early age and develop you, while here it is kind of isolated, you have to make things happen.
>
> (Mark)

A longitudinal view on music careers and working patterns

We now move on to exploring the LDLHE data. Comparing the destinations at six months and 3.5 years after graduation of the LDLHE respondents (Table 9.8), first, it is noticeable that music graduates are more likely to be self-employed/freelance and be in further study. Also across all students the number in full-time work increases between the two time periods and hence the number in study and unemployment has fallen but the number in part-time work and self-employment, has increased and this is especially true for music graduates.

While this general view shows a strengthening of full-time employment, it is important to consider in which sectors job stability has increased. Table 9.9 shows that the proportion with a graduate job has increased between six months and 3.5 years for all subjects – with the proportion in a creative job only increasing for non-creative graduates and decreasing slightly for other creative and music students. The proportion of music students in music and performing arts sector jobs has increased slightly between six months and 3.5 years from 17 per cent to 20 per cent. Examining the non-creative sectors shows the proportion of music students in education has increased from 20 per cent to 31.5 per cent (36 per cent of music students in the education sector at 3.5 years were in further study at six months).

The graduates interviewed were still between one and two years from graduation, so would not correspond to the 3.5 year samples used by HESA:

> However, in the interviews they highlighted and mentioned career strategies and long-term trajectories which closely related to the role played by the education sector (as a back-up plan) but also to the need of job stability and long-term planning. It is a performance degree ... focused on the music itself, but I always thought there should be also something else, a fallback position, which I do not think lots of musicians think about; lots of them are solely focused on the music ... it is risk management from my point of view, if the playing does not work out I need to think of something else.
>
> (Mark)

For some, a long-term career strategy was a response to a lack of vision or direction in the career opportunities offered by universities. This was especially true for students who did not pursue the performing career path:

Table 9.8 Destinations: comparing six months and 3.5 years of LDHLE respondents

	6 months			3.5 years		
	Non-creative	*Other creative*	*Music*	*Non-creative*	*Other creative*	*Music*
Full-time employment	51.38	46.53	33.63	69.52	58.54	47.35
Self-employed/freelance	1.24	6.28	9.44	3.05	9.56	18.67
Part-time/unpaid employment	7.68	12.02	10.21	7.94	11.78	11.52
Work and study	13.41	8.19	11.12	5.71	3.65	7.04
Further study only	15.98	12.06	25.57	7.37	5.51	8.38
Unemployed	5.26	8.86	5.71	3.59	6.51	4.9
Other	5.06	6.07	4.32	2.82	4.45	2.14

Table 9.9 Jobs in creative and others sectors (six months vs. 3.5 years) of the LDLHE respondents

	6 months			3.5 years		
	Non-creative	Other creative	Music	Non-creative	Other creative	Music
% Graduate job	70.93	61.88	60.03	78.57	70.79	76.28
% Creative job	11.84	49.26	35.87	12.78	48.02	35.03
Creative	11.85	49.32	36.00	12.84	48.45	35.18
Advertising	2.66	4.55	5.52	2.86	5.47	4.57
Architecture and design	1.66	6.99	0.34	1.33	4.76	0.37
Design, designer fashion and crafts	0.63	17.92	0.43	0.62	15.55	1.45
Film, TV, radio and photography	0.7	6.27	6.81	0.76	6.11	4.02
Music and performing arts	0.81	5.38	17	0.94	7.5	20.05
Publishing	0.84	3.49	1.94	1.01	3.1	1.43
Software, computer games and electronic publishing	3.96	3.31	2.74	4.63	4.32	2.21
Libraries, museums and art galleries	0.6	1.41	1.23	0.69	1.64	1.09
Non-creative	88.15	50.68	64.00	87.16	51.55	64.82
Science, technology and engineering	11.78	4.16	2.9	11.57	6.41	4.18
Health and social welfare	28.09	3.9	6.41	25.67	5.13	6.83
Education	11.3	6.37	20.26	16.07	12.72	31.53
Financial, property and business	16.31	9.86	8.71	17.04	8.2	6.65
Public administration	5.04	2.05	1.73	5.94	2.4	2.61
Other	15.62	24.33	23.99	10.87	16.69	13.03

it was not made very clear to us what other career options there were in music, part of me going to advertising was me trying to find a realistic option, because at no point did they say you can be a composer, here are the contacts you need to make, the network you need to be part, or if you want to work in the record industry ... there was none of that direction from a music point of view, so that probably forms part of why I was determined to find a career path myself.

(Laura)

This issue was less relevant for students wanting a career in performance as opportunities seem more available/obvious for them within their degree

Part of the attraction of the course at the conservatoire and part of the reason I stayed a second year was that built into the course they had several professional development opportunities, which included professional experience schemes with several professional orchestras based in the city.

(Maria)

Teaching/education was on the one hand perceived as a blessing (as it offered economic support and interaction within people's practice) but on the other it was also looked down on:

the teaching, I am blessed as I got a great relationship with students, and if I wanted full-time work teaching, I could get it, but I restrict myself to two days' teaching because I find [it] not very stimulating and creatively stifling, so it would be quite hard.

(Sandra)

I wish I was performing more ... and teaching was almost looked down upon I felt and now I bump into people now and they go 'oh you are teaching too' so people are doing it but I do not think they saw themselves doing it.

(Maria)

I thought about teaching ... I definitely have not discarded that idea but I want to give this a go before and see if I can get into doing postgraduate studies, so teaching is a bit of back-up plan but something that I am sure I would enjoy doing.

(Anna)

Respondents to the LDLHE survey are asked how many jobs they had, if they had been unemployed for a month or more, how many spells and total months of unemployement for those with at least one spell of more than one month. Table 9.10 suggests music students on average have had more jobs than non-creative and other creative (note that music students are more likely to hold more than

Table 9.10 Multiple jobs and unemployment

	No. of jobs since graduation		Unemployed 1 month or more		Months unemployed	
	N	mean	N	mean	N	mean
Non-creative	28,260	2.36	29,721	29.87	8,915	6.17
Other creative	3,718	3.30	3,930	45.36	1,788	7.13
Music	433	3.38	451	42	190	6.25

one job at a time with 32 per cent of music students at 3.5 years holding more than one job, compared to 10 per cent of non-creative and 18 per cent of other creative graduates). A high proportion (42 per cent) of music students have experienced at least a month's unemployment (slightly lower than other creative graduates) and on average those unemployed had six months of unemployment between graduation and the LDLHE survey.

The issue of unemployment and transition between academia and the world of work was also expressed in our interviews:

> Currently I teach music that takes more of my time and I perform and I have a little music company that I founded straight after university.
>
> (Sandra)

> I got to the end of my degree and I felt exhausted so I think I spent three–four months just staying at home not doing much.... It was a big step for me to decide to be self-employed. I did apply and was getting interviews at corporate stuff but it did not suit my nature, I was looking at jobs in arts management and some teaching roles, anything to do with the arts.
>
> (Maria)

> You have to do a lot for free before you start getting stuff that will pay ... because you need that experience on your CV and then the initial salary is very low ... so you might have to work several jobs simultaneously ... most musicians fill as much time as possible with teaching because it is the most available employment and in a way it is the most flexible ... you cannot really have a music career without teaching.
>
> (Anna)

Salaries and economic rewards

The average salary[5] has increased between six months and 3.5 years (Table 9.11). Music students earn slightly more than other creatives at 3.5 years (but marginally less at six months) and have a bigger increase in salary than other creative and non-creatives. Although the cell sizes for music students are very small so results need to be interpreted with caution.[6]

Table 9.11 Average salaries (in £ sterling) by subject group (six months vs. 3.5 years)

	6 months		3.5 years		% change
	N	mean	N	mean	
Non-creative	11,182	20,344	19,094	22,764	11.9
Other creative	1,097	16,824	2,129	18,867	12.1
Music	104	16,547	239	19,550	18.1
Total	12,383	19,958	22,000	22,297	11.7

Graduates interviewed were particularly aware of their weak starting position in the job market and of the need for further support and time to develop their practice and networks:

> The major barriers are, finding an income that supports living rent free rather than going home and live with your parents, although I know friends who have done that and are building up work from home, secondly particularly to be an orchestral musician, while there are a lots of jobs around compared to the number of graduates there are still very few.
>
> (Anna)

> I did not want to have to rely on the insecurity of not knowing where the next month rent is coming from … so it was a conscious decision for me music is a passion, a hobby…. For me I can still go out now and gig two three times a week, if I do not want to, or I cannot, I do not have to take the gig to eat and pay the bills.
>
> (Mark)

> I actively chose a career path that pays rubbishly, but continuing with why I chose music in first place, I chose a career that I thought I am going to enjoy and be good at, that why I have done it not from a money point of view.
>
> (Laura)

If we look specifically at creative versus non-creative jobs we can see that music individuals have the biggest increase in both creative and non-creative jobs with all subjects having a greater average salary for creative than non-creative jobs.

On average, while earning less than non-creative graduates, music graduates earn more than other creative graduates – although the gap is less within creative jobs. Non-creative graduates seem to earn more across both non-creative and creative graduates.

There is a clear acknowledgement from the music graduates interviewed that a career in music might not provide the level of salary of other sectors or might not even be enough to support their living:

Table 9.12 Salaries and creative occupations (in £ sterling), 6 months vs. 3.5 years

	6 months		3.5 years		% change	
	Creative	Non-creative	Creative	Non-creative	Creative	Non-creative
Non-creative	20,882	20,259	22,981	22,732	10.1	12.2
Other creative	17,637	15,945	20,040	17,830	13.6	11.8
Music	17,908	15,803	21,062	18,743	17.6	18.6
Total	19,873	19,976	22,032	22,349	10.9	11.9

even if it was not just music but dance or theatre, I want to be in an industry that is creative … there is pressure when you come out of university, it is a lot money to study for three years, and you put pressure on yourself to find a job when you can earn, I am not going to earn a lot of money not for a while I am not driven my money but I am probably driven more by creativity and having fun.

(Anna)

I do not know if I will ever end up with a permanent orchestra job or with enough freelance work to live off it is a bit of a gamble but for the moment I got to try until I fail.

(Maria)

I was at the assessment for a job outside the sector, the pay was incredible for the time, I was almost feeling like I was selling myself, but in my mind I knew, if I do that job I can do gigging and what I wanted to do, but I got a phone call from here [performing arts venue], it paid probably half as much as what I was going for, but it was in the career, in direct relation with what I wanted to do … I could use the value of it to carry on.

(Mark)

Migration and geographies of work

Comparing region of employment between six months and 3.5 years there is an obvious increase in the proportion working in London and for music a specific increase in the number in the south-east.

Interviewees also mentioned the difficulty of remaining in the location of study without parental support, a trend identified in Faggian *et al.* (forthcoming). The importance of support at the outset of their career is key especially for self-employed musicians

It was very hard time for me, it was straight out university, I am a lonely child living away from home, a bit of a decision making: do I stick down here and make a go at it or go back home and try and carve something out?

(Mark)

I am very blessed because my parents are Londoners and I live with them and I acknowledge that it is a financial safety blanket ... so that enabled me to start being self-employed without immediately needing an income which is fairly unique, I know a lot of my colleagues went home for a period afterwards, but I had a bonus of being in London. That was a real benefit.

(Sandra)

The proportion of music students in a creative job in London has increased from 45 per cent to 46 per cent and in the south-east increased from 5 per cent to 10 per cent, while for non-creative jobs the proportion in London has increased from 15 per cent to 24 per cent and in the south-east 13 per cent to 14 per cent.

One interviewee mentioned the importance of London in their music career

I wanted to be in London, a lot of the work that I am getting in singing at the moment is working in young professional scheme with them, who are helping me to guide me for a year, to be in London I thought it was a good idea for that kind of things ... I always wanted to move to London ... the job has been a good way to ease into London.

(Maria)

However, they also mentioned the importance of being mobile and following the job opportunities available:

I think your career is much more important than your location when you are a graduate point of view, further down the line it might be more important ... but as a graduate you cannot be tied down and I am not the kind of person who would be.

(Anna)

I am applying for auditions UK-wide, because you have to go where there is work, this is my philosophy, I do not think I can afford to be picky and choosy ... I am going to try and make it anywhere ... I was also interested in exploring opportunities in Europe.

(Maria)

Conclusions

Using HESA data and qualitative interviews, this chapter has attempted to provide a better understanding of the transition of music graduates from higher education into the world of work. It provides an important reflection on the initial steps of music graduates in building a career and a network to enter the professional world.

The data presented highlight a complex picture of different academic practice (especially distinguishing between graduates from conservatoires and graduates from other higher education institutions) as well as different ways of entering work, and creative careers in particular. From the quantitative data it seems that the position of music as a discipline in older and more prestigious institutions allows for more opportunity (less unemployment) for music graduates. It also allows for investment in further training and retraining. However, while music graduates leave university in a stronger position than other creative graduates, they still face the difficulties brought by portfolio careers and multiple-job handling. Here networks become key to sustaining their livelihood and to projecting them into a professional career. Networks are used to mobilise resources that enable them to start freelancing and get established.

From the qualitative interviews, it is possible to highlight two further areas for future research and consideration: the role played by networks in facilitating the transition from higher education to work and the role played by the higher education departments and their employability agendas.

In reference to the role of networks, graduates interviewed highlighted how the contacts established during higher education (often within extracurricular activities) are still key to their current work. Individuals use these contact to mobilise opportunities:

> I met other musicians via the jazz society from other universities ... having made those contacts, I can now contact them for gigs, and through those networks you meet endless more ... all of the musicians that I use now in gigs there is some contact from having met someone at university, so you can almost trace it back and a lot of venue owners and people who run events ... I still use those contacts now.

Music graduates were aware of the importance of investing in those networks while at university and also of their place-based nature and the importance of nurturing them. Graduates seem to invest in developing their social capital while studying in order to be able to tap into future work and are also aware of the weak nature of some of these ties and how they need to be sustained over time.

> I worked so hard for three years while at university to build such a networks and reputation on the strength of my ability to come in and read and substitute people and my reliability, if I went away for six months or a year this network would not be there when I would be back.
>
> (Maria)

Another area of further research and investigation relates to the attitude and understanding of employability and career transitions in academia. Recent literature has highlighted the importance of creating awareness among students about the challenges of music careers (Gembris 2004). Furthermore, there has been a push to introduce professional development opportunities and activities in students' curricula (Barnes and Holt 2000) that aim to enhance their employability, as well as new teaching methods to enhance independent learning (Lebler 2007) and complementarity with other skills and careers (Bennett and Stanberg 2006).

As one interviewee in our project suggested:

> everybody can get a music degree but not everyone can have music degree with experience … I needed to make myself more attractive to a potential employer, it was a big eye opener.

(Mark)

Some of the interviewees praised the opportunity offered by the university and their career services; however, there was also a lack of understanding on the part of these services as to what is important to know to enter a music career.

> I am not sure how much they really know about the professional music industry and I think no one really knows until they tried to enter it. I think that kind of information gets passed on from your singing teacher or instrumental teacher. It is difficult for the career service which is working in such a massive university to know exactly what it entails.

(Laura)

Overall, interviewees experienced more opportunities for career development outside the classroom, so the same student, while admitting that 'I can never remember having a conversation with a lecturer about what will I do after university, like never', conceded that her involvement in the university jazz society meant that 'I learnt all the stuff I do for my company there. I took them on tour, I ran gigs, I met musicians and I made contacts, that really helped me' (Sandra). So, from the conversation with graduates it was clear that, as Pitts (2003. 292) said, learning, personality and opportunity thus become intertwined in students' experience of a music degree and these aspects of the "hidden curriculum" assume a powerful role' towards their future career.

Lastly, graduates seem to call for 'more real world exposure to the risks of being a musician', particularly to mediate the changes taking place from being in the world of higher education to entering the world of work. The quantitative data show that music graduates perform better in the longitudinal survey, therefore suggesting there is a long-term adjustment. However, the short-term data and interviews reveal the trauma and adjustment required; as one of the interviewee suggests: 'there is a big safety net in the higher education setting that quickly gets taken away without you realising instantaneously as soon as you finish.'

Notes

1 Interviewees were recruited through mail-outs to recent alumni among graduates from two UK Russell Group universities, one conservatoire and one new university. The communications enabled us to recruit five recent (between one and two years from graduation) graduates. Interviews were transcribed and coded and are used in the text to discuss findings emerging from the HESA data. The names of the interviewees have been changed to respect anonymity.

2 For more information on the Joint Academic Coding System (or JACS) see www.hesa. ac.uk/index.php?option=com_content&task=view&id=158&Itemid=233.
3 Although six months may seem relatively early on in graduate careers, it is still a useful indicator of both longer-term labour market success (Elias *et al.* 1999) and assimilation into the graduate labour market. Elias *et al.* (1999) found that students employed six months after graduation were more likely to be in graduate jobs three and half years later, while graduates unemployed six months after leaving university tended to have lower earnings and lower job satisfaction later on in their careers (McKnight 1999).
4 Graduates were categorised as 'bohemian graduates' according to the following criteria: if they were single honours students and their subject fell under any of the creative categories; if they were a joint honours student and their first or both subjects were creative (those whose second but not first subject were classed as bohemian were classified as 'non-bohemian'); if they were a joint honours student with three subjects and two or three of the subjects were creative (even if the first subject was not creative).
5 The 3.5-year salary level has been deflated (using the Consumer Price Index) to the price levels at six months (January 2008).
6 These changes have to be viewed with caution as the six-month and 3.5-year values don't necessarily include the same students. The response rate is much higher at 3.5 years (79 per cent) than six months (51 per cent).

References

Aguilar, M. (1998) Education of the Professional Musician. Online, available at www. mca.org.au/r18300.htm (accessed 2 July 2002).

Ball, L., Pollard, E. and Stanley, N. (2010) *Creative Graduates, Creative Futures*. London, Creative Graduates Creative Futures Higher Education Partnership and the Institute for Employment Studies.

Banks, M. (2007) *The Politics of Cultural Work*, Basingstoke, Palgrave Macmillan.

Barnes, J. and Holt, G. (2000) *Making Music Work: Professional Integration Project: Fostering Professional Skills among Those Studying Music in Higher Education*, London, Royal College of Music.

Bennett, D. (2007) Utopia for Music Graduates: Is It Achievable, and How Should It Be Defined? *British Journal of Music Education* 24, 179–89.

Bennett, D. (2008) *Understanding the Classical Music Profession: The Past, the Present and Strategies for the Future*, Aldershot, Ashgate Publishing.

Bennett, D. and Stanberg, A. (2006) Musicians as Teachers: Developing a Positive View Through Collaborative Learning Partnerships, *International Journal of Music Education* 24, 219–30.

Cattani, G. and Ferriani, S. (2008) A Core/Periphery Perspective on Individual Creative Performance: Social Networks and Cinematic Achievements in the Hollywood Film Industry, *Organization Science* 19, 824–44.

Comunian, R. (2012) Exploring the Role of Networks in the Creative Economy of North East England: Economic and Cultural Dynamics, *Encounters and Engagements between Economic and Cultural Geography*, 143–57.

Comunian, R. and Faggian, A. (2011) Higher Education and the Creative City, in Anderson, D. and Mellender, C. (eds), *Handbook of Creative Cities*, London and New York, Edward Elgar, 187–207.

Comunian, R., Faggian, A. and Jewell, S. (2011) Winning and Losing in the Creative Industries: An Analysis of Creative Graduates' Career Opportunities across Creative Disciplines, *Cultural Trends* 20, 291–308.

Comunian, R., Faggian, A. and Li, Q.C. (2010) Unrewarded Careers in the Creative Class: The Strange Case of Bohemian Graduates, *Papers in Regional Science* 89, 389–410.

DCMS (1998) *Creative Industries Mapping Document*, London, Department for Culture, Media and Sport

Elias, P., McKnight, A., Purcell, K. and Pitcher, J. (eds) (1999) *Moving On: Graduate Careers Three Years after Graduation*, Manchester, CSU/DfEE.

Erickson, B.H. (2001) Good Networks and Good Jobs: The Value of Social Capital to Employers and Employees, in Lin, N., Cook, K. and Burt, R.S. (eds), *Social Capital: Theory and Research.*, New York, Aldine de Gruyter, 127–58.

Faggian, A., Comunian, R. and Li, Q.C. (forthcoming) Interregional Migration of Human Creative Capital: The Case of 'Bohemian graduates', *Geoforum.*

Faggian, A., Comunian, R., Jewell, S. and Kelly, U. (2013) Bohemian Graduates in the UK: Disciplines and Location Determinants of Creative Careers, *Regional Studies* 47, 183–200.

Faulkner, R.R. (1973) Career Concerns and Mobility Motivations of Orchestra Musicians, *Sociological Quarterly* 14, 334–49.

Freakley, V. and Neelands, J. (2003) The UK Artist's World of Work, *Research in Dance Education* 4, 51–61.

Frey, B.S. (1994) The Economics of Music Festivals, *Journal of Cultural Economics* 18, 29–39.

Gembris, H. (2004) A New Approach to Pursuing the Professional Development of Recent Graduates from German Music Academies: The Alumni Project, in Davidson, Jane W. (ed.), *The Music Practitioner: Research for the Music Performer, Teacher and Listener*, Aldershot, Ashgate, 309–18.

Gill, R. (2002) Cool, Creative and Egalitarian? Exploring Gender in Project-Based New Media Work in Europe, *Information, Communication and Society* 5, 70–89.

Gill, R. and Pratt, A. (2008) In the Social Factory? Immaterial Labour, Precariousness and Cultural Work, *Theory, Culture and Society* 25, 1–30.

Granovetter, M.S. (1973) The Strength of Weak Ties, *American Journal of Sociology* 78, 1360–80.

Hearn, G. and Bridgstock, R. (eds). (2010) *Education for the Creative Economy: Innovation, Transdisciplinarity, and Networks*, New York, Peter Lang.

Higgs, P., Cunningham, S. and Bakhshi, H. (2008) *Beyond the Creative Industries: Mapping the Creative Economy in the United Kingdom*, London: NESTA.

Hracs, B.J. (2009) Beyond Bohemia: Geographies of Everyday Creativity for Musicians in Toronto, in Edensor, T., Leslie, D., Millington, S. and Rantisi, N.M. (eds), *Spaces of Vernacular Creativity: Rethinking the Cultural Economy*, London, Routledge, 75–88.

Hracs, B.J. (2012) A Creative Industry in Transition: The Rise of Digitally Driven Independent Music Production, *Growth and Change* 43, 442–61.

Jones, C. (2002) Signaling Expertise: How Signals Shape Careers in Creative Industries, in Peiperl, M.A., Arthur, M.B. and Anand N. (eds.), *Career Creativity: Explorations in the Remaking of Work,* Oxford: Oxford University Press, 209–28.

Jones, C. (2010) Finding a Place in History: Symbolic and Social Networks in Creative Careers and Collective Memory, *Journal of Organizational Behavior* 31, 726–48.

Juuti, S. and Littleton, K. (2010) Musical Identities in Transition: Solo-Piano Students' Accounts of Entering the Academy, *Psychology of Music* 38, 481–97.

Juuti, S. and Littleton, K. (2012) Tracing the Transition from Study to a Contemporary Creative Working Life: The Trajectories of Professional Musicians, *Vocations and Learning* 5, 5–21.

Lebler, D. (2007) Student-as-Master? Reflections on a Learning Innovation in Popular Music Pedagogy, *International Journal of Music Education* 25, 205–21.

Lorenzen, M. and Frederiksen, L. (2005) The Management of Projects and Product Experimentation: Examples from the Music Industry, *European Management Review* 2, 198–211.

Martin, P.J. (2006) Musicians' Worlds: Music-Making as a Collaborative Activity, *Symbolic Interaction* 29, 95–107.

McKnight, A. (1999) Graduate Employability and Performance Indicators, First Destinations and Beyond, in Elias, P., McKnight, A., Purcell, K. and Pitcher, J. (eds), *Moving On: Graduate Careers Three Years after Graduation*, Manchester, CSU/DfEE.

Menger, P.M. (1999) Artistic Labor Markets and Careers, *Annual Review of Sociology* 25, 541–74.

Oakland, J., MacDonald, R.A. and Flowers, P. (2012) Re-defining 'Me': Exploring Career Transition and the Experience of Loss in the Context of Redundancy for Professional Opera Choristers, *Musicae Scientiae* 16, 135–47.

Oakley, K. (2009) From Bohemian to Britart: Art Students over 50 Years, *Cultural Trends* 18, 281–94.

Parkes, K.A. and Jones, B.D. (2011) Students' Motivations for Considering a Career in Music Performance, *Update: Applications of Research in Music Education* 29, 20–8.

Pitts, S.E. (2003) What Do Students Learn When We Teach Music? An Investigation of the 'Hidden' Curriculum in a University Music Department, *Arts and Humanities in Higher Education* 2, 281–92.

Spence, M. (1973) Job Market Signaling, *Quarterly Journal of Economics* 87, 355–74.

Tams, S. and Arthur, M.B. (2010) New Directions for Boundaryless Careers: Agency and Interdependence in a Changing World, *Journal of Organizational Behavior* 31, 629–46.

10 Tastes, ties and social space

Exploring Sheffield's folk singing world

Fay Hield and Nick Crossley

Musical taste and its association with social position have been key foci of sociological research in recent years, following the groundbreaking work of Pierre Bourdieu (1984) and Richard Peterson (1992; Peterson and Kern 1996; Bennett *et al.* 2009; Bryson 1996, 1997; Chan and Goldthorpe 2007; Savage 2006). Within this body of research we find a growing strand focused upon social networks (DiMaggio 1987; Erickson 1996; Lewis *et al.* 2008; Lizardo 2006, 2011; Mark 1998, 2003; Relish 1997; Steglich *et al.* 2006; Upright 2004). Noah Mark (1998), in particular, has explained the abovementioned association between tastes and social position by reference to mutual influence within networks.

This network strand significantly advances our understanding of tastes, their acquisition, effects and distribution. However, the data used in this work are mostly from large sample surveys with a wide focus not restricted to music. Though advantageous for some purposes, this approach is limited. Standard sampling strategies filter out dependencies between respondents, which means filtering out networks in anything but a very basic, ego–net format. Furthermore, information about alters is often sparse and does not extend to their tastes, such that the investigation of social influence and the transmission of tastes is, at best, indirect. And measures of taste are superficial and undifferentiated. Respondents express their liking for a small number of vague genre categories, on Likert scales, and their commitment to these genres is gauged, if at all, by their having listened to recordings or attended a live music event within a (usually generous) time period. This sets the threshold for 'strong liking' at a low level, failing to distinguish between those who attend an occasional high-profile gig and those who are more actively involved in a grassroots 'music world' (on worlds see Becker 1982; Lopes 2002; Finnegan 1989; Martin 2005, 2006; Bottero and Crossley 2011, 2014; Crossley 2015).

Indeed, there is no acknowledgement of the collective nature of musical activity, captured by the concept of worlds. Respondents are addressed as individuals and their tastes treated as discrete individual attributes. We are given no sense of the way in which tastes are defined and contested by enthusiasts, creating ever finer distinctions and attendant identities and rituals. Likewise, there is no recognition of the different contexts in which music is produced/consumed or the fact that tastes may extend beyond genre to cover such contexts: e.g. a preference for small sweaty clubs over big halls, live over recorded music, participatory over non-participatory events, etc. This raises the question of how well, if at all, the abovementioned ideas regarding tastes and ties apply to grassroots music worlds?

In this chapter we address this question, drawing upon research which has approached the relationship between tastes, ties and socio-demographics through a case study of a grassroots music world: the local folk-singing world in Sheffield (UK). Through a detailed investigation of this world we aim to capture details and explore complexities which, we believe, elude the large sample surveys.

We have various sources of data. As an insider with 30 years of experience of active engagement, the first-named author brings an autoethnographic perspective to bear (on autoethnographic method see Maréchal 2010). In addition, she conducted extensive ethnographic research over four years between 2006 and 2010 (Hield 2010). This involved participant-observation at ten events in Sheffield; participant diaries completed by 27 singers; a focus group with 16 participants; and interviews with seven professional folk singers living in the area.

Further to this, both authors conducted a survey of participants, which, alongside basic demographic information, asked about their participation in 77 folk-related events in the Sheffield area between April and June 2012 inclusive, allowing them to add further local events attended during the specified period. Respondents were approached, initially, via the owners of 40 Sheffield-based, folk-related e-mail lists. They were invited to participate and provided with a (SurveyMonkey) link to the questionnaire. The sample generated by this strategy was boosted by a number of targeted e-mails to key figures in the Sheffield folk world, by the first-named author, with a request to pass on details of, and a link to, the survey. Overall, 188 usable responses were generated, and 101 events, with at least one attendee, were identified.

All survey respondents were anonymous. Following ethnomusicological convention, however, we use real names when describing the world and when drawing upon qualitative sources. The rationale for this is twofold. Performers often like to be credited for their work and maintaining anonymity within a localised community, where roles and voices could easily be identified, despite the use of pseudonyms, is all but impossible in any case.

As this suggests, we adopt a mixed-methods approach to analysis, combining formal social network analysis (SNA) both with more conventional quantitative methods and with qualitative, ethnographic methods. SNA allows us to capture the networked nature of the Sheffield folk world and the existence of distinct 'blocks' of both participants and events within it. The more conventional quantitative approach allows us to demographically profile the network, testing out the abovementioned ideas regarding associations between taste and social position. The qualitative material adds depth and detail to both and also allows us to capture the agency of individual participants who, within a context of relational influence, carve their own 'pathways' (Finnegan 1989) through the folk world.

Generation proves to be a key demographic element in the picture we paint, both in our general characterisation of the folk world and in relation to the differentiation of blocks within it. The picture is complex and nuanced, however, and we hope that we manage to do justice to that fact. We begin with an exposition of Mark's argument.

Mark on taste, ties and niches

Mark begins with the observation, borne out across a number of surveys, that preferences for at least some types of music tend to be strongly correlated with particular socio-demographic variables. Some music is typically preferred by the young, for example; some by particular ethnic groups; and some, as Bourdieu (1984) and Gans (1999) suggest, by those who enjoy higher or lower levels of economic and/or cultural capital. Mark expresses this by suggesting that different musical genres, and we would add music worlds, occupy specific niches in 'social space'.

As Mark conceives of it, following Blau (1977), social space has multiple dimensions, each representing a significant form of status differentiation: e.g. age, income, education and, less obviously, given their categorical nature, gender and ethnicity.[1] Each member of society has a position along each of these dimensions, in virtue of their age, income, etc., and so do tastes. Tastes are located in social space via the mean values for their adherent populations. If the mean age of rock fans is 40, for example, then 'rock' would be located at 40 along the age dimension, and if their mean annual income is £28,000 then rock will be located at point 28 along the income dimension. Or rather, since mean values take no account of dispersion, Mark recommends taking two points 1.5 standard deviations either side of the mean. This has the effect of marking out musical niches in the manner of a box (see Figure 10.1) or, when all dimensions are taken into consideration, a (multi-dimensional) 'hyper-box'. Where tastes have a wide appeal the box will be big but some niches will be very compact.

Mark explains the tendency for tastes to cluster within specific niches in two steps. First, he argues that individuals' musical tastes are shaped by mutual influence within friendship networks. He says almost nothing about the mechanisms involved in this process and does not offer independent evidence that it happens. However, there is a growing body of evidence which supports the idea. A number of surveys indicate that actors tend to have similar musical tastes to those with whom they enjoy a relationship ('taste homophily'[2]) and statistical models, with appropriate controls, identify influence as a key determinate of such patterns (Erickson 1996; Relish 1997; Steglich *et al.* 2006; Upright 2004). Second, he argues that the social networks which shape tastes are themselves shaped by what Lazarsfeld and Merton (1964) call 'status homophily': that is, the tendency, poorly explained in much of this work but empirically demonstrable, for individuals to disproportionately form ties with others of a similar social standing to themselves (e.g. a similar age, gender, ethnicity, occupational status, education, etc.).

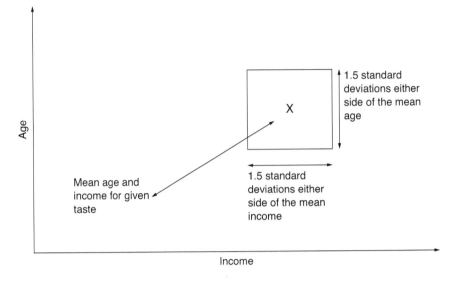

Figure 10.1 Mapping taste niches in social space: a hypothetical and simplified (two-dimensional) example.

This is a diffusion model of taste. Tastes originate somewhere in social space, within the small population of a pioneer world, and they spread outwards from this point of origin through social networks. However, they do not spread evenly in all directions, tending rather to concentrate in particular regions of social space, particular niches, because ties of sociable contact and influence occur much more often between actors of a similar social status.

Mark's model can explain the elite status of certain tastes identified by Bourdieu (1984), Gans (1999) and others (see also Mark 2003). If social elites mix disproportionately with other elites, influencing and being influenced by them, then we would expect certain tastes to become associated with these elites. Similarly, the model resonates with the emphasis upon youth and social class in much early work on sub-cultures, and more recent work on music and ethnicity (e.g. Clarke *et al.* 1993; Rose 1994; Gilroy 1992) As both Shibutani and Dewey observe, closure around status groups minimises cultural transmission and influence between them, resulting in distinct cultures:

> Variations in outlook arise through differential contact and association; the maintenance of social distance – through segregation, conflict or simply the reading of different literature – leads to the formation of distinct cultures. Thus people in different classes develop different modes of life and outlook, not because of anything inherent in economic position, but because similarity of occupation and limitations set by income level dispose them to certain restricted communication channels.
>
> (Shibutani 1955, 565–6)

[S]egregated classes develop their own customs, which is to say their own working morals.... There is no common ground, no moral understanding, no agreed upon standard of appeal.

(Dewey 1988, 58–9)

Furthermore, the status of particular groups 'rubs off' on their tastes. Opera, for example, is perceived and classified as 'high culture' because its audience is drawn primarily from high-status groups. Conversely, jazz was denigrated throughout its early history because of its association with poor blacks (Kofsky 1998).

However, Mark allows that some individuals, as recent debates on middle-class omnivorousness suggest, have diverse tastes and he seeks to explain this by reference to social networks and niches too. Specifically, he argues that individuals who occupy a position in social space where a high number of niches overlap will be more likely to be omnivores because they are likely to be exposed to a higher number of musical forms through their various friendships.

This latter argument risks circularity – actors at particular points in social space tend to have wide-ranging tastes, Mark argues, because they are influenced by (other) actors in that space, who tend to have wide-ranging tastes. Furthermore, the argument does not explain why omnivores tend to be located higher up the socio-economic axis of social space, as most studies suggest. We do find a (network-related) explanation of this, however, in Erickson (1996, see also DiMaggio 1987). She observes that many middle-class occupations require that their incumbents interact positively with a wide range of people from different backgrounds. This, she argues, necessitates a command over a range of taste cultures. Elites use some forms of culture to mark their distinction from others and solidify their domination but they also need to coordinate their activities with their 'subordinates' and, indeed, to coordinate their subordinates, and this requires a popular touch. Politicians, who interact with fellow international leaders in high-cultural contexts but must also pass as 'ordinary' when engaging with voters, provide an obvious example of this. Movement between social circles, Erickson argues, exposes middle-class actors to a wide range of influences and gives them an incentive to acquire competence in a range of cultural forms – which, in turn, increases the likelihood of them acquiring the taste for such diverse forms.

Mark's theory is important, interesting and persuasive. As it stands, however, it is thin on detail and insensitive to complexities in the process it hypothesises. In what follows we aim to add depth, detail and complexity to his model via an exploration of a local musical world. We begin by introducing our case study.

Sheffield's folk world

While 'traditional' or 'folk' repertoires may be performed in many contexts, including classical recitations, community choirs and rugby matches, the folk music world involves a discrete set of actors who identify with what they commonly call 'the folk scene'. These actors form a network, both directly, through mutual acquaintance, and indirectly, through mutual participation in various folk events which are themselves important elements of the folk world. Defined thus, the folk world can be identified and analysed at local, national and international levels. Furthermore, it can be differentiated according to styles and the emphasis put upon, for example, singing, dancing and instrumentation. Our focus here is upon folk singing in Sheffield, a city which boasts a strong folk singing community and high levels of participation, attracting claims in the national specialist press that 'Sheffield has become the new centre of English folk music' (Nickson 2006).

The folk events referred to above assume a variety of forms and are differentiated in a number of ways. On a national level they include large festivals like Glastonbury, which increasingly include folk bands on their roster, and also high profile, dedicated national folk festivals such as the Cambridge Folk Festival. These events involve complex staging, with public address (PA) and lighting systems. And professional folk bands often perform alongside artists representing a wide range of other genres, to equally heterogenous audiences. Audiences for professional, touring folk bands, who often play in Sheffield and its surrounding area, may be less heterogenous, in terms of their tastes, but levels of professionalism, staging devices and performer–audience interactions are much the same, particularly in larger theatres such as the City Hall or Library Theatre.

Local singing sessions and singarounds, by contrast, take place in very different performance spaces and are structured according to very different conventions. Occasionally included in festival programmes but more often functioning independently as regular events within local communities, sessions and singarounds dispense with technicalities of professional staging and PAs, and dissolve distinctions between performer and audience (MacKinnon 1993). They do this in subtly different ways, however. The Kelham Island Singing Session, in Sheffield, for example, meet on the fourth Sunday of the month in the back room of a real-ale pub. Informally led by a core group of three or four people, 20–40 singers meet to share songs. The evening starts around 8 p.m. when one of the core singers, Jess Arrowsmith, strikes up a rousing chorus song, and the rest of the group joins her on the chorus. Another singer from the group takes the next turn to lead. Singing and talking alternate throughout the evening, with people pitching in with a song as the mood takes them. At Raise the Roof, a singaround, by contrast, though everyone present is similarly welcome to sing, the turn of the singer moves incrementally round the room ensuring everyone has an equal opportunity to lead – hence 'singaround'. Both events favour chorus songs, ensuring maximum participation from those present and participation in the act of singing is the organising ethos, in contrast to the performance–reception structure of the larger gigs mentioned above.

Other events strike a balance between these forms of performance and find a way of combining elements of both. The Sheffield Sessions Festival organisers, for example, use a PA and staging for their headliner gigs, but also provide opportunities for audience participation through sessions. And folk clubs typically offer a blend. At the Beehive Folk Club, for example, invited guests appear for a paying audience. Unlike bigger concerts, however, the guest set is preceded by performances from 'floor singers' – members of the audience who sing one or two songs each. Combined with the efforts of many guest performers to break down audience–performer distinctions through personalised song introductions and interaction with audiences before and after their performance, these events provide a unique form of participatory entertainment (for more on staging devices see Mackinnon 1993).

In addition to performance structures there is a wide variety in repertoire type. The question 'What is a folk song?' is debated by those involved in the folk world as ardently as by academic observers (for perspectives from each period of folk song resurgence see Sharp 1907; Harker 1985). The events in Sheffield represent a broad range of interpretations. The singers at Sheffield Ballads Club, for example, perform repertoires from or related to sources collected around the mid-nineteenth to early twentieth century (for a fuller discussion on English ballads, see Atkinson 2002), while American interpretations of folk and con-temporary social-political commentary (see Rahn 2001), found in the early work of Bob Dylan, and also pop songs, particularly including the Beatles' repertoire, are sung at Royal Folk. Representing two further strands, The Greystones affords a space for contemporary singer-songwriters to perform, while well-known local singer, Vikki Appleton-Fielden, writes and performs comic parodies of tradi-tional songs at Raise the Roof among other places.

These song types project different ideals. Tradition, social commentary and participation figure in most folk repertoires to varying degrees but the emphasis differs. Thus, at Sheffield Ballads, the preservation of tradition through perform-ance is primary; at Raise Your Banners the political content of songs and the protest element involved in singing them is key; and at Raise the Roof, public participation is higher on the agenda.

Context shapes the way singers perform. However, the same songs are often performed in different contexts and, in this sense, context and repertoire vary independently of one another, each constituting a distinct axis of differentiation and taste. For example, traditional ballads can be performed both within the singing session context and upon a Glastonbury stage. Similarly, singer-songwriters can appear both in highly mediated environments and within an acoustic session. Indeed the same person may perform the same song in different contexts, adapting their style as they perceive to be appropriate.

Jon Boden, for example, is the lead singer of Bellowhead, an internationally acclaimed band who have appeared on *Later … With Jools Holland* and have been playlisted on BBC Radio 2. With Bellowhead, Jon performs 'Byker Hill', a song of north-east mining origin, within a 12-piece band arrangement (Bellow-head 2012). In addition, however, Jon occasionally attends the Kelham Island Singing Session; here he sings the song unaccompanied, with audience participa-tion on the chorus. In Figures 10.2 and 10.3 Jon can be seen in each of these contexts. The images illustrate the structural differences described above, includ-ing staging and seating practices, but these are not only physical differences, they also affect the approach to sonic behaviour. Folk participants are attuned to

Figure 10.2 Jon Boden performs with Bellowhead.

Figure 10.3 Jon Boden at Kelham Island Singing Session (far right, side profile).

these variations and, as we elaborate below, carve their own pathway through the options available.

These and other such distinctions are not registered in the surveys referred to in the introduction to our chapter. If folk music is referred to at all it is as a single, undifferentiated genre. They matter academically, however, because they matter within the folk world, to participants who orient to them when carving out their pathways through the folk world. We return to these pathways. First, however, we must consider the networked character of the folk world and its location in social space.

The folk world as a network

While a taste for folk music may be satisfied, for some people, through recordings and an occasional gig, others are drawn to participate in the many local events and clubs referred to above, and often to a series of local events. This creates a two-mode network of participants linked to events as we see in Figure 10.4, which visualises the ties of participation captured in our survey. The grey circular nodes are participants, the black square nodes are events, and participants are linked by connecting lines to those events which they attended.

This is not only a network of participants to events, however. As Feld's (1981, 1982) work on network foci suggests, such events generate ties and thereby networks between participants by drawing them together in the same places, at the same times and in a context framed by their shared interests (see also Lizardo 2006, 2011). This facilitates and encourages the formation of participant-to-participant networks. Furthermore, the movement of participants between different events creates a flow of gossip and resources between those events, effectively generating an event-to-event network. Thus, as with many two-mode networks (Breiger 1974), we may decompose the network represented in Figure 10.4 into two single-mode networks (Figures 10.5 and 10.6).

We present a more sophisticated analysis of our two-mode network and its single-mode derivatives later in the chapter. For present purposes, note that it is highly cohesive. Each participant enjoys contact, on average, with 96 others (although the standard deviation (SD) of 45 is high) and 51 per cent of all possible contact between participants is realised. In addition, a further 42 per cent of pairs are linked by only one intermediary. Likewise, each of our events is connected by at least one common participant to 36 other such events, on average (SD = 23), with 36 per cent of all possible connections between events actualised. We would expect ideas, innovation, gossip and perhaps other resources to move very quickly and efficiently through this network. Moreover, the work of Coleman (1990) and Burt (2005) suggests that such cohesion tends to cultivate mutual support, commitment incentives and a sense of trust, solidarity and collective identity.

Our qualitative data also point to cohesion. Although it is unlikely that everybody attending an event, and particularly a large or one-off event, would either know or get to know everybody else at that event, participants indicate that their

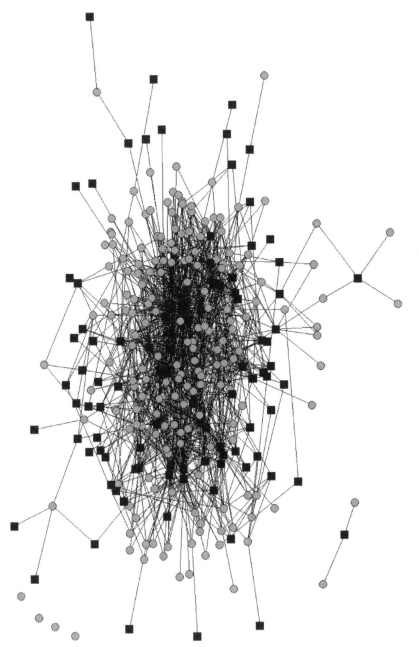

Figure 10.4 The Sheffield folk world as a two-mode network of participants and events.

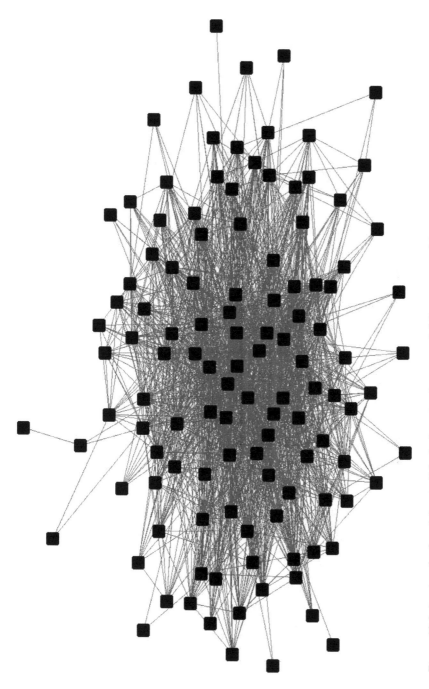

Figure 10.5 A network of participants, linked where they have attended four or more of the same events (isolates removed).

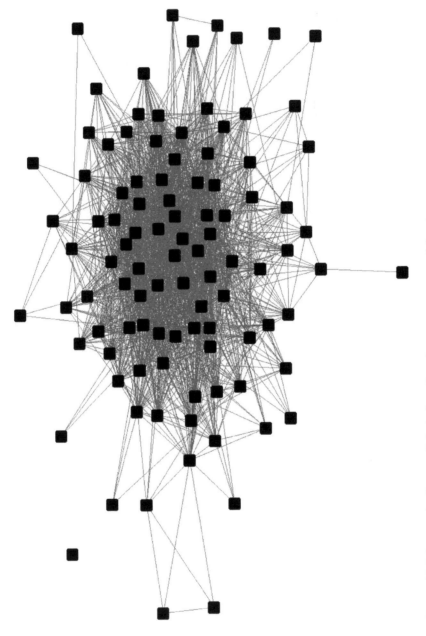

Figure 10.6 A network of events, linked where they share one or more participants.

involvement in the folk world has led to the formation of many new and significant friendships. The folk world is a site of sociability and friendship as well as music:

> Most friends are folkies, though not all sing.
>
> (Peter Burdett, diary, 2007)

> After 13 years [my friends] are mostly on the folk scene, and most of them sing somewhere.
>
> (Bob Butler, diary, 2007)

> Probably most of the friends I've made over the past twenty years are singers of one sort or another (which gives you a notion of the narrowness of my social circle...).
>
> (Raymond Greenoaken, diary, 2007)

The observation that 'most' of the interviewees' friends are involved in the folk world suggests, as Finnegan's (1989, 58) analysis of the Milton Keynes folk world also found, that much of our participants' time is given over to participation, an observation they confirm:

> I don't have time to be involved in anything outside the folk scene.
>
> (Bob Butler, diary, 2007)

> [I]t's almost my only reason for going out in the evenings – folk clubs and concerts.
>
> (Peter Burnett, diary, 2007)

Significant involvement in any music world draws heavily upon participants' time, energy and money, all of which are scarce resources, leaving them with reduced scope to develop further interests and ties. This, moreover, can have the effect of locking them into the world. As Crossley (2008a) has said of gym participants, the concentration of friendships within a particular social world provides positive incentives for continued participation (i.e. friendship) and negative sanctions for withdrawal (i.e. likely loss of a primary friendship group).

Furthermore, in many cases involvement is closely interwoven with identity. Even those with relatively low levels of attendance often attach considerable importance to their involvement. Attendee of various unaccompanied singing sessions, Jerry Simon, for example, finds that singing is a very big part of his life; 'though perhaps more in terms of importance rather than the number of evenings singing per week' (diary, 2007). Similarly, professional singer, Gavin Davenport, describes his participation as 'a crucial part of me, and of the community that I feel myself a part of' (diary, 2007). Raymond Greenoaken, singer and editor of *Stirrings* magazine (see below), specifies the 'spiritual' value of participation in the folk world:

[I] can't imagine a meaningful life without it; but nor could I imagine making any money out of it. So at a material level it's very unimportant, but at a, um, spiritual level it's the very stuff of life.

(Diary, 2007)

These observations serve as a useful corrective to the tendency in some academic work, including, in practice if not in theory, Mark's, to reduce taste to mere expressed preference for a musical genre (see also Hennion 2004). The taste for folk is an activity bound in various ways with a wider lifestyle, friendship network and identity. Rather than merely seeing it as a way to fill leisure time, folk singers include their singing and wider participation within their sense of their place in the world (for further discussion on the impacts of 'serious leisure' see Stebbins 1996, 2007).

In addition, networks shaped, via focal events, by tastes may themselves further shape tastes in various ways. First, as noted above, ties can 'lock' participants into worlds, entrenching and deepening a taste that may otherwise have been short-lived and shallow. Second, discussion and exchange of recordings may sensitise the individual's hearing to previously inaudible nuances. Third, competition for in-group status may incentivise greater commitment (Riesman 1950). Finally, a critical and connected mass of enthusiasts will facilitate organisation of activities that would not otherwise be possible, exposing participants to new musical forms and potentially transformative experiences (Crossley 2008b, 2009, 2015).

Folk world and social space

Having introduced the folk world and briefly explored its networked character we turn now to its location in social space. Following Mark we have sought to specify the demographic profile of participants. Before we introduce these data, however, it is necessary to outline the hypotheses that informed our survey and the thinking that lay behind them.

Like the wider UK and US folk worlds, the Sheffield folk world emerged in the context of the late 1960s–early 1970s folk revival, which had a strong root, via student societies, in the universities and which was nested in the wider student movement of that time (see MacKinnon 1993, Boyes 1993, Brocken 2003 and Sweers 2005). The revival had a strong root in the universities. Folk music was rediscovered and revived through university societies. Jenny Day, one of the original organisers of the monthly Raise the Roof club in the 1980s describes how she got involved:

I am of an age to have done Singing Together and Country Dancing at junior school [late 1940s]. The dances were fairly simple ceilidh dances and the songs were mostly folk songs. Some rather strange for [children]....
[There was a b]it of a gap between 12 to 16 and then when Ron went to college [1960s] he roomed next door to a guy who played the guitar and he

took up the guitar himself. His colleague was mainly a jazz musician but in the summer time played at holiday resorts and learned many folk songs which Ron picked up. We then started a folk club in Scarborough and have been interested ever since.

(Jenny Day, email correspondence, 2013)

Jenny was familiar with folk music from school but it was later, after a gap, when 'Ron went to college' in the 1960s, at the start of the folk revival, that her current interest was sparked. Significantly, she is also a longstanding political activist, reflecting the association of the folk revival with the politics of the student movement during the 1960s (on the US experience, see Eyerman and Jamison 1998)

The formative role of the folk revival in relation to the contemporary folk world led us to hypothesise a concentration of 55–65 year olds among our survey participants. Developing Mark's ideas, we contend that tastes are, among other things, generational. Actors acquire tastes through interaction with friends and friends tend to be of a similar age. More importantly, core musical preferences and related identities tend to be formed during youth, when actors have a greater opportunity to participate in music-related activities and to make music central to their lives and identities. Enthusiasm and identification often persist but research on older music enthusiasts suggests that most pursue the styles of their youth (e.g. Bennett 2006, 2013; Bennett and Hodkinson 2012; Gibson 2010; Smith 2009). Given that those who were in their late teens during the folk revival, in the late 1960s and early 1970s, will be in their late fifties and early sixties now, therefore, we would expect a majority of folk enthusiasts to be in that age bracket.

This hypothesis is further informed by ethnographically based knowledge of the relative closure and underground nature of the folk world (Hield 2010). A general lack of promotion outside the specialist media keeps smaller folk events beneath the radar of those not already involved. And the specialist press is mostly only available at folk events, so one must already be involved to gain access to it. Specialist media function well to diversify experience for those already involved in the folk world (see below) but they do not support discovery of and entry into that world. This tends to insulate the folk world from uniniti-ated outsiders and makes personal connection the key means of access and recruitment to it. The information necessary for entry is almost exclusively avail-able through direct connection to other participants and event organisers, which, to reiterate, is more likely where a potential participant is of the same generation as these gatekeepers.

There are exceptions. Participants are in some cases recruited by means of larger, publicised and more open events. The Peace in the Park festival and Shef-field Green Fair, for example, both attracted new, younger audiences and also participants with a longstanding interest in folk who do not commit to regular folk club attendance. Furthermore, parents often transmit their love of folk to their children, countering the tendency to generational closure. Hield (2010) has found significant ethnographic evidence for this in the Sheffield case and it is more generally observable at the level of such high-profile 'folk families' as the Waterson: Carthys, the Lakemans and the Unthanks, and also by the recent relaunch (in Sheffield) of Ashley Hutchins' Albion Band by, among others, his son. We return to this. For the moment it must suffice to say that we do not expect these countervailing factors to be so strong as to cancel out the age skew that we have hypothesised.

Given the importance of university campuses in the story of the folk revival we further hypothesise that the highly educated will be disproportionately represented in the Sheffield folk world. The folk revival comprised collective action by students (predominantly) and it was most accessible, geographically and socially, to those who frequented and felt at home on a university campus (i.e. students). In addition, given the ethnic homogeneity of university populations during the 1960s, we would expect participants to be disproportionately white.

Our survey data support these hypotheses. Although the mean age of our respondents is 51, the 55–65 age group is significantly overrepresented (see Figure 10.7). Likewise the highly educated (see Figure 10.8). Furthermore, although our ethnicity question was flawed,[3] it appears that the whole sample were white European.

Given the under-representation of women in many music worlds (e.g. Bayton 1998, Cohen 1997, Finnegan 1989) and Bourdieu's (1984) insistence upon the importance of economic capital we also asked about gender and income bracket. Women made up 45 per cent of respondents, suggesting a slight gender imbalance but the income distribution had no particular skew, even when the unwaged

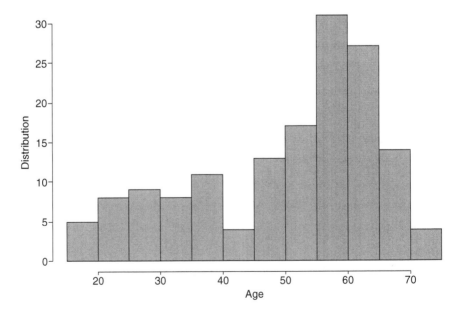

Figure 10.7 The age distribution of the Sheffield folk world.

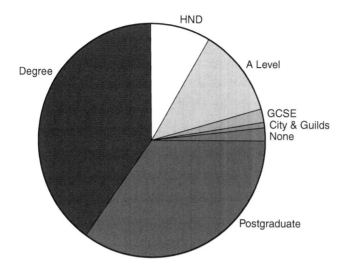

Figure 10.8 Highest formal educational qualification.

(students and retirees) were controlled for. Folk enthusiasts do not appear to be recruited from any particular income bracket – although, of course, their income distribution may not match that of the wider population.

These findings match a survey of folk club audiences conducted in the 1990s by Niall MacKinnon (1993), suggesting that the demographic type has remained throughout the period from 1970s to the present day. Our sample is older but that is to be expected given the passage of time and the fact, indicated by our ethnographic data, that older participants typically have a long history of involvement.

Pathways and emergent conventions

Our findings support Mark's theory, as we have developed and applied it. The folk world occupies and recruits from within a specific niche in social space, at least in terms of age, education and ethnicity. This is important but these broad associations mask complexities which require further investigation. As noted above, the folk world is internally differentiated and participants must negotiate these distinctions and carve out their own pathway through. We suggest in the final section of this chapter that this process too is shaped by location in social space. Before we discuss this, however, it is important to illuminate its nuances and complexity.

As indicated in our survey, participants are often members of more than one club. In many cases this is necessary to provide them with the frequency and regularity of involvement that they desire. Some events, such as Cobden View and The Rock, meet weekly, for example, but many, such as Raise the Roof, Royal Traditions and Kelham Island Singing Session, are monthly, so that singers who wish to sing more than once a month need to attend more than one of these events.

Involvement in folk events can be fluid. In contrast to certain other singing groups, such as community choirs and barbershop choruses, there is no requirement to come to each meeting. Singers and audiences can attend sporadically. There are no negative sanctions dissuading this. However, many groups have regular, core members. And regular attendance and commitment are rewarded with status (Smith 1987).

Nobody can attend everything, however. The sheer quantity of events, the inevitable time clashes between some and the limits to individual time, energy and money all require participants to make choices and forge what Finnegan (1989) calls 'pathways' through the folk world. These pathways are shaped by variation in the stylistic and participatory conventions of particular events, and their correspondence (or not) to finer taste distinctions within the broader category of folk singing. Many clubs claim that everyone is welcome to sing and that they can sing whatever they like:

> We encourage anyone to sing, we don't mind what they sing.
>
> (Jenny Day, diary, 2007)

> The rule is – sing whatever you want to sing.
>
> (Bob Butler, diary, 2007)

However, the demand that competing and conflicting tastes be accommodated and coordinated has inevitably given rise to different performance and repertoire conventions at specific events. Furthermore, events acquire reputations for particular conventions, tending therefore to disproportionately attract participants with a preference for those conventions and setting in motion a self-fulfilling prophecy whereby different events reflect different sub-divisions of the more generic 'taste for folk'.

Participants, not surprisingly, attend those events whose conventions are to their taste. People who like singing ballads and who identify with more traditional notions of folk might be drawn to the Sheffield Ballads Club, for example, whereas those who prefer more pop influenced folk find a home at Acoustic Rotherham. In addition, they fit their contribution at a particular event to the conventions of that event:

> I went for things with choruses as that's what they usually sing.
>
> (Philip Shaw, diary 2007)

And if they are unfamiliar with the conventions of a regular event many hang back to gauge what is appropriate before fully joining in:

> The only way to know if your style or repertoire type fits with the group ideal is to listen to other performers to get the feel of the audience.
>
> (Paul Davenport, email, 2013)

I try not to go first so I can get a feel for the usual songs. Then I'll pull out whatever feels right – if people are singing chorus songs, so will I.

(Paddy Rose, email, 2013)

If we visit a new club I always try to gauge what is appropriate and what is not. I choose what I play accordingly. Even when I play at [my regular club] I don't have a set plan as to what I'm going to play and decide literally on the spot depending on what others are playing or what is the mood of the room.

(William McFarlane, email, 2013)

There are quite a few new performers at the Crookes Club and about three of four weeks ago a group of five or six younger people came along (I think they might be students as it is a student area). Me being me, I got chatting to them and asked if they played. They said yes but wanted to see what sort of things people played before committing to playing. I am very pleased to say that they have been every week since and one or two have now started to play and join in.

(William McFarlane, email, 2013)

Furthermore, participants often judge their performance retrospectively by reference to the responses of others, using this information to guide any future participation:

I judge it by the applause, the encouragement I receive to attend and sing, compliments I receive and the interest people show in what I sing.

(Bob Butler, diary, 2007)

And where there is a rift between personal taste and that of the group, and a singer feels that their style doesn't fit, they might decide not to participate.

[I] attended a social/folk gathering where the material being sung was very 'Mid-Atlantic' and the dominant people were clearly into a more 'pop' style. So declined the offer to contribute because repertoire would not have been suited to the ambience.

(Paul Davenport, email, 2013)

However, in such cases the network allows people to be directed to more appropriate events: one event serving as a portal to others. If a singer shows a preference for a certain type of music, others with knowledge of events which cater for such tastes may pass on this information. Once within the world participants have access to a good information network regarding a wide range of events. Navigation may require perseverance, however. Newcomers who feel they don't fit in can fall out of the musical world before finding a place that suits them.

This process is further facilitated by the mediated networks of the folk world. A key information source for those more actively involved and present at the events where it is sold is *Stirrings*, a quarterly magazine which supports 'folk roots and acoustic music in South Yorks and beyond' (Stirrings 2013). The approximately 62-page magazine includes a diary of upcoming events, CD reviews, advertisements and articles of interest to the folk community. Its directory lists 51 regular sessions and 47 folk clubs in their area of coverage. In addition, national and international magazines provide information regarding recording artists, events and activities further afield, with festivals in particular drawing audiences from around the country. And the national folk world has a strong on-line presence, including fROOTS forum, TradSong (both discussion groups) and Mudcat Café (repertoire sharing site).

Evolution of the event network

Neither individual event conventions nor the event network are set in stone. Both are maintained through practice and potentially subject to change. Events typically catering to the taste for one type of folk music may evolve such that they cater for another if the composition of its participants and their tastes change. And where specific tastes are not catered for, new events can be launched, drawing from the wider network while simultaneously reconfiguring it. The network is constantly evolving. While clubs like Raise the Roof have been running in some form for over 30 years, for example, other events have closed and new events have been established. For example, Bright Phoebus was created by a group of professional folk musicians in the area who wanted to form a semi-regular club, with a house band, to promote large-scale gigs in the city centre. In this way the local folk world becomes more internally diverse and differentiated, reflecting but also cultivating a range of finer grained aesthetic distinctions, including, for example, the taste for chorus-heavy songs (Raise the Roof, Kelham Island Singing Session) and for Irish material (Irish Heartland, Fagans). Each event fills a niche in the market, while remaining closely linked to other events.

The emergence of new events can cause competition and conflict. Tensions occasionally arise when a one-off concert is programmed for the same evening as a regular event, for example, creating direct competition. On the whole, however, organisers of regular events do not seem to view one another as rivals, not least because the flow of many of the same people through different events prevents an us-and-them situation from emerging. Links between events, formed by shared audiences, which are especially common where events draw upon the similar stylistic and performance conventions, ease tensions and encourage cooperation and mutual support. Dissimilar events with fewer common participants are more inclined to conflict and compete. However, such competition is more ideological than economic. Factions do not expect to attract the same participants and so do not compete over who attracts whom.

Many participants enjoy a variety of different event sub-genres. Jemma Gurney, for example, goes to a number of contexts; she enjoys singing sessions but also attends both larger concerts at the City Hall and community festivals like the Sheffield Green Fair. Singers with wide repertoires, like William McFarlane, enjoy attending a number of different kinds of events:

> My repertoire is quite varied so I have something suitable for every occasion depending on where I am playing. A lot of what I play and sing is blues based and I am known for playing steel slide guitar or even a bit of ragtime. However, I do also sing unaccompanied and have even written a song of my own which I have performed at Paul and Liz's ballad session.
>
> (William McFarlane, email, 2013)

The loose nature of folk event membership enables people to move freely between events acting as culture brokers between friendship- and style-based clusters (Noyes 1995). As the notion of clusters suggests, however, individual pathways tend to coalesce in collective patterns (and are not therefore as individual as they may seem). A cluster of like-minded friends and fans has formed around events organised by Jess and Richard Arrowsmith, for example, including singing sessions at the Kelham Island Tavern and the Hillsborough Hotel, and also local gigs for their bands, Crucible and The Melrose Quartet. Similarly, Bright Phoebus and Royal Traditions have common organisers so share a mailing list and attract a core audience from the same pool of people.

These clusters reflect tastes and pathways. This raises the question whether, like the broader taste for participation in the folk world, they occupy distinct positions in social space. If position in social space affects the music worlds that actors participate in, then it might also shape their pathway through a given world. In what follows we offer evidence to suggest that it does.

Folk generations

We noted above that the taste for folk is often passed through families (Smith 2009, 2012 suggests something similar in the world of Northern Soul). The children of 1960–70s singers have enjoyed a direct introduction to the inner workings of the folk world, often from a young age. And in some cases they have been able to widen the appeal of folk within their own generational cohort, recruiting younger members to the folk world. The tastes of younger folk enthusiasts have not always been identical to those of the parental generation, however, so that at least some of the new events emerging within the event network represent not only new taste niches within the folk world but also a younger demographic.

The University of Sheffield's folk music and dance society, CeilidhSoc, for example, was formed in the 1990s by a group of students who had often been introduced to folk music by their parents. Out of this group, Jess and Richard Arrowsmith, Gavin Davenport and Helena Reynolds formed the band Crucible. As noted above, this group established sessions and local concerts, forming the focus for one of the noticeable clusters in the Sheffield folk world network.

The younger generation are more likely to play or sing as a group in sessions, feeling more comfortable in this environment, and they are more likely to pursue careers as professional performers. The older generation, by contrast, participate more in amateur performance contexts and often enjoy the opportunity for a solo slot afforded at many traditional folk clubs. Differences are not categorical. Younger people attend folk clubs and older people attend sessions. However, there is a tendency to separation along these lines.

Furthermore, the political leaning of the groups tends to differ, with the longer-established folk clubs retaining a traditional socialist discourse, while the younger generation – at Sheffield's Green Fair, for example – though often left leaning, adopt a more contemporary political style. And political identity is foregrounded to a greater extent by the older generation. While it is rare for in-depth political discussion to take place within folk clubs, political parodies concerning current affairs and reference to contemporary or historical politics can be incorporated into singers' introductions. Singers may express support for the political content of a song, for example, or dissociate themselves from it. And they often assume similar views on behalf of their audience. An example of this is found in Gordon Hoyland's introduction to 'A Few Jovial Sportsmen' at Folk at Home:

> I'll give you one of my hunting songs. If anyone takes offence please feel free to go [audience laughs]. It doesn't faze me at all, I think they need to be sung anyway.
>
> (Field recording, 2008)

The assumption of political homogeneity in such claims is resented by some, particularly younger participants, and politicised introductions are less prevalent in the events organised and favoured by them. As Smith (2009, 2012) found in relation to the world of Northern Soul, age can a source of (gentle and subtle) division.

Such differences are often subtle but they make participants feel more or less at home within different kinds of folk event:

> In Sheffield we fit in fortunately, due to our long standing and in association with our son and friends. But, it is becoming very difficult for older performers to get gigs because there is now a perceived belief that younger is better. Last year we ran a concert at the festival in Sheffield called, 'Rarely Heard' in which a number of older performers played. These were 'names' back in the '70s but now many felt forgotten or lacking in confidence to 'compete' with the younger set.
>
> (Paul Davenport, email, 2013)

> I think the reason that the Crookes club has such a diverse cross-section of ages is because it is more an acoustic music club than a traditional folk club in the strictest sense. Therefore, the cross-section of music played there is also very diverse. Performers don't feel that they can't play a particular song

or tune because it is not regarded as traditional. However, there is also a reasonable amount of traditional and new folk songs and tunes played there.

(William McFarlane, email, 2013)

As a final step in our analysis we elected to see whether these ethnographic observations regarding generational differences show up in the network structure captured in our survey. We began by performing a hierarchical cluster analysis on our actor–events matrix, seeking out clusters of both participants and events, and bringing the results together in the manner of a two-mode blockmodel. We decided upon a three-block partition of participants and a five-block partition of events, deriving inter-block densities by calculating the total number of events attended in a particular event block, by each distinct participant block, and dividing by the number of events that could theoretically have been attended, given both the number of participants and the number of events in the respective blocks. For sake of clarity the results were then multiplied by 100 to give percentages. The results are given in Table 10.1.

It is immediately obvious that Participant Block 1 is defined by relatively low levels of participation across all event blocks and Event Block 1 by relatively low levels of attendance from participants across all blocks. In the case of the participant blocks we explored this further by comparing mean events attended (see Figure 10.9). Using UCINET's network-friendly ANOVA algorithm we confirmed that the difference between these means is statistically significant at the 0.01 level. Participants in Block 1 are distinguished by their relatively low levels of participation.

The comparison of means also suggests a quantitative difference in network attendance between Participant Blocks 2 and 3, with participants in Block 2 having higher levels of attendance. However, the difference between these two blocks is not restricted to sheer levels of attendance. Table 10.1 points to a different pattern in events attended. Specifically, Participant Block 2 has a much higher rate of participation in Event Block 2 but a significantly lower rate of participation in Event Blocks 3 and 4.

Though it is not possible to account for every event in every block, the events in Blocks 2, 3 and 4, respectively, fit the picture suggested by our ethnographic observations. Block 2 includes many of the types of events that younger

Table 10.1 A two-mode blockmodel of the Sheffield folk world (%)

	Events				
	Block 1 (n = 67)	Block 2 (n = 17)	Block 3 (n = 3)	Block 4 (n = 9)	Block 5 (n = 5)
Participants					
Block 1 (n = 79)	1	6	14	2	4
Block 2 (n = 48)	3	38	44	13	38
Block 3 (n = 61)	2	9	56	21	42

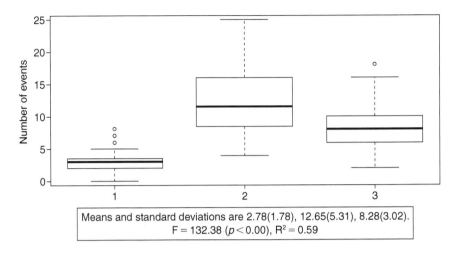

Figure 10.9 Number of events attended by block.

participants found less to their taste, according to our ethnographic data, and Block 3 includes all of the events which they organised to better cater to their own tastes.

This raises the question of the socio-demographic composition of our participant blocks and, in particular, whether the age profiles of Blocks 2 and 3 differ significantly, as we would predict on the basis of the ethnographic observation. They do. As Figure 10.10 shows, Block 3 members are, on average, 13 years younger than Block 2 members. Furthermore, as Table 10.2 shows, this is not the only demographic difference. Where males outweigh females in Blocks 1 and 2, the reverse is the case in Block 3. Moreover, Block 3 is distinct in having

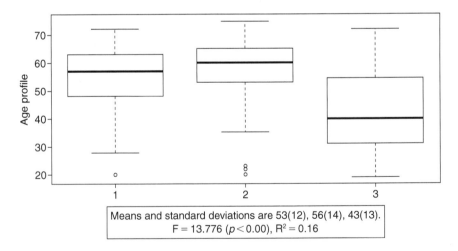

Figure 10.10 The age profile of the three participant blocks.

Table 10.2 Other relevant block demographics

	Gender		Highest educational qualification			Employment status		
	Male	*Female*	*Below degree*	*Degree*	*Postgraduate*	*Employed*	*Retired*	*Other*
Block 1	34	20	15	24	15	32	16	6
Block 2	29	17	15	17	14	19	23	4
Block 3	21	29	9	18	24	41	5	5

a high proportion of postgraduates within its ranks. And Block 2 is distinguished by its high proportion of retirees. Blocks 2 and 3 occupy different niches in social space.

This analysis identifies tendencies rather than hard and fast divisions. However, they are interesting tendencies which correspond to the ethnographic findings discussed above. And together these findings point to the complexities in the relations between taste and social networks referred to at the start of the chapter.

Conclusions

In this chapter we have explored the relationship between networks, tastes and their niche positions in social space by way of a detailed analysis of Sheffield's folk singing world. Our analysis offers some support for and development of Mark's (1998, 2003) analysis, suggesting both that worlds occupy particular positions in social space, on account of network influences, and that pathways through worlds may be similarly shaped. The interplay of tastes and ties is more complex than this suggests, however, and we have sought to draw out some of these complexities. Taste has more facets than typical survey modules capture and not only in the respect of breaking down into ever finer sub-genre categories. It extends, for example, to performance styles and context-conventions. And it runs much deeper than the notion of 'preference' might suggest, in some cases consuming all of an individual's spare time and forming a crucial part of their identity and meaningful orientation towards the world.

Furthermore, though tastes certainly are transmitted through networks, this process too is complex and tastes are changed in ways which then act back upon networks. Networks shape tastes and their distribution but tastes evolve as an effect of other factors too and they shape networks, not least as participants, guided by their tastes, forge pathways through music worlds and, in some cases, where dissatisfied by the range of events available, mobilise their contacts to establish new ones.

Notes

1 We mean less obvious in the sense that it is difficult to think of categorical attributes such as gender and ethnicity in terms of a continuous axis or scale. Notwithstanding this conceptual matter, however, there is good evidence that both gender and ethnicity affect participation in music worlds. Specifically, gender seems to function as a barrier to participation for women, across a range of worlds, while ethnicity is often a significant factor affecting music taste and the specific worlds in which social actors engage.
2 Taste homophily is a variant upon what Lazarsfeld and Merton (1964) call 'value homophily' and which they distinguish from 'status homophily'. We turn to status homophily later in the chapter.
3 The question was open-ended, which led to some confusion. However, only two responses suggested anything other than a white respondent. One said 'alien', which was probably a joke. The other said 'mixed', which could have implied mixed race but in a context where some respondents said 'mixed, English-Irish' may have meant that. That one respondent replied 'the usual' reinforces our sense of ethnic homogeneity.

References

Atkinson, D. (2002) *The English Traditional Ballad: Theory, Method, and Practice*, Aldershot, Ashgate.

Bayton, M. (1998) *Frock Rock*, Oxford, Oxford University Press.

Becker, H. (1982) *Art Worlds*, Berkeley, University of California Press.

Bellowhead (2012) 'Byker Hill', *Broadside*, Navigator Records, Navigator073.

Bennett, A. (2006) Punk's Not Dead, *Sociology* 40, 219–35.

Bennett, A. (2013) *Music, Style and Aging*, Philadelphia, PA, Temple University Press.

Bennett, A. and Hodkinson, P. (eds) (2012) *Ageing and Youth Cultures*, New York, Berg.

Bennett, T., Savage, M., Silva, E. and Warde, A. (2009) *Culture, Class, Distinction*, London, Routledge.

Blau, P. (1977) A Macrosociological Theory of Social Structure, *American Journal of Sociology* 83(1), 26–54.

Bottero, W. and Crossley, N. (2011) Worlds, Fields and Networks, *Cultural Sociology* 5(1), 99–119.

Bourdieu, P. (1984) *Distinction*, London, Routledge.

Boyes, G. (1993) *The Imagined Village: Culture, Ideology and the English Folk Revival*, Manchester, Manchester University Press.

Breiger, R. (1974) The Duality of Persons and Groups, *Social Forces* 53(2), 181–90.

Brocken, M. (2003) *The British Folk Revival 1944–2002*, Aldershot, Ashgate.

Bryson, B. (1996) Anything but Heavy Metal, *American Sociological Review* 61(5), 884–99.

Bryson, B. (1997) What about the Univores? *Poetics* 25, 141–56.

Burt, R. (2005) *Brokerage and Closure*, Oxford, Oxford University Press.

Chan, T. and Goldthorpe, J. (2007) Social Stratification and Cultural Consumption: Music in England, *European Sociological Review* 23(1), 1–19.

Clarke, J., Hall, S., Jefferson, T. and Roberts, B. (1993) Subcultures, Cultures and Class, in Hall, S. and Jefferson, T. (eds), *Resistance Through Rituals*, London, Routledge, 9–79.

Cohen, S. (1997) Men Making A Scene, in Whiteley, S. (ed.), *Sexing the Groove*, London, Routledge, 17–36.

Coleman, J. (1990) *Foundations of Social Theory*, Cambridge, MA, Belknap Press.

Crossley, N. (2008a) (Net)Working Out: Social Capital in a Private Health Club, *British Journal of Sociology* 59(3), 475–500.

Crossley, N. (2008b) Pretty Connected: The Social Network of the Early UK Punk Movement, *Theory, Culture and Society* 25(6), 89–116.

Crossley, N. (2009) The Man Whose Web Expanded: Network Dynamics in Manchester's Post-Punk Music Scene 1976–1980, *Poetics* 37(1), 24–49.

Crossley, N. (2011) *Towards Relational Sociology*, London, Routledge.

Crossley, N. (2015) *Networks of Sound, Style and Subversion: The Punk and Post-Punk Musical Worlds of Manchester, London, Liverpool and Sheffield 1976–1980*, Manchester, Manchester University Press.

Dewey, J. (1988) *Human Nature and Conduct*, Carbondale, Southern Illinois University Press.

DiMaggio, P. (1987) Classification in Art, *American Sociological Review* 52(4), 440–55.

Erickson, B. (1996) Culture, Class and Connections, *American Journal of Sociology* 102(1), 217–51.

Eyerman, R. and Jamison, A. (1998) *Music and Social Movements*, Cambridge, Cambridge University Press.

Feld, S. (1981) The Focused Organisation of Social Ties, *American Journal of Sociology* 86, 1015–35.

Feld, S. (1982) Social Structural Determinants of Similarity among Associates, *American Sociological Review* 47, 797–801.

Finnegan, R. (1989) *The Hidden Musicians: Music-Making in an English Town*, Cambridge, Cambridge University Press.

fRoots, (2013) Online forum, available at www.froots.net/phpBB2/ (accessed 17 April 2013).

Gilroy, P. (1992) *There Ain't No Black in the Union Jack*, London, Routledge.

Gans, H. (1999) *Popular Culture and High Culture*, New York, Basic Books.

Gibson, L. (2010) Popular Music and the Life Course, PhD thesis, Department of Sociology, University of Manchester.

Harker, D. (1985) *Fakesong: The Manufacture of British 'Folksong', 1700 to the Present Day*, Milton Keynes, Open University Press.

Hennion, A. (2004) Pragmatics of Taste, in Jacobs, M. and Hanrahan, N. (eds), *Blackwell Companion to the Sociology of Culture*, Oxford, Blackwell, 131–44.

Hield, F. (2010) English Folk Singing and the Construction of Community, PhD thesis, University of Sheffield.

Kofsky, F. (1998) *Black Music, White Business*, New York, Pathfinder.

Lazarsfeld, P. and Merton, R. (1964) Friendship as Social Process, in Berger, M., Abel, T. and Page, C. (eds), *Freedom and Control in Modern Society*, New York, Octagon Books, 18–66.

Lewis. K., Kaufman, J., Gonzalez, M., Wimmer, A. and Christakis, N. (2008) Tastes, Ties and Time, *Social Networks* 30, 330–42.

Lizardo, O. (2006) How Cultural Tastes Shape Personal Networks, *American Sociological Review* 71, 778–807.

Lizardo, O. (2011) Cultural Correlates of Ego–Net Closure, *Sociological Perspectives* 54(3), 479–87.

Lopes, P. (2002) *The Rise of a Jazz Art World*, Cambridge, Cambridge University Press.

MacKinnon, N. (1993) *The British Folk Scene: Musical Performance and Social Identity*, Buckingham, Open University Press.

Maréchal, G. (2010) Autoethnography, in Mills, Albert J., Durepos, Gabrielle and Wiebe, Elden (eds), *Encyclopedia of Case Study Research*, Vol. 2, Thousand Oaks, CA, Sage Publications, 43–45.

Mark, N. (1998) Birds of a Feather Sing Together, *Social Forces* 77(2), 453–85.

Mark, N. (2003) Culture and Competition: Homophily and Distancing Explanations for Cultural Niches, *American Sociological Review* 68(3), 319–45.

Martin, P. (2005) The Jazz Community as an Art World, *Jazz Research Journal* 2. Online, available at at www.equinoxpub.com/journals/index.php/JAZZ.

Martin, P. (2006) Musicians Worlds, *Symbolic Interaction* 29(1), 95–107.

Mudcat Café (2013) Traditional music and folklore collection and community. Online, available at http://mudcat.org/ (accessed 17 April 2013).

Nickson, C. (2006) Folk Industry. *fROOTS* 276, 39–41.

Noyes, D. (1995) Group, *Journal of American Folklore* 108, 449–78.

Peterson, R. (1992) Understanding Audience Segmentation: From Elite and Mass to Omnivore and Univore, *Poetics* 21, 243–58.

Peterson, R. and Kern, R. (1996) Changing Highbrow Taste: From Snob to Omnivore, *American Sociological Review* 61(5), 900–7.

Radbourne, J., Glow, H. and Johanson, K. (eds) (2013) *The Audience Experience: A Critical Analysis of Audiences in the Performing Arts,* Chicago, Intellect.

Rahn, M. (2001) The Folk Revival: Beyond Child's Canon and Sharp's Song Catching, in Rubin, R. and Melnick, J. (eds), *American Popular Music*, Amherst, University of Massachusetts Press, 193–210.

Relish, M. (1997) It's Not All Education, *Poetics* 25, 121–39.

Riesman, D. (1950) Listening to Popular Music, *American Quarterly* 2(4), 359–71.

Rose, T. (1994) *Black Noise*, Middletown, CT, Wesleyan University Press.

Savage, M. (2006) The Musical Field, *Cultural Trends* 15(2–3), 159–74.

Sharp, C. (1907) *English Folk-Song: Some Conclusions*, Taunton, Barnicott and Pearce.

Shibutani, T. (1955) Reference Groups as Perspectives, *American Journal of Sociology* 60(6), 562–9.

Smith, J.L. (1987) The Ethogenics of Music Performance: A Case Study of the Glebe Live Music Club, in Pickering, M. and Green, T. (eds), *Everyday Culture: Popular Song and the Vernacular Milieu*, Milton Keynes, Open University Press, 150–72.

Smith, N. (2009) Beyond the Master Narrative of Youth, in Scott, D. (ed.), *The Ashgate Research Companion to Popular Musicology*, Aldershot, Ashgate, 427–48.

Smith, N. (2012) Parenthood and the Transfer of Capital in the Northern Soul Scene, in Bennett, A. and Hodkinson, P. (eds), *Ageing and Youth Cultures*, New York, Berg, 159–72.

Stebbins, R.A. (1996) *The Barbershop Singer: Inside the Social World of a Musical Hobby*, London, University of Toronto Press.

Stebbins, R.A. (2007) *Serious Leisure*, London, Transaction Publishers.

Steglich, C., Sjijders, T. and West, P. (2006) Applying SIENA: An Illustrative Analysis of the Coevolution of Adolescents' Friendship Networks, Taste in Music and Alcohol Consumption, *Methodology* 2(1), 48–56.

Stirrings (2013) 154, Cover.

Sweers, B. (2005) *Electrick Folk: The Changing Face of English Traditional Music*, Oxford, Oxford University Press.

Traditional Song Forum, Discussion Group, (2013) Online, available at http://launch.groups.yahoo.com/group/Tradsong/ (accessed 17 April 2013).

Upright, C. (2004) Social Capital and Cultural Participation, *Poetics* 32, 129–43.

11 On jazz worlds

Siobhan McAndrew, Paul Widdop and
Rachel Stevenson[1]

As a music form, jazz is inherently social. This has been well described by prominent sociologists. Howard Becker, whose work has been so influential for the sociology of culture, has also worked since his teens as a semi-professional jazz musician. His book on jazz, co-authored with sociologist and musician Robert Faulkner, begins thus:

> Every night, all over the United States and in many other parts of the world as well, this scene takes place. Several musicians walk into a club, a bar, a restaurant, a place for a party. They get their instruments out, warm up, and then without much discussion begin to play.... These players might never have met, though, depending on the locale, that's not very likely.... [Nevertheless] they do just fine.
>
> (Faulkner and Becker 2009, 14–15)

Jazz has always relied on a pool of skilled musicians combining flexibly depending on the nature of the work at hand. They share tacit knowledge regarding musical and performance conventions so that they can adapt to the occasion, relying on standards particularly when rehearsal time is limited. Furthermore, jazz is very difficult to learn through formal study alone. Skills are developed through absorbing an aural tradition and playing with others: musicians must be able to adapt to the harmonic and rhythmic context in which they are working, and learn how to make the right choices about their place within a wider ensemble, skills best learned through doing. Accordingly, jazz musicians and bands create music within communities and music worlds which are 'essentially reticulate in structure', and therefore can be explained using the concepts and tools of social network analysis (Krinsky and Crossley 2014).

Because of the importance of connections and groups in jazz, social network analysis offers a promising set of concepts and methods which we use here to look at the case of British jazz. Our aim here is to examine how British jazz networks are structured, using a rich resource covering British jazz musicians who are or have been established in the jazz world. Outside a select few, many work as teachers, jobbing musicians and recording session musicians capable of playing across a number of genres. Faulkner and Becker describe the semi-professional and professional musicians in their study as 'ordinary musicians' (Faulkner and Becker 2009, 29). The group analysed here generally work as full-time musicians, and among their cohort tended to be exceptional; however, the temporal focus in this chapter is broad enough that among their peers and set against the long-run context most do appear 'ordinary'. Because of the scope of the data and our interest in relationships, we analyse these musicians and their careers less as cases of individual talents and occasional geniuses working in isolation, and more as the product of musical ecologies and sets of relationships. This is consistent with the work of psychologist and jazz pianist Keith Sawyer, who has written of how 'in jazz the group has the ideas, not the individual musicians' (Sawyer 2008: x).

Why social network analysis of jazz?

Jazz is highly amenable to social network analysis for a number of reasons. Jazz is a complex genre, requiring considerable musical proficiency, largely acquired tacitly following formal music training, for even a basic performance standard. A thorough knowledge of harmony, blues and modal and pentatonic scales is required for competent improvisation. Performing musicians need to be able to learn tunes and their implicit accompaniments quickly by ear, to memorise a large number of standards, and ideally sight-read from lead sheets. They should also be able to play tunes in any key depending on others', particularly vocalists', preferences. They also need to be aware of their limitations with regards to difficult tunes, and to negotiate a set-list within their range of competence extremely quickly. With this set of skills they will be able to play well with others with little to no rehearsal together (Faulkner and Becker 2009, 76–98). Even with these skills, a competent jazz musician may require a minimum repertoire of 300 songs, perhaps more (Faulkner and Becker 2009, 95). The rise of recorded music, and the popularity of pop and rock, has also meant that the broader market for jazz musicians at dance halls, weddings and parties has shrunk enormously in favour of DJs; jazz has accordingly become more intellectualised over the past 60 years, as a 'form of art music' increasingly experienced in arts venues and concert halls (Faulkner and Becker 2009, 105). In sum, whether historically as a popular form or currently as an art form, competence in jazz requires significant musical knowledge acquired face-to-face through playing with others, with training typically beginning by late childhood.

Second, success as a professional musician requires building and maintaining diverse and extensive networks so that income sources are secured. Professional musicians can be roughly divided into two main types: session musicians, usually termed 'sidemen' in jazz; and leaders, often termed 'royalty musicians' in the rock world, who in the past earned a substantial proportion of their income through composed or arranged works which sold a large number of recordings. Sidemen earn flat fees, or occasionally a regular wage, when hired to record or tour with lead musicians or a group comprised of a fixed line-up, generally signing royalty waivers or reassigning copyright for their contribution to arrangements. Sidemen spread their risk by building a strong reputation in their chosen instruments, adaptability across genres, and multiple income sources, for example through teaching, arranging and non-musical work as well as musical performance. Leaders bear more risk. Some musicians are naturally more entre-preneurial and adept at organising and motivating others, as well as talented at self-promotion. They are not necessarily great soloists, although often are. In jazz, such musicians are characteristically summarised as 'soloist, composer, arranger, bandleader', while sidemen seek security and rewards by becoming 'musicians' musicians', with a reputation for professionalism and collegiality. The distinction is a little blurred in jazz: sidemen do form groups and make recordings highly appreciated by aficionados, while leaders generally begin their careers as sidemen to others. Even the most successful musicians may choose to guest with others. Jazz biographers often differentiate the discographies of their subjects depending on whether they recorded a particular record as a leader or as a sideman, suggesting both that the distinction is important, and that many musi-cians have worked as both during their careers.

Partly to deal with sparsity of demand, band leaders offer their musicianship in a variety of ensemble sizes. In economic terms this serves to differentiate their ser-vices: a duo of a soloist and accompanist offers similar but not identical music to the soloist, and a third musician added to the duo offers a different musical experi-ence again. This modularity of band availability, depending on the preferences of the gig promoter or function organiser and their ability to pay, depends on a ready supply of connected musicians capable of playing together with little rehearsal. For both leaders and sidemen, reputation matters. Social networks enable supply to be responsive and to internalise the risk of incompetence and of unprofitability: both bandleaders and sidemen count on personal reputations and knowledge of standards to ensure a good night's (paid) work. Faulkner and Becker clarify:

> a musical community grows up around a network of jobs players can com-fortably get to and from in an evening of driving ... players from many places find themselves playing together, not regularly but now and then ... patterns of work create a sort of community among them, as reputations travel and occasional performances together create some at least minimal acquaintance with each other's knowledge and abilities...

> [P]layers can sound like they have rehearsed, though they haven't, because the vagaries of the hiring process eventually bring many of them together repeatedly in the same kind of situation requiring roughly the same kind of music.... They may not have rehearsed, but they have played the same things together many times, in various combinations, and thus have developed what might be called network-specific repertoires.

> (Faulkner and Becker 2009, 185, 200)

The importance of networks for learning and performing jazz has been noted elsewhere by social scientists. Douglas Heckathorn and Joan Jeffri used jazz communities to illustrate the possibilities provided by respondent driven sampling, explaining that 'the population under study must be linked by a contact pattern: members of the community under study must know one another. Jazz musicians fulfil this requirement because they generally perform together and develop their skills working together' (Heckathorn and Jeffri 2003, 50).

Third, jazz has been attractive to social network analysts partly because good quality data are available. Parsonage describes jazz as 'the first musical genre to be disseminated primarily through the "culture industry"' (Parsonage 2005, 61). In other words, its history is relatively recent and runs in tandem with the rise of recorded music, so that we have access to discographies giving extensive information about the network of recording musicians.

Finally, the network as an organisational form is associated with innovation and the generation of new knowledge. New musical ideas and styles, like knowledge more broadly, are non-excludable and non-rival. Networks help those involved with knowledge creation to appropriate the benefits of their innovative activities, for example through fostering secrecy and limiting access to information, or through allocating opportunities, status and moral rights in a social world; they accordingly provide what economists call an 'appropriability mechanism'. Furthermore, while individual musicians develop distinct styles through absorbing influences via their formal and informal learning, this is not just a property of the individual: different times and places give rise to particular musical innovations and distinct sounds, both producing and transmitting novel styles through networks of musicians and bands. Such stylistic innovations are characteristics of the music community as well as individual musicians. Connections with other musicians and the local jazz community, and personal reputation within that community, are critical both for the individual musician and the music arising.

Existing literature and theoretical motivation

For all these reasons, social network analysts have been drawn to the study of jazz using large datasets. One notable contribution is Gleiser and Danon's examination of community structure in jazz, written as a contribution to the complexity science literature (Gleiser and Danon 2003). They sought to uncover the effects of city location and racial segregation on community structure. They found a rank-size distribution of centrality which suggested the jazz network was scale free, suggesting that there might be 'fundamental laws regarding the social interactions that lead to the formation of community structures' (Gleiser and Danon 2003, 10). Drawing on the Red Hot Jazz Archive database of bands active between 1912 and 1940 (Alexander n.d.), they defined a link as existing between individual musicians if they had played in the same band, and between bands, where two bands are connected if they have a musician in common. An obvious issue is that jazz band longevity can mean that two musicians play in the same band decades apart, so that there is in fact no personal link between musicians. Furthermore, some social scientists and complexity theorists have become sceptical of scale-free networks being found where in fact the rank-size distribution more properly fits a log-normal or alternative distribution to the power law; and the quest for 'fundamental laws' may be a futile quest (Clauset *et al.* 2009). Nevertheless, this was an important foray into the use of data from discographies for social network analysis.

A major contribution, one which has attracted considerable interest in the social networks field and more broadly in organisational sociology, is Damon Phillips's study of data from the Brian Rust and Tom Lord discographies. Phillips examined discographical data across 67 cities where jazz (including ragtime) was recorded between 1897 and 1933. Rather than examining individuals or bands, he treated cities as nodes, and built a statistical model to predict 'citation counts' of tunes and songs featuring on original recordings by city, and rerecordings by original recordings. He found that both highly central cities (such as New York and Chicago) *and* highly disconnected cities (such as Sydney) allowed musicians to be differentiated, with songs from both attracting higher numbers of rerecordings. Highly central cities focus demand and so musicians and groups differentiate themselves stylistically to capture some of this demand; they have a greater claim to legitimacy through 'membership of the category of jazz' (Phillips 2011, 8). As a result, bands including clear stylistic identifiers in their names tended to do better in recording terms if they hailed from more central cities. By contrast, highly disconnected cities are more able to foster unique and interesting styles without musicians and audiences alike being tempted away in the short term by proximate and more conventional musical rivals. As Phillips summarises, 'disconnected producers have a novelty, foreignness, or exoticism advantage' (Phillips 2011, 6). This finding that there may be an optimal level of distance is important for research into innovation-based social systems, including cultural markets and technological systems (Phillips 2011, 2).

These papers inform our analysis as follows. First, we wish to explore the features of the network associated with creativity and success. Second, we wish to differentiate links between individuals, and links between individuals and bands, to see how accounting for this duality adds to our understanding of jazz. Our primary datasource is *Who's Who of British Jazz*, the directory of British jazz compiled by jazz trumpeter and writer John Chilton. This was the first published work devoted solely to the careers of British jazz musicians, covering hundreds of musicians omitted from previous reference works. The most recent edition includes entries for 980 musicians, their collaborations and band memberships, numbering 3,804 in total. In addition to those musicians with their own directory entry, a further 2,540 are named as collaborators. This wider group includes musicians (such as semi-professionals) who do not win their own entry; folk musicians such as Ewan MacColl and June Tabor; pop, rock, soul, blues and R&B musicians such as Dina Carroll, Elvis Costello, Eric Clapton, and Gabrielle; classical musicians such as Aaron Copland and Willard White; and renowned American swing and jazz musicians such as Dizzy Gillespie, Duke Ellington, Fats Waller, Frank Sinatra, and Glenn Miller. The core group spans a period from the First World War to the present day, from Brylo Ford (*c*.1890–?)

to Jamie Cullum, who came to fame just before the most recent edition of the directory in 2004.

Chilton gathered information directly from musicians, supplementing it with evidence from contemporary newspapers and magazines, to create as complete a historical record as possible (Chilton 2004, vii). It provides excellent coverage of musicians and bands which did not record widely – the more ordinary musicians – and also supplies a good deal of biographical information unavailable if relying on discographical data. The source also allows us to distinguish named links between individual musicians, and musicians' links with bands. Since performance almost entirely takes place in a 'band' context, this may seem unimportant; however, as we have already mentioned, the longevity of some bands means that band members may never have met. Furthermore, training and family links matter, as does friendship and mentorship, for musicians' careers. Our approach trades sample size for detail, resulting in what we describe as a 'middle-N' study.

A typical entry is structured thus:

> Dankworth, 'Alec' Alexander William. Born: London, 14 May 1960, double bass. Son of John Dankworth and Cleo Laine, brother of singer Jacqueline (Jacqui). Played clarinet before taking up double bass. At seventeen studied at the Berklee School of Music in the USA. Worked often with his parents for ten years from 1981 ... but also with Tommy Chase, Dave O'Higgins, Tommy Smith, Jean Toussaint, Buddy De Franco, Stephane Grappelli, Michael Garrick, etc. In September 1986 began long musical association with Clark Tracey line-ups, and in the late 1980s commenced another durable connection with the Pizza Express Modern Jazz Sextet.... During the 1990s played in the Dankworth Generation Band, in the London Jazz Orchestra ... and did prolific freelance work, including a brief stint with Freddie Hubbard.
>
> (Chilton 2004, 98)

The semi-structured approach allows us to capture information on date and place of birth, family background, education, instrument competence and musical relationships, with both named musicians and band affiliations. We treat the directory as a 'whole network', as a population rather than a sample; we can summarise it as follows. Figure 11.1 illustrates the rise and relative decline of jazz in Britain in terms of the number of jazz musicians listed in the directory. Following jazz's entry to Britain in 1918–19 (Martin and Waters 2011, 124), a small number of musicians born in the 1890s began moving into jazz, drawn by the growing popularity of swing bands; the dance craze of the 1930s heralded the heyday of the big band and provided even more opportunities for musicians. After a peak with the 1920s cohort, which came to adulthood and professional life from the early 1940s, jazz in Britain began to face stylistic competition from rock 'n' roll in the 1950s and pop in the 1960s. Further, 'steady gigs' in hotels and nightclubs, and demand for music for weddings and other private functions,

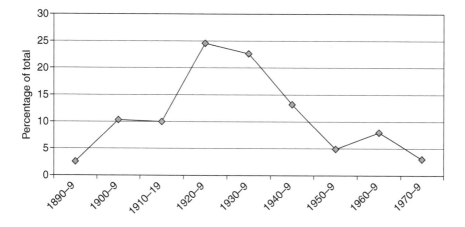

Figure 11.1 Distribution of the 980 musicians listed in Chilton (2004) by birth cohort.

began to decline as disc jockey services increasingly provided effective competition. With this dissipation in demand, jazz performance changed over time: bands became smaller, while from the late 1970s a market emerged for tribute bands devoted to the arrangements and styles of well-known bands and leaders of the past. Some examples include the Alex Welsh Tribute Band, Don Lusher's Ted Heath Tribute Orchestra, Peter York's Gene Krupa Tribute and Celebrating the Jazz Couriers quintet, formed in 2000 by Martin Drew and Mornington Lockett as a tribute to the Jazz Couriers, co-led by Tubby Hayes and Ronnie Scott.

The structure of the data allows us to draw out some career themes, as summarised in Table 11.1. Women comprise 4 per cent, although the proportion has risen for each birth cohort, from almost zero in the earliest cohorts to 21 per cent of those born from 1970. Because the 1920s cohort came of age in the 1930s and 1940s, a large proportion served in the armed forces, with a number choosing to join to train as boy musicians in military bands. Twenty per cent received a formal music or higher education, with this proportion rising from less than 10 per cent for those born in the 1890s to 80 per cent for those born in the 1970s or 1980s. For the earliest birth cohorts, compulsory secondary education ended at age 14 and university education was limited, even for those with middle-class backgrounds. Of those attending university or music college the majority studied music, with the jazz courses at Goldsmiths College and Leeds College of Music popular choices. At some point, 14 per cent emigrated, although not always permanently; 9 per cent immigrated to Britain, largely from the Caribbean. During their career, 54 per cent toured overseas, with jazz circuits often transnational in nature, while 12 per cent worked on cruise ships, an employment source which tends to be mentioned only in passing in the jazz literature, but which provided a useful source of income, often leading to the breaking up of established bands so

Table 11.1 Jazz musicians' characteristics – summary

Musician characteristics	Percentage (%) or mean/standard deviation
Male	96.0
Music school or higher education	20.2
Church music background	2.6
Served in the armed forces	27.8
Performing bandleader	61.8
Recording bandleader	11.7
Emigrated from Britain	13.5
Immigrated to Britain	8.7
Toured overseas	53.8
Worked on cruise ships	12.4
Age began learning music	10.9 (4.1)
Composer	27.1
Arranger	19.8
Known for playing one instrument	41.8
Known for playing two instruments	27.6
Three instruments	18.7
Four or more instruments	11.9
Vocalist	17.2

that the bandleader could take the contract. One important employer was the bandleader Geraldo, who was head of light entertainment for the Entertainments National Service Association (ENSA) during the Second World War, organising musicians known as 'Geraldo's Guards'. After the war he ran an agency supplying Cunard with musicians known as 'Geraldo's Navy', alongside several orchestras (McKay 2005, 261). Before the advent of mass air travel, working in a cruise ship band on the transatlantic lines also offered access to the latest styles in New York.

In terms of musicianship, 42 per cent are described as playing one instrument (including voice) and 28 per cent two, with these instruments often cognate (such as alto and baritone saxophones). In many cases the instrument or instruments for which they were known was not the instrument they first learned, with a switch made partly through preference, partly in response to market demands and on occasion following injury or trauma, such as when Sammy Stokes lost his embouchure while playing in the Stalag VIII B Band, thereafter becoming a vocalist and bassist. It is apparently more important for musicians to be highly competent on one or two instruments, and known for that competence, than to be versatile but slightly less adept on very many (an exception being the saxophonist and multi-instrumentalist Art Christmas, with 10). Vocalists make up 17 per cent, although many vocalists also play other instruments; 72 per cent of the female musicians are vocalists, while 17 per cent of the vocalists are female – they do not monopolise jazz singing by any means.

Unfortunately, the career summaries do not report the age when musical training began in every case or in standard terms; some refer to beginning 'in early childhood' with the ages of beginning learning in the jazz tradition, first gig, or first professional performance seen as important alternative beginnings. Of the 341 where age is given, there is a surprisingly wide spread (from three to 22) with the mean 11 years of age. Two themes emerge from the set of biographies: communal learning at an early stage figures heavily; and later starts do not appear to inhibit those committed to making music a career.

Finally, the diversity of career types is instructive. Many members of the earlier cohorts began performing as children. Jack Hylton (1892–1965) began at seven as 'the Singing Millboy'; Pat Dodd (1909–91) accompanied silent movies from 14. Nine musicians began their careers as children playing in their father's band. Jack Bentley (1913–94) joined the army as a musician at 14. Les Carew (1908–94) joined the local mill as an apprentice before becoming a professional musician. Bill Ashton (b. 1936), Dudley Moore (1935–2002), Zoe Rahman (1971) and six others all studied at the University of Oxford; Dave Gelly (b. 1938), Colin Purbrook (1936–99), Steve Lodder (b. 1951), and 11 others all studied at the University of Cambridge. Alternative well-paid and secure careers were surely open to them. Art Themen (b. 1939) has combined careers as a leading jazz musician and orthopaedic surgeon. Spike Wells worked as a solicitor alongside his music career before taking holy orders; Billy Wiltshire (b. 1916) also became a minister. Malcolm Everson (1942–91) qualified as an architect. Others moved into the hospitality industry: three musicians ran hotels at some point during their careers, and two ran pubs. Billy Wiltshire and Pete Deuchar (*c.*1930–?) both worked as professional cyclists, Buddy Featherstonhaugh (1909–76) as a motor racing driver, Jimmy Walker (b. 1926) as a driving instructor. Ten worked as booking agents. Dave Carey (1914–99) opened an instrument shop; Billy Amstell (b. 1911), Harry Hayes (1909–2002) and Ivor Mairants (1908–98) also ran music shops. Eric Lister (1926–88) ran a motor car business, art gallery and health food shop in London, all while leading his own band.

Exploratory network analysis

We now explore the network of jazz musicians, first by visualising the 980 given their own entry by Chilton. While the links named in the full directory relate the musicians to the wider music ecology of jobbing and semi-professional jazz musicians as well as rock, classical and folk musicians, we restrict network membership here to those who have achieved their own entry. Figure 11.2 summarises the network. The vast majority are connected to a single large component: this is a highly connected network. We have scaled the nodes by in-degree centrality, whereby musicians who are named more often in others' entries are larger; and located them using the spring embedding algorithm in NetDraw 2.089, whereby the most connected nodes are at the centre.

As is ubiquitous in network studies, there is an apparent core–periphery pattern here with a relatively dense core and more loosely connected periphery; the discrete core–periphery analysis tool provided by UCINET suggests (although cannot do so conclusively) that the core comprises 24 per cent of the group and the looser periphery 76 per cent. On our definition of the network as a

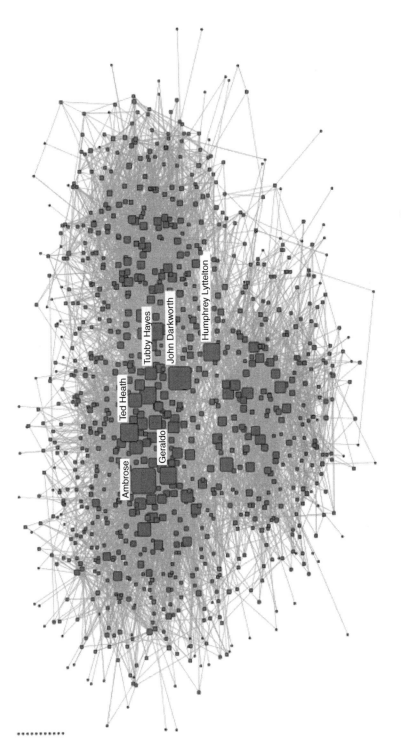

Figure 11.2 Network of the 980 musicians individually listed in Chilton (2004), scaled by in-degree centrality.

whole network of those with entries in Chilton's *Who's Who*, only 11 musicians are isolates. Because of the importance of collaboration and ensemble playing in jazz, in most of these cases this is because links are cited to other musicians without their own entries, or to bands rather than individuals.

It also appears that there are at least two distinct communities within the main component, with links somewhat sparse at the centre, where we generally expect to find the most central actors in a network. Table 11.2 reports the highest-ranking musicians in terms of degree centrality. Ambrose and Geraldo, both bandleaders during the era of swing jazz, and who both set up music agencies, rank highly. Saxophonist and club owner Ronnie Scott, broadcaster and trad jazz exponent Humphrey Lyttelton, and John Dankworth (who, with Ronnie Scott, introduced bebop to Britain) also feature in the top ten. Tubby Hayes, considered the first British-born jazz musician to reach truly world-class standards in jazz (Orgill 2008, 4), ranks fourteenth. However, Hayes died at 38, so that the time available for him to forge links was much reduced.

Similar tables for eigenvector centrality or betweenness centrality are given in the Appendix to this chapter: they provide some interesting points of similarity and difference. In terms of betweenness centrality, the top 20 rankings are similar to those for degree centrality: Ambrose ranks first, Dankworth second, and Lyttelton third, while 14 of the top 20 feature in both Table 11.2 and Table 11.A1. The most notable difference is that Tubby Hayes falls to 34 by this measure. There are further differences between the ranking for degree centrality and eigenvector centrality: Dankworth now ranks first and Ambrose second, while Tubby Hayes rises to seventh. Humphrey Lyttelton falls to twentieth. This may partly arise because the betweenness measure uses unsymmetrised data and the eigenvector centrality measure uses symmetrised data. However, the results also suggest that these leading musicians occupy distinct positions in the network. Dankworth has many links and is positioned close to those with many links; Lyttelton has many links and forms a 'shortest path' between many nodes; while Hayes has slightly fewer links, is positioned close to the highly linked, but has less capacity than Dankworth or Lyttelton to act as a 'broker' between disparate nodes. This is not necessarily a negative characteristic; brokerage can be draining of time and energy, and there is some evidence that brokers between different subgroups tend to be trusted less (Gladstone and O'Connor 2013).

Two-mode network analysis: the duality of musicians and bands

We now move on to consider how musicians are linked to bands. Bands are both comprised of their members, and also define the musicians who play in them. This notion of duality has been theorised by Ronald Breiger: groups partly define the individuals who belong to them; individuals are also defined by their patterns of memberships (Breiger 1974). Applying this concept to music worlds, a band or ensemble partly defines the musicians who belong to it, while each musician is individually defined by their network of band memberships. Data on band

Table 11.2 Jazz musicians ranked by normalised degree centrality (first 20 places)

Rank	Musician	Degree centrality	Rank	Musician	Degree centrality
1	Ambrose (1896–1971)	3.882	=10	Freddy Randall (1921–1999)	1.907
2	John Dankworth (1927–2010)	3.473	=10	Lew Stone (1898–1969)	1.907
3	Ted Heath (1900–69)	2.724	13	Vic Lewis (1919–2009)	1.839
4	Stan Tracey (b. 1926)	2.588	14	Tubby Hayes (1935–73)	1.805
5	Humphrey Lyttelton (1921–2008)	2.554	15	Harry Gold (1907–2005)	1.771
6	Ronnie Scott (1927–96)	2.486	16	Digby Fairweather (b. 1946)	1.634
7	Geraldo (1903–74)	2.451	=17	Bobby Wellins (b. 1936)	1.600
=8	Frank Weir (1911–81)	1.975	=17	Ken Colyer (1928–88)	1.600
=8	Jack Parnell (1923–2010)	1.975	19	Harry Hayes (1935–73)	1.532
=10	Kenny Wheeler (b. 1930)	1.907	20	Alex Welsh (1929–82)	1.464

memberships is 'two–mode' in nature, with discographies a rich source, unlike the one-mode network data on relationships between musicians which can also be gathered from surveys, personal histories and biographies. To explore how the concept of duality and two-mode network analysis is useful for understanding British jazz, we graph our musicians-by-bands data in Figure 11.3.

In Figure 11.3, the darker, square nodes represent bands, while the lighter, circular nodes are musicians. Both are scaled by two-mode network degree centrality. The graph is laid out using multidimensional scaling whereby more *dissimilar* (namely less connected) nodes are closer together: this is to enable labelling of the most central musicians and bands. To aid visualisation further, we have also removed the most peripheral nodes, namely isolates and nodes which participate only in a one-core or two-core. To put it differently, every musician here is a member of at least three bands, while every band has at least three musicians represented, which serves to reduce the number of nodes from 4,784 to 687, and makes the diagram easier to read.

Tables 11.3 and 11.4 present the most central musicians in the two-mode network, and the most central bands, measured by two-mode degree centrality. A musician is more central if they play for more bands, while a band is more central if it has hosted more musicians. This analysis is insightful for the following reasons. Table 11.3 presents a very different set of musicians from that in Table 11.2: it lists the most active sidemen, as well as those flexible leaders who have led a larger number of ensembles. Accordingly, Chicago-style Dixieland cornettist and broadcaster Digby Fairweather (b. 1946), New Orleans trad jazz trombonist Mike Pointon (b. 1941) and prolific bandleader, trumpeter and free jazz exponent Kenny Wheeler (b. 1930) rank jointly first. In terms of bands, Table 11.4 shows that the National Youth Jazz Orchestra (NYJO), running since 1965, is the most central by some margin. The large prewar swing bands and orchestras are not heavily represented here, which is slightly surprising. Indeed, the number of bands in Table 11.4 associated with the armed services and BBC – including the Skyrockets and Squadronaires – is highly suggestive of a critical and infrastructural role for the public sector, in its broadest sense, in the organisation of British jazz. Relatedly, McKay has noted the role of the NYJO in formalising jazz education in Britain, alongside the movement of jazz into higher education music courses, Arts Council schemes to embed professional jazz musicians in schools, and the inclusion of jazz as an option on the secondary education music syllabus (McKay 2005, 234). Such patterns are suggestive of jazz moving partly into the public sector; its credibility as an academic subject may well have assisted further legitimation, for example with regard to claims for subsidy for live performance.

In the final part of this chapter, we turn to the question of how network position relates to artistic success. It is plausible that the most central musicians represent the best-resourced: those whose careers have flourished and who have access to most musical ideas. Alternatively, it may be that musical innovation and creativity of the type rewarded in awards contests is associated with a certain level of marginality: the most innovative musicians may well 'stand on the

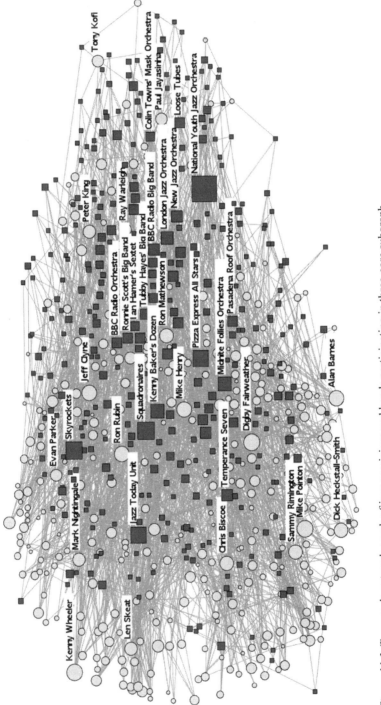

Figure 11.3 Two-mode network graph of jazz musicians and bands participating in three-core subgraph.

Table 11.3 Top 20 musicians by two-mode degree centrality

Rank	Musician	Degree centrality	Rank	Musician	Degree centrality
=1	Digby Fairweather (b. 1946)	0.007	=9	Shanti Paul Jayasinha (b. 1963)	0.005
=1	Mike Pointon (b. 1941)	0.007	=9	Chris Biscoe (b. 1947)	0.005
=1	Kenny Wheeler (b. 1930)	0.007	=9	Buddy Featherstonhaugh (1909–76)	0.005
=4	Ron Mathewson (b. 1944)	0.006	=9	Jimmy Deuchar (1930–93)	0.005
=4	Alan Barnes (b. 1959)	0.006	=9	Len Skeat (b. 1937)	0.005
=4	Mike Henry (b. 1955)	0.006	=9	Ray Warleigh (b. 1938)	0.005
=4	Ron Rubin (b. 1933)	0.006	=9	Sammy Rimington (b. 1942)	0.005
=4	Jeff Clyne (1937–2009)	0.006	=9	Mark Nightingale (b. 1967)	0.005
=9	Guy Barker (b. 1957)	0.005	=9	Evan Parker (b. 1944)	0.005
=9	Peter King (b. 1940)	0.005	=9	Dick Heckstall-Smith (1934–2004)	0.005

Table 11.4 Top 20 bands by two-mode degree centrality

Rank	Band	Degree centrality	Rank	Band	Degree centrality
1	National Youth Jazz Orchestra (est. 1965)	0.04	=10	New Jazz Orchestra (1963–70)	0.016
2	Skyrockets (c.1941–50s)[1]	0.026	=10	Clyde Valley Stompers (1952–63; 1981)	0.016
=3	Pizza Express All Stars (est. 1980)	0.024	=13	BBC Radio Big Band (1964)	0.015
=3	Charlie Watts' Big Band (1985–7)	0.024	=13	Loose Tubes (1984–90)	0.015
=3	Squadronaires (1940–64)[2]	0.024	=15	Bob Wilber's Big Band (1980s/90s)	0.014
6	Jazz Today Unit (1950s)	0.023	=15	BBC Radio Orchestra (1965–91)	0.014
=7	Midnite Follies Orchestra (1978–90s)	0.02	=15	Alex Welsh Band (1958–82)	0.014
=7	Kenny Baker's Dozen (1950s; 1993)	0.02	=15	Humphrey Lyttelton's Band (est. 1948)	0.014
9	London Jazz Orchestra (est. 1988)	0.018	=20	Pasadena Roof Orchestra (est. 1969)	0.013
=10	Temperance Seven (est. 1955)	0.016	=20	Harry South's Big Band (c.1964–70s)	0.013

Notes
1 Formally the No. 1 Balloon Centre Dance Orchestra during war years.
2 Formally the Dance Orchestra of HM Royal Air Force during war years. The New Squadronaires adopted its name and style, working as a civilian band from 1964 to 1997. It was renamed as The Squadronaires and heavily reformed in 1997. The RAF also established a large dance band known as the Royal Air Force Squadronaires in 1985.

shoulders of giants', with access to musical and financial resources through proximity to the 'core' or most central actors, as well as other communities, which enables the pursuit of new and disruptive forms. Such actors have different, non-standard skills and attempt riskier work as a route to success. The concept of 'optimal marginality' was developed by Neil McLaughlin with an application to innovation in psychoanalytic theory (McLaughlin 2001). More recently, Uzzi and Spiro have extended this framework to enable study of creativity among Broadway artists in an attempt to theorise the conditions under which too much embeddedness leads to groupthink and inbreeding (Uzzi and Spiro 2005). In addition to the sociological literature cited above, McAndrew and Everett have summarised literature in the economics tradition on creativity and innovation which suggests that network embeddedness can lead to a lack of creativity and staleness (McAndrew and Everett forthcoming; Baumol *et al.* 2009, 714–15, 724–5). Relatedly, Phillips compared the importance of centrality as an indicator of credibility, compared with disconnectedness as a source of originality (Phillips 2011).

We use as a measure of success the number of times a musician was named in *Melody Maker*'s annual readers' jazz poll, which ranked musicians and bands in a number of categories: musician of the year, best trumpeter, pianist, male vocalist, female vocalist and so forth.[2] We have been able to gather data from 1957 to 1974; accordingly, we remove those from the dataset who had died before 1957, as well as those who did not reach 18 by 1974, namely 19 per cent of the original dataset. Our outcome variable is a count of the total number of first and runner-up prizes each musician won between 1957 and 1974.

Table 11.5 gives the name and number of 'mentions' (awards plus shortlistings) achieved by the top ten ranking musicians. Despite his short life, saxophonist and multi-instrumentalist Tubby Hayes leads by some way, followed by saxophonist John Dankworth, clarinettist Tony Coe, trumpeter Humphrey Lyttelton, and pianist Dave Lee. We also provide a network graph in Figure 11.4 where the nodes are sized by number of awards and shortlistings won.

The Chilton directory allows us to include a number of predictors: gender, number of instruments played, whether the musician is a vocalist or not, and

Table 11.5 Top ten award-winners by number of *Melody Maker* readers' poll awards, 1957–74.

Rank	Musician	Number of awards/shortlistings
1	Tubby Hayes	66
2	John Dankworth	40
3	Tony Coe	31
4	Humphrey Lyttelton	28
5	Dave Lee	26
6	Joe Harriott	25
7	Bruce Turner	22
8	Don Rendell	20
9	Stan Tracey	20
10	Sandy Brown	19

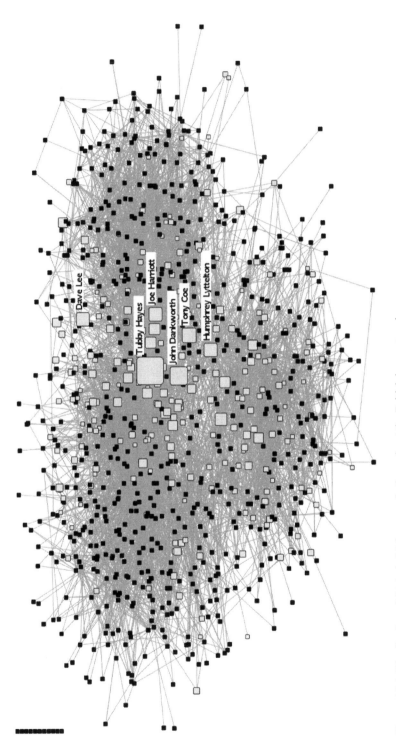

Figure 11.4 Distribution of *Melody Maker* awards throughout the British jazz network.

Note
More central nodes are located towards the centre of the diagram. Darker nodes represent having won no prizes. Lighter nodes have won at least one prize, while larger nodes represent having won more prizes.

some indicators of career type and educational background. We know whether musicians have been educated formally at a music college or university. We know whether the musicians are known as composers. We also know whether musicians toured overseas, and whether they worked on cruise ships. Year of birth is included as a continuous measure to take account of whether later generations are more likely to win prizes.[3]

We can also see how network position relates to the ability to win prizes. Here our interest is in optimal marginality. Phillips used as a measure of centrality Burt's effective network size, while his measure of disconnectedness was the effective network size of each city in the network complement.[4] The effective network size takes account of *redundancy* in ties to others, while his measure of disconnectedness is valuable in that it takes account of variation in centrality among the relatively disconnected and isolates, the latter of which are often otherwise excluded in regression analyses. Phillips criticised the near-standard use of degree centrality and the square of centrality to capture the differential effects of relative isolation and centrality, arguing for a more subtle measure of disconnectedness as opposed to isolation.

Here, because of the substantial network size, it is difficult to extract the network complement from the data and to replicate Phillips's method. Accordingly, we use a set of simpler measures to capture centrality and connectedness at the individual level. In any case, it is intuitively plausible that having more ties can indicate problems as well as opportunities – the need to be 'on call' to a number of bandleaders, for example, or excessively high mobility, or lack of control over career. We look to capture this by a measure of *network constraint*: those with a lower score are more likely to be a source of unique information or set of relationships, since they have links to others who are not already linked to each other. Phillips's intuition regarding disconnectedness appears plausible; again we use a simpler measure, namely a continuous measure of the extent to which a given musician is a member of the core as opposed to the periphery.[5] In core–periphery networks, core members tend to be connected to other core members while peripheral members tend not to be connected to other peripheral members (Borgatti *et al.* 2013, 225); in other words, a measure of coreness takes account of how far a node is 'at the centre of things'. It is therefore possible to have relatively high degree centrality in terms of number of links while not necessarily being at the centre of things. Table 11.A3 in the Appendix illustrates that the coreness measure correlates with both one-mode and two-mode degree centrality, but relatively weakly. Kenny Wheeler ranks highest in terms of coreness, while many of the highly central, at least in terms of degree centrality, rank relatively low among the 980: John Dankworth ranks at 313, Ambrose at 333, Geraldo at 812 and Humphrey Lyttelton at 881.

Musicians' ties to bands are taken into account by including two-mode degree centrality, and – while taking Phillips's critique seriously – we nevertheless include a squared term, which aims to capture the extent to which both relatively fewer links to bands and extremely high numbers of links (for example, through prolific work as a sideman) affect esteem among jazz aficionados. Here, we partly address Uzzi and Spiro's suggestion that information from both unipartite (one-mode) and bipartite (two-mode, or affiliation) networks is valuable.

Finally, we consider model specification. Of the 'eligible' musicians, 68 per cent do not win an award, nor are they shortlisted, while a small number win repeatedly. Our outcome measure is therefore positively skewed with a large proportion of zeroes. Here, we choose a conditional or two-part model, modelling the achievement of being shortlisted or winning *any* award using a logistic regression model, and then running a linear regression model of the *extent* of success (using a suitably transformed measure of the number of awards).[6] For this, we assume conditional mean independence of the errors and explanatory variables.

Our results are as follows, summarised in Table 11.6. Birth year is significant for being shortlisted or winning at least one award: those born later in the century are more likely to clear that hurdle. Being female rather than male is not significant, perhaps because there is a specific category for 'best female vocalist' which allows women to be granted symbolic success in an otherwise highly competitive and male-dominated environment. Surprisingly, having received formal music school or university education is not associated with being shortlisted for or winning at least one award; however, being known as a composer is a predictor. Having served in the armed forces has no effect. Surprisingly, having worked on the cruise ships and overseas touring do not have significant effects; neither does number of instruments played.

Finally, we can look at the differential effect of the various measures of connectedness. Degree centrality measured by links with other musicians is positive and significant. The squared centrality term is negative, indicative of there being an optimal level of marginality: musicians are more likely to win or be shortlisted for an award if they are neither highly marginal nor highly central. The measure of network constraint is negative as expected. This suggests that while network closure matters for jazz through fostering trust, certainty and common standards, so does the bridging of structural holes (Burt 2004) for accessing novelty and attracting the esteem of aficionados. Coreness however, has a positive but insignificant effect. Neither the term for two-mode network centrality nor the squared term are significant, perhaps because the variety of bands played with has no separate effect from that for one-mode centrality.

We now turn to the model predicting how successful the musicians are in terms of the *number* of awards they either win or are shortlisted for. Here, birth year is insignificant – those born in the earlier part of the century are as likely to win as those growing up later. Women win slightly fewer awards, although this result is not significant.. Interestingly, those with formal music or higher education do less well. In this case, being known as a composer has no effect while having worked on the cruise ships is associated with more success, as is a record of service in the forces.

The various measures of connectedness have interesting effects in this model. The term for centrality is negative and significant, while the squared term is positive and significant, suggesting that it is better to be less connected but that there are benefits to being either relatively more marginal or highly central.

Table 11.6 Logistic and Robust Regression Results of Model Predicting Jazz Musicians' Prizes in the Melody Maker Readers' Poll, 1957-1974.

Variable	Logistic regression model predicting whether musician wins/is shortlisted for **any award**, 1957–1974		Robust regression model predicting **number of awards/ shortlistings won**, 1957–1974	
	Coefficient	p-value	Coefficient	p-value
Constant	−63.118 ***	0.000	−0.146	0.219
Birth year	0.032 ***	0.000	0.000	0.118
Female	0.312	0.527	−0.004	0.341
Higher education	0.288	0.228	−0.004 *	0.065
Composer	0.337 *	0.083	0.000	0.974
Worked on cruise ships	−0.012	0.976	0.008 *	0.051
Toured overseas	0.178	0.281	0.000	0.967
Served in armed services	0.026	0.887	0.004 **	0.030
Number of instruments played	0.092	0.232	0.000	0.484
Degree centrality	1.938 ***	0.000	−0.327 ***	0.000
Centrality squared	−0.407 **	0.007	0.473 ***	0.000
Network constraint	−0.912	0.019	−0.015 ***	0.000
Coreness	3.879	0.345	−0.016 ***	0.000
Two-mode centrality	157.760	0.490	1.260	0.483
Two-mode centrality squared	−28710.028	0.524	48.468	0.890
N	822		822	
LR chi²(14)	98.13	F (14, 807)	16320.15	
Prob > chi²	0.000	Prob > F	0.000	
Pseudo R²	0.111			

Notes

Dataset created by authors from Chilton (2004); analysis, authors' own.

* Significant at the 0.1 level; ** significant at the 0.05 level; *** significant at the 0.01 level.

Again, the term for network constraint is negative and significant – those connected to people who are not linked to each other perform better, suggesting that again, bridging brings benefits. The measure of coreness is negative, but insignificant. The measures for two-mode centrality are again insignificant. While the results are partial and mixed, there does seem to be some evidence here for optimal marginality at least in terms of the number of awards for which musicians were shortlisted or have won, during the 1957–74 period. These findings at the individual level have some consistency with Phillips's findings at the city level.

In terms of the effect of connectedness to bands, playing in more bands is not associated with either additional or less success once centrality has been taken into account. Compared with many genres, jazz audiences do pay tribute to accomplished sidemen, with musicians' musicians often running their own bands for short projects while established bandleaders are often happy to guest with others. Further qualitative research would help unpack 'duality' in the jazz world.

We should consider the question of causality. We do not directly measure talent, and it is plausibly an important missing variable here, determining musicianship, connectedness and success alike, and the lack of which results in 'omitted variable bias'. Our interpretation, however, is that talent is made, not born, and that our measures of education, work as a composer and of having worked on cruise liners serve as good proxies for differential ability. Our interpretation also springs from theoretical grounds. Social and musical connections help turn raw talent into professional ability; they generate the norms which govern effective musicianship, the tacit knowledge which sets high musical standards, and the allocation mechanism whereby musicians converge to the roles in which they are most competent. Our interpretation then depends on a strong but defensible assumption that the direction of causality does run from connectedness to success rather than the opposite; in future work this could be examined more precisely.

Conclusion

In this chapter, we have discussed why social network analysis is so useful for the study of jazz worlds. Drawing on network data extracted from an important directory of British jazz musicians, we examined the structure of the British jazz network, in particular the value of different indicators illustrating the position of bandleaders and sidemen. We calculated a number of measures of centrality before examining the relationships between musicians and bands as a bipartite network. We then examined the drivers of success among British jazz musicians as measured by the esteem provided by *Melody Maker*'s readers for its end of year readers' polls awards. The results from the two-stage analysis are apparently fragile but suggestive of 'optimal marginality' – the more successful were less likely to be highly central, and more likely to have links with a diverse group of musicians. They are consistent with those of Damon Phillips at the city level, and Uzzi and Spiro from their study of Broadway artists.

Our wider aim was to show the possibilities of social network analysis for the study of jazz. Jazz discographies and directories offer immense opportunities for primary data collection and subsequent analysis, for example with regard to the analysis of communities within the wider network and their association with distinct styles, the position of female jazz musicians and the introduction of temporal and spatial information. The analysis here has been necessarily exploratory and broad in scope. We hope that scholars of jazz studies will adopt (and where appropriate, interrogate) these methods tactically to advance the field using mixed-methods approaches. In this way, detailed understanding of forms, identity and meaning can combine with selective use of technical analysis to provide a fuller account of jazz worlds in Britain.

Appendix

Here we provide the top-ranked musicians by betweenness centrality in Table 11.A1, namely the extent to which the musicians connect other musicians into the network as a whole. We also provide a list of the top-ranked musicians by eigenvector centrality in Table 11.A2, or the extent to which musicians connect to the most highly connected. In Table 11.A3, we show how our different measures of connectedness correlate.

Table 11.A1 British jazz musicians ranked by normalised betweenness centrality (first 20 places)

Rank		Betweenness centrality	Rank		Betweenness centrality
1	Ambrose (1896–1971)	8.335	11	Chris Barber (b. 1930)	2.306
2	John Dankworth (1927–2010)	7.250	12	Kenny Wheeler (b. 1930)	2.133
3	Humphrey Lyttelton (1921–2008)	6.501	13	Bobby Wellins (b. 1936)	2.072
4	Stan Tracey (1926–2013)	4.081	14	Digby Fairweather (b. 1946)	1.996
5	Ronnie Scott (1927–96)	3.732	15	Don Rendell (b. 1926)	1.995
6	Harry Gold (1907–2005)	3.017	16	Lew Stone (1898–1969)	1.995
7	Ted Heath (1900–69)	2.966	17	Nat Gonella (1908–98)	1.962
8	Geraldo (1903–74)	2.876	18	Keith Smith (1940–2008)	1.957
9	Frank Weir (1911–81)	2.676	19	Bobby Mickleburgh (b. 1920)	1.949
10	Freddy Randall (1921–99)	2.506	20	Kenny Baker (1921–99)	1.873

Table 11.A2 British jazz musicians ranked by normalised eigenvector centrality (first 20 places)

Rank	Musician	Eigenvector centrality	Rank	Musician	Eigenvector centrality
1	John Dankworth (1927–2010)	30.125	11	Vic Lewis (1919–2009)	17.155
2	Ambrose (1896–1971)	28.867	12	Bobby Wellins (b. 1936)	15.301
3	Ronnie Scott (1927–96)	27.003	13	Alan Skidmore (b. 1942)	15.178
4	Ted Heath (1900–69)	25.391	14	Hank Shaw (b. 1926)	14.769
5	Stan Tracey (1926–2013)	24.654	15	Kenny Baker (1921–99)	14.638
6	Kenny Wheeler (b. 1930)	21.468	16	Tony Crombie (1925–99)	14.462
7	Tubby Hayes (1935–73)	20.305	17	Mike Gibbs (b. 1937)	12.910
8	Jack Parnell (1923–2010)	19.489	18	Ronnie Ross (1933–91)	12.745
9	Frank Weir (1911–81)	19.437	19	Benny Goodman (1927–74)	12.511
10	Geraldo (1903–74)	17.494	20	Humphrey Lyttelton (1921–2008)	12.503

Table 11.A3 Correlation matrix of degree centrality, network constraint, coreness and two-mode degree centrality

	Degree centrality	*Constraint*	*Coreness*	*Two-mode degree centrality*
Degree centrality	1			
Constraint	−0.280*** 0.000	1		
Coreness	0.218*** 0.000	−0.090*** 0.005	1	
Two-mode degree centrality	0.228*** 0.000	−0.075** 0.020	0.251*** 0.000	1

Notes

$N=970$. Dataset created by authors from Chilton (2004); analysis, authors' own.

* significant at the 0.1 level.

** significant at the 0.05 level.

*** significant at the 0.01 level.

Notes

1 The dataset on which we draw here was built in collaboration with research assistants Duncan Lockhart and Mariken Schipper. We are extremely grateful for their patient and painstaking work.

2 Data on *Melody Maker* end of year readers' polls awards were captured from 'The Melody Maker Jazz Polls: British Section 1960–1974', http://archive.is/I7xa. Data for 1957–9 were originally published by David Taylor at his 'Modern British Jazz' website at http://vzone.virgin.net/davidh.taylor/mmpolls3.htm, and confirmed by personal communication.

3 In a further specification we included a squared term, which was not significant; it was removed in the interest of parsimony.

4 The 'network complement' is the network of ties that do *not* exist between members of a group.

5 A categorical distinction between core members and peripheral members is intuitively more appealing, with musicians typologised into core members and periphery members. However, Borgatti *et al.* warn that the algorithm for this method in UCINET may not yield robust solutions, and that the algorithm should be run successively from different starting configurations (Borgatti *et al.* 2002: help file). Doing so did not yield good agreement between the results, which suggested that there was not a very clear split among the musicians, and that a continuous measure would be preferable.

6 A Poisson specification failed to converge while the lambda term in a Heckman correction model was not significant, suggesting a double-hurdle model would be preferable: musicians form a pool of which some are considered worthy of recognition, and conditional on being worthy of recognition, *Melody Maker*'s readers decide how many times they are recognised due to the extent and distinction of their work. This model assumes that the first and second stages are independent (as implied by the Heckman model results). We use a robust regression specification for the second hurdle, and transform the count of awards by calculating the inverse hyperbolic sine: IHS of $x = \log(x + (x^2 + 1)^{1/2})$.

References

Alexander, S. (n.d.) The Red Hot Jazz Archive: A History of Jazz before 1930, online at www.redhotjazz.com/ (accessed 7 July 2013).

Baumol, W.J., Schilling, M.A. and Wolff, E. (2009) The Superstar Inventors and Entrepreneurs: How Were They Educated? *Journal of Economics and Management Strategy* 18(3), 711–28.

Borgatti, S.P., Everett, M.G. and Freeman, L.C. (2002) *UCINET for Windows: Software for Social Network Analysis*, Cambridge, MA, Analytic Technologies.

Borgatti, S.P., Everett, M.G. and Johnson, J.C. (2013) *Analyzing Social Networks*, London, Sage Publications.

Breiger, R.L. (1974) The Duality of Persons and Groups, *Social Forces* 53(2), 181–90.

Burt, R. (2004) Structural Holes and Good Ideas, *American Journal of Sociology* 110(2), 349–99.

Chilton, J. (2004) *Who's Who of British Jazz*, London, Continuum.

Clauset, A., Shalizi, C.R. and Newman, M.E.J. (2009) Power-law Distributions in Empirical Data, *Society for Industrial and Applied Mathematics Review* 51(4), 661–703.

Faulkner, R.R. and Becker, H.S. (2009) *Do You Know…? The Jazz Repertoire in Action*, Chicago, University of Chicago Press.

Gladstone, E. and O'Connor, K. (2013) Smart, but Shifty: Trustworthiness and the Contingent Appeal of Brokers, Working Paper, Johnson Graduate School of Management, Cornell University.

Gleiser, P.M. and Danon, L. (2003) Community Structure in Jazz, *Advances in Complex Systems* 6(4), 565–74.

Heckathorn, D.D. and Jeffri, J. (2003) Social Networks of Jazz Musicians , in *Changing the Beat: A Study of the Worklife of Jazz Musicians*, vol. 3: *Respondent-Driven Sampling: Survey Results*, National Endowment for the Arts Research Division Report No. 43, Washington, DC, Research Center for Arts and Culture, 48–61.

Krinsky, J. and Crossley, N. (2014) Social Movements and Social Networks: Introduction, *Social Movement Studies: Journal of Social, Cultural and Political Protest* 13(1), 1–21.

Martin, H. and Waters, K. (2011) *Essential Jazz: The First 100 Years*, Stamford, CT, Cengage Learning.

McAndrew, S. and Everett, M. (forthcoming) Music as Collective Invention: A Social Network Analysis of British Composers, *Cultural Sociology*.

McKay, G. (2005) *Circular Breathing: The Cultural Politics of Jazz in Britain*, Durham, NC, Duke University Press.

McLaughlin, N. (2001) Optimal Marginality: Innovation and Orthodoxy in Fromm's Revision of Psychoanalysis, *Sociological Quarterly* 42(2), 271–88.

Orgill, E.R. (2008) Blue Hayes: An Analysis of the Performance Style of Jazz Saxophonist Tubby Hayes, PhD dissertation, University of Michigan (Ann Arbor, MI, University Microfilms International).

Parsonage, C. (2005) *The Evolution of Jazz in Britain 1880–1935*, Aldershot, Ashgate.

Phillips, D. (2011) Jazz and the Disconnected: City, Structural Disconnectedness and the Emergence of a Jazz Canon 1897–1933, *American Journal of Sociology* 117(2), 420–83.

Sawyer, K. (2008) *Group Genius: The Creative Power of Collaboration*, New York, Basic Books .

Uzzi, B. and Spiro, J. (2005) Collaboration and Creativity: The Small World Problem, *American Journal of Sociology* 111(2), 447–504.

Index